"Graham Johnston's book considers a very important theme—briskly written, amply illustrated, and quite revealing. I have been preaching for over twenty-five years and benefited enormously from reading the book."
J. John, speaker and writer

"Preaching to a Postmodern World provides a clear and helpful approach to communicating Christian truth in our postmodern context."
Susan Perlman, associate executive director, Jews for Jesus

"Graham Johnston has written a very helpful and practical book that both understands the shift in outlook and offers ways to connect to postmodern people.
Rev. Peter Corney, executive director, Arrow Leadership Australia Ltd.

Preaching to a Postmodern World

A Guide to Reaching
Twenty-first-Century Listeners

Graham Johnston

Dear Gary —
This past year has been
such a blessing for me to
work with you at Trinity.
Thanks for all your help, encouragement
and friendship.

Jim Linder
5/25/04

Baker Books

A Division of Baker Book House Co
Grand Rapids, Michigan 49516

© 2001 by Graham MacPherson Johnston

Published by Baker Books
a division of Baker Book House Company
P.O. Box 6287, Grand Rapids, MI 49516-6287

Third printing, February 2004

Printed in the United States of America

Library of Congress Cataloging-in-Publication Data

Johnston, Graham MacPherson, 1960–
    Preaching to a postmodern world : a guide to reaching twenty-first-century listeners / by Graham MacPherson Johnston.
    p.   cm.
    Includes bibliographical references.
    ISBN 0-8010-6367-1 (pbk.)
    1. Preaching. 2. Postmodernism—Religious aspects—Christianity. I Title.
    BV4211.2 .J58   2001
    251—dc21   2001025687

For current information about all releases from Baker Book House, visit our web site: http://www.bakerbooks.com

Contents

To Dad
Thanks for showing me the way

Foreword

When you invite an amateur to speak, his first question is usually "What will I talk about?" If you ask a professional to speak, her question is "Who is my audience?" The most important single factor in whether or not you are an effective communicator lies in whether or not you doggedly pursue a third question: "Who are my listeners?"

For some reason, though, those of us called to teach and preach often fail to raise this important part of the equation. Too often our big question is "What's my content?"

Let's face it. We don't teach the Bible. We teach *people* the Bible. As vital as it is to know content, it's not enough. We must know our audiences.

Perhaps we feel we know our listeners. Pastors have a distinct advantage over other communicators. As ministers move among their people, they get to know them. Or they should. They know their names, how many children they have, what they do to earn a living. They know couples who exist in wretched marriages, and parents whose kids have taken off for the far country to lease a condo there.

But hearers are more than their vital statistics. They are denizens of a culture they hardly understand, and in fact may not even realize is there. (After all, if you asked a fish to tell you about its existence, it might not even mention the water.) Yet Christian communicators who want to know their audience must be aware of the culture that shapes them, motivates them, and often lures them away from God.

Graham Johnston describes the water in which we exist. He describes in detail the culture. He points out what it does to us. Better still, he provides some workable leads on how to communicate the life-giving Word to men and women swimming in the currents of the twenty-first century.

If you really want to know the answer to "Who is my audience?" this book will tell you. Investing a few hours reading it can help you communicate more effectively. Your hearers will be glad you read it. So will you.

Haddon Robinson
Gordon-Conwell Theological Seminary
South Hamilton, Massachusetts
June 2001

Introduction

How is biblical preaching changing now that a recent Barna Report survey shows us two-thirds of Americans no longer believe in objective truth? What will powerful preaching sound like as this twenty-first century continues to unfold?

To get an idea, look at the movie *Contact* and its central question: "Could there be life somewhere else in our universe?"[1]

Jodie Foster, who plays the film's heroine, is a research scientist optimistic of life in the universe, but openly skeptical to life in the form of a personal God. She represents the classic modernist, relying on science as the arbiter of what's true. Then in a reversal of fortune, she travels through time and space to encounter intelligent beings from another galaxy, only to find herself awkwardly having to defend her personal encounter in ways that defy the common boundaries of scientific explanation.

Before a congressional hearing, she offers this defense: "I had an experience . . . I can't prove it. I can't explain it, but everything I know as a living being and everything I am tells me it's real. I was given something wonderful . . . something that changed me forever. A vision of the universe that tells us undeniably how tiny and insignificant and how rare and precious we all are. A vision that tells us that we belong to something that is greater than ourselves. That we are not . . . none of us is alone. I wish I could share that . . . I wish that everyone if only for one moment could feel that awe, that humility, that hope."

The message brims with optimism: We are not alone in the universe, and our lives possess meaning.

It's a message the postmodern culture gets. In the same way that Foster's character made the shift from a scientific rationalism to an experiential and intuitive base of understanding, our culture has shifted from once clinging to certainty, to now valuing relativistic thinking and a lack of absolute truth. Welcome postmodernity, theologian Diogenes Allen observes. "[O]ur intellectual culture is at a major turning point," he says. "A massive intellectual revolution is taking place that is perhaps as great as that which marked off the modern world from the Middle Ages. The foundations of the modern world are collapsing, and we are entering a post-modern world."[2]

Today postmodernity says: All you can believe is what's in your own heart, count on intuition and faith, give up on the idea of truth, have an experience instead.

This shift in Western thinking is like the air that we breathe, agrees William Willimon: It affects the way we perceive the world, think of ourselves, and how we understand reality or what is. Just because this revolution didn't begin with some battle cry does not make it any less dramatic. He adds: "Sometime between 1960 and 1980, an old, inadequately conceived world ended, and a fresh, new world began." That, they say, calls for "a renewed sense of what it means to be Christian, and more precisely, of what it means to be pastors who care for Christians in a distinctly changed world."[3]

For the biblical expositor as well as the home Bible study leader, this raises unique problems in how to communicate God's message. After all, to many pastors' chagrin, the postmodern mindset is not exclusive to the unchurched. It's shared by those folks who fill church sanctuaries each Sunday. This cultural gap must be bridged, within the church and outside it, so that the Christian worldview engages the listener's worldview in a life-altering divine encounter.

To start, know that the Christian outlook is neither wholly modern nor postmodern. So Christianity has not changed—just the issues and questions faced by the people in the pews today. As Helmut Thielicke puts it, "The Gospel must be constantly forwarded to a new address because the recipient is repeatedly changing place of residence."[4]

Today, then, preachers must think not only on the message but also on the nature of the hearers. Our times beg the question, "Is the message of Christ being heard, not just preached?"

If biblical communicators fail to perceive the significant ideological shifts affecting humanity, the church may wake up to discover that preachers are merely talking to themselves about matters only the deeply committed comprehend.

Insight into the postmodern worldview, however, will better equip you to address today's listener with clarity and relevance in two ways. First, understanding the assumptions, beliefs, and values of your listeners will enable communicators to connect in areas of common ground and shared interest. Second, since preaching carries a prophetic voice that cries out when things run contrary to Christ and His Word, it allows you to challenge.

But how do you connect, and how do you best challenge the post-modern listener?

Risk Your Life

Gaining a knowledge of postmodernity doesn't mean you must compromise the message to suit the hearer, risk being corrupted, or lose your moorings in Christ. But who hasn't feared the often-quoted trap Dean Inge describes: "He who marries the spirit of the age soon becomes a widow"?[5]

This is perhaps the greatest tension the contemporary church wrestles with—how to reach the present age without selling out to it.

"[The Christian message] can fail," acknowledges theologian Lesslie Newbigin, "by failing to understand and take seriously the world in which it is set, so that the gospel is not heard but remains incomprehensible because the Church has sought security in its own past instead of risking its life in a deep involvement with the world. It can fail, on the other hand, by allowing the world to dictate the issues and the terms of the meeting. The result then is that the world is not challenged at its depth but rather absorbs and domesticates the gospel and uses it to sacralize its own purposes."[6]

After all, God's truth transcends culture; for God's truth to penetrate today's culture we have only to find ways to bridge the biblical and the postmodern worlds—to speak meaningfully to people where they are.

Think like a Missionary

My appeal is that biblical communication to a postmodern culture should be approached in the same way that a missionary goes into a foreign culture. No missionary worth his or her salt would enter a field without first doing an exhaustive study of the culture he or she seeks to reach. The time has come for today's preachers to don the missionary garb.

"The better seminaries have long included courses in the missions curriculum to help prospective missionaries 'read' the culture they are about to enter," observes Don Carson. "But such courses are rarely required of students in the pastoral track. The assumption is that these students are returning to their own culture, so they do not need such assistance. But the rising empirical pluralism and the pressures from globalization ensure that the assumption is usually misplaced. Apart from isolated pockets, Western culture is changing so quickly that the church now struggles to understand what is going on. Indeed, it is less and less easy to speak of 'Western culture' in such a monolithic fashion: there is a plethora of competing cultures in most Western nations, and many pastors will minister to several of them during their ministry. Indeed, in many metropolitan areas, pastors may find themselves ministering to several of them at once."[7]

For many, any change is hard. "All innovation is open to question and different assessments," says author and theologian Os Guinness. "The darker side of this innovative genius is the church's proneness to compromise with the spirit of its age. But from the adaptations of the early church—for example, Augustine's translations of the language and ideas of Platonism, down to the innovations of eighteenth-century Methodism and nineteenth-century revivalism—Christians have been tirelessly determined to innovate and adapt for the sake of the Gospel. . . . In sum, innovation is not a problem."[8]

So resistance has its reason, Guinness concludes, because there can be danger when the focus on methodology comes at the expense of sound theology. His bottom line, "Critical discernment is essential."[9]

Weigh Style, Skill, and Spirit

There are those who might suggest this is an either-or situation, that we must be divided by the tension between a reliance upon Scripture or upon communication skills.

The folks who believe preaching draws its power exclusively from the mystical outworking of God's Word see any focus on communication skills as only detracting from the divine empowerment in the Bible. "Just preach the Word, and that's all you need," they say. Or, "We don't need any more books telling us how to preach. Just proclaim the simple gospel."

Yet what many effective preachers fail to recognize is that their own communication skills come sharply honed. Their preaching carries with it more than mere faithfulness to the text, even though they are unaware of their presentation skill. This is why some outstanding preachers do not teach others to preach well. The elements that make their preaching soar work on an unconscious level. In business circles, these types of people are called "unconscious competents."

What's deemed as a lack of the gift of teaching in some other fellow, may, indeed, be nothing more than inadequate training in communication. In fact that's what propelled noted speaker and pastor Steve Brown to pen his own work on preaching, where he states openly that he wanted to discuss good communication because he's heard so much poor communication in church pulpits.[10]

However, divine empowering and good communication are not mutually exclusive. The resolution between communication skills and the empowering work of the Spirit is not found in an overdependence upon better techniques, nor an overreliance upon God's Word "not to return void." It's best found in developing a discerning balance.

One of my favorite illustrations of this is straight from the everyday life of theologian Bruce Waltke who used to act out the story of David and Goliath with his primary age children. Waltke, of course, played Goliath, while his little boy and girl formed a collective David. The son was enamoured with David's sling, crudely fashioned from a belt and a Ping Pong ball. The boy would rush ahead of his sister, slinging the Ping Pong ball at Dad. Waltke's daughter, meanwhile, relished everyone's full attention as she shouted at the top of her lungs, "I come against you in the name of the Lord."

But Goliath could not be vanquished by a stone alone, nor by only shouts against him.

Waltke insisted that both responses take place—the slinging of the stone and the cry of God's empowerment—to defeat the foe. One without the other, he told his children, was inadequate.

So it is in teaching. The balance of good communication needs the presence of God's Spirit to achieve God's purposes. Good communication need not be seen as adversarial to the work of the Holy Spirit. To the contrary, communication skills complement the preaching of God's truth, not undermine it.

My purpose is to examine both sermon development and delivery in light of our postmodern generation. Mine is not a theological treatise on postmodernity, nor an attempt to address exegetical procedures of sermon preparation. My working assumption is that biblical teaching would demonstrate a proper exegesis while maintaining attention to the changing culture. I hope to surface issues on the effects of postmodernity upon biblical preaching, with the understanding that this subject is far wider and more complex than can be addressed in one writing.

We must start somewhere, though. As theologian Lesslie Newbigin affirms, "I am trying to talk about the Gospel—good news about something which happened and which, in that sense, does not change. The way of telling it, of understanding it, however, does change."[11]

Here is to maintaining the biblical message while investigating fresh means of how to communicate God's message.

1 | "Toto, We're Not in Kansas Anymore"

For many in ministry the reaction to the postmodern shift can be either a shrug as if to suggest "who cares?" or a nervous twitch that reveals "this whole thing is beyond me." Postmodernity, after all, is one of those topics that's bandied about, yet can seem grasped only by intellectuals trying to define how the concept shapes our society or affects our twenty-first-century mindset.

Yet as rock icon Bob Dylan sang, "The times they are a-changin'." Indeed, postmodern times are here, and it doesn't look like they're going away.

Theologian Diogenes Allen affirms this: "The principles forged during the Enlightenment (1600–1780), which formed the foundations of the modern mentality, are crumbling."[1]

How did we get here? Twentieth-century philosopher Ludwig Wittgenstein captured the age's conclusion when he wrote, "We feel that even when all possible scientific questions have been answered, the problems of life remain completely untouched."[2]

The rock group Supertramp framed this Enlightenment dilemma in its 1979 hit "The Logical Song":

> When I was young, it seemed that life was so
>   wonderful,
> a miracle, oh it was beautiful, magical.
> And all the birds in the trees, well they'd be singing
>   so happily,
> oh joyfully, oh playfully, watching me.

But then they sent me away to teach me how to be
sensible, logical, oh reasonable, practical.
And then they showed me a world where I could be so
dependable, oh clinical, oh intellectual, cynical. . . .
At night, when all the world's asleep
the questions run too deep
for such a simple man.
Won't you please, please tell what we've learned?
I know it sounds absurd,
please tell me who I am. . . .

The crisis of modernity, you see, was a failure of the head to address the questions of the heart. Modernity could not adequately deal with one basic question: "Tell me who I am?"

So postmodern people have began approaching belief in God, truth, and the Bible differently. But has the church reciprocated in its approach?

No, Martin Robinson observes. Many preachers have not been trained nor educated in communicating to postmodern listeners. "We find a church in a desperately difficult situation," Robinson says. "It has not been able to adapt. . . . Things thought unquestionable in the 1950s and '60s are now completely unsustainable."[3]

The church can choose to bury its head in the sand or, equally disastrous, attempt to turn back the clock to the good old days. Neither option works. The former is unadvisable, and the latter impossible.

The way forward for the Christian faith will be for evangelical Christians to stop shrugging or twitching at the mention of postmodernism, and get on with engaging the culture with God's timeless message in a critical and thoughtful manner. A good starting place is to understand three overarching implications for biblical preaching to twenty-first-century listeners.

Expect Differing Worldviews from the Pew

The first implication is that there's variety in the perspectives of your listeners. In fact, preaching aims for a target and if you didn't realize it ours happens to be moving. You can no longer assume, for example, that your regular church listeners subscribe to a Christian worldview. Look at the changes this past century in evangelistic preaching. The rage in the late seventies through the eighties was a confrontational apologetic that played up the rationale and intellectual integrity of the gospel.

The approach was effective, particularly on university campuses where the rhetoric of scientific rationalism thrived.

In the nineties, however, scientific rationalism began losing its grip. People started tuning out, and ministries sought to reinvent their approach from a less analytical or confrontational manner to a more relational one.

"For modern pulpits, faith often became unwittingly a synonym for rationalism," explains homiletician Craig Loscalzo. "We thought we were the children of Abraham, but discovered we were merely the children of Descartes."[4]

One of the clear and present dangers for Christian belief is being wed to the Enlightenment and encased in an approach to ministry that allows Christianity to be viewed as a thing of the past.

"The transition from the modern era to a postmodern era poses a grave challenge to the church in its mission to its own generation," acknowledges Stanley Grenz. "Confronted by this new context, we dare not fall into the trap of wistfully longing for a return to the early modernity that gave evangelicalism its birth, for we are called to minister not to the past but to the contemporary context, and our contemporary context is influenced by postmodern ideas. . . . It would be tragic if evangelicals ended up as the last defenders of the now dying modernity. To reach people in the new postmodern context, we must set ourselves to the task of deciphering the implications of postmodernism for the gospel."[5]

That doesn't mean labeling yourself a postmodernist preacher. Don Carson cautions, "Christianity cannot wholly embrace either modernity or postmodernity, yet it must learn certain lessons from both; it must vigorously oppose many features of philosophical pluralism, without retreating to modernism."[6]

It also doesn't mean expecting your listeners—whether churched or unchurched—to define their thinking as either "postmodern" or "Christian."

Many pastors would be surprised at how postmodern some long-standing members seem. Postmodern thinking creeps into our lives not necessarily through conscious choices but through a steady stream of bombardment via movies, magazines, song, and television. Our congregations gather each Sunday and nod at the appropriate spots in the sermon, but in their hearts many parishoners hold deep-seated beliefs and values more in keeping with a postmodern worldview than with a biblical one.

"We can no longer assume that our preaching takes place within a more or less 'Christian culture,'" Craig Loscalzo says. "The great narratives of Judeo-Christian belief, the pivotal stories of the Bible's characters, the epoch of the life and ministry of Jesus Christ, either are not known or do not carry the meaning-making significance they did to previous generations."[7]

Doug Webster argues that it's no longer enough for preachers to offer people moral instruction and biblical stories. Now people need to be taught how to think and view the world "Christianly." He says, "The Protestant church itself is in need of evangelization, since it has been heavily influenced by radical pluralism, individualism, and relativism."[8]

A 1994 report from the Barna research and polling association shows that a startling 62 percent of born-again Christians, not just churchgoers, say they don't believe in the existence of absolute truth. Interestingly, Barna's national poll of the wider community revealed even more people (close to 75 percent) reject the notion of absolute truth.

This comparison, however, demonstrates that the beliefs of the people in the pews are not far away from those on the streets.[9] In reply to this crisis of belief, Charles Colson calls for a response in the pulpit: "We cannot content ourselves with business as usual, preaching soothing sermons to a shrinking number of true believers."[10]

The average congregation is probably more postmodern than many pastors would dare imagine. "People have changed address," comments Australian Anglican minister Peter Corney, "and unless we work out where they are, we will fail to communicate with them."[11]

The implication extends to both the evangelist who addresses crowds in school auditoriums or community centers, and the local pastor who ministers to the faithful in the pews every Sunday: Just because you have an audience doesn't mean your listeners share a biblical worldview.

See the Opportunities and the Unprecedented

The second implication for preaching is that the cultural shift toward postmodernity may provide new opportunities for the Christian message to be preached in an unprecedented fashion.

As David Goetz declares, "Postmodernism has stuck a needle in the ballooned arrogance of the Enlightenment. Science and technology, we're learning, are not God."[12] Secular humanism, the church's long-standing foe, is meeting its demise and reason as the sole arbiter of knowledge is being dethroned. In this wake of modernity's comeuppance, many people will be experiencing a vacuum of beliefs. It's into this void the Christian message can go forward; in fact, the door is left open for faith to regain a place of importance in our society.

A glance at the newsstand shows this. Spiritual issues, once relegated to obscurity, are now on the public agenda. They also made for cover stories of some of the most widely read newsmagazines throughout the nineties:

"The Power of Prayer" (*Life,* March 1994)

"Is the Bible Fact or Fiction?" (*Time,* December 18, 1995)

"The Search for the Sacred: America's Quest for Spiritual Meaning" (*Newsweek,* November 28, 1994)

"The Search for Jesus" (*Time,* April 8, 1996)

"Faith and Healing" (*Time,* June 24, 1996)

"Does Heaven Exist?" (*Time,* March 24, 1997)

All this interest in matters of faith and spirituality prompted one sarcastic letter that asked the editors of *Time* magazine, "Why don't you guys just change your name to *Christianity Today?*"[13]

The growing hunger over spiritual matters that's accompanied the postmodern shift shows up in other media too. It was once said that the greatest taboo in television wasn't sexuality but spirituality. The one word that no one dared mention on TV—God—now is popular with viewers throughout the week, and on both daytime and prime time hit shows like *Oprah, 7th Heaven,* and *Touched by an Angel.*

At the bookstore, best-sellers reflect the same popularity of spiritual matters: the *Chicken Soup for the Soul* series, *Return to Love, The Celestine Prophecy,* and the *Left Behind* series each affirm virtues and God's power and love.

Indeed, the cultural shift from modernity's rationalism and empiricism has spawned what has been named the age of "neopaganism" or "neomysticism." Spirituality and faith, once taboo subjects in a period of scientific rationalism, now are deemed vital to human development.

To evangelical Christians, some of the conclusions being drawn in the name of faith are alarming (Christ as a New Age Master, for example). But one should still be able to see that the present situation allows for all kinds of openings to speak the Christian faith.

One Christian thinker, Diogenes Allen, sees tremendous opportunities as a result of the demise of modernity: "A culture that is increasingly free of the assumptions of the Enlightenment view of science, religion, morality, and society is a culture that is increasingly free of assumptions that prevent one from coming to an appreciation of the intellectual strength of Christianity."[14] As disturbing as postmodernity might appear, it is equally exciting in light of the renewed interest in matters of faith.

Granted, an inherent danger exists that the Christian faith will be consumed by our culture. Biblical communicators need to be aware and guard themselves from allowing society to shape Christian core beliefs and values.

"Pluralism and pragmatism have secularized the church," Allen cautions. "Mainliners seek cultural respectability and political correctness, while marketers seek popularity. We are becoming secularized by the culture we are trying to reach with the gospel, and in this respect mainliners and evangelicals look alike. . . . Loss of cultural respectability and popularity should not concern a church that ought to be more worried about losing its soul than about gaining the whole world."[15]

The teaching handed down by Christ of being in the world but not of it is an ever-present tension in the area of ministry and preaching. This present age carries with it both the danger of seduction and the possibility for renewal.

What Worked Then May Not Now

When Stanley Kubrick released the film *2001: A Space Odyssey* in 1968, he changed the way we view movies. He never made the declaration to do so, but *2001* delighted and thrilled audiences with space travel so believably real there was no going back to hokey special effects. Previous generations had always suspended their disbelief to enjoy rocket ships controlled by visible wires and men in ape suits. But after an introduction to something more sophisticated what worked for their generation would not cut it with the next.

The same can be said of preaching in the twenty-first century. What proved effective in communicating the gospel to a modern audience may not work in a postmodern culture.

The thing to keep in mind, as authors Clyde Fant and William Pinson Jr. observe in their thirteen-volume anthology *20 Centuries of Great Preaching,* is this: The great sermons of the past "lacked sparkle and punch today precisely because they were written for another generation. . . . 'Great preaching is relevant preaching.'"[16]

Practicing the Principles: Two Burdens

So these three implications of postmodernism leave preachers with two burdens: Reach the listener, a fellow human being, with the message of Christ, and at the same time uphold the Word of God, faithfully and with integrity. The best biblical communicators will not sacrifice either burden but will allow these dual desires to fuel one another.

It's worthless to engage people and not bring them to face God's truth, and likewise, it is absurd to declare to the world "good news" with an indifference as to whether the listener responds. To lose either of these burdens results in not being heard or in having nothing to say.

The dilemma preachers will continue to face is pandering to their listeners (telling them only what they wish to hear), or droning out the message in an expressionless tone (telling people what they need in a way they won't receive anyway).

After all, our postmodern generation has a tendency to employ what previous generations considered sacred in a banal and senseless fashion. This can be a means of ridiculing the beliefs that lie behind the symbol or it could also be that the symbol has simply lost any substantial meaning. For example, the cross of Christ is used as a fashion accessory that one wears purely for decoration; current bands share such names as *Jesus and the Mary Chain, The Superjesus*, and *Jesus Jones;* and teenagers wear T-shirts with JOHN 3:16 or JESUS LOVES YOU emblazoned across the front. These displays have no grounding in an active faith. They are meaningless icons and slogans of a bygone era.

Living in the global village of Western society, today's listeners, both young and old, have a familiarity with elements of the Christian faith that has brought about a contempt. Who hasn't heard a televangelist on TV; or seen a billboard that reads JESUS SAVES AT THE DISCOUNT WAREHOUSE? Western civilization wallows in fragments of Christian cliches and paraphernalia.

This saturation reduces Christianity to slogans and meaningless phrases. The Christian faith becomes just another part of the pop culture like Astro Boy, Bozo the Clown, or Speed Racer. People today don't know what Christianity is all about even though they may think they do. Instead, they consider it old hat. They've heard it all before, and know what the church will say before it even speaks.

Sometimes, we preachers prove them right.

It's like a scene I love from the movie *Crocodile Dundee* where Mick Dundee, hero of the Aussie outback, checks into a New York hotel room, looks around, and spies a TV in one corner. "Television," he says. "I haven't watched TV for twenty years." He turns on the set only to find the opening credits of *I Love Lucy* rolling across the screen. "Yep," he mumbles to himself as he turns off the set, "pretty much what I remember."

How many times have people returned to our churches after twenty years only to discover nothing's changed? We're singing and saying the same things, and they walk away thinking, "Yep, pretty much what I remember."

It's incumbent upon preaching to demonstrate how the message of Christ has value and meaning.

Unfortunately, Mark Filiatreau points out in his article "'Good News' or 'Old News'?" the church has a perception problem—and the gravity of a perception problem in postmodern times is immense, he says, since perception and reality are deemed indistinguishable. "The world sees a Christianity that is angrily defensive," Filiatreau writes. "Everyone knows what we are against—relativism, abortion, and homosexuality—but few know what we are for, besides traditional values. Largely lost to the world's eyes is a Christian spirit of mercy and love, not to mention an appreciation for the mystical character of God."[17]

As Colson stated, are you content with business as usual in the face of this concern? Will you keep on speaking, without knowing for sure that anyone out there's really listening?

The task, of course, is to engage people anew, with a fresh voice so that even in this millennium, the gospel will remain the good news rather than yesterday's news. In the process, postmodernity will beg the question: "Will we as preachers be known for being lovers of the truth or lovers of people?"

As a young Bible student I was reared to be wary of those less committed to God's Word—those who favored feel-good stories to the sometimes unpleasant demands of the gospel. Then during my postgraduate homiletic training under Haddon Robinson, I heard a fascinating story from the life of Norman Vincent Peale, one of those known for his wholesome-but-never-harsh-enough-to-offend stories.

Dr. Peale had established a center in his name to further training in ministry for men and women. Oddly enough, though, he hired an evangelical man to direct the operations. One day, Dr. Peale and the director found themselves alone and the director thought he would seize the opportunity. He turned to his boss and asked, "Dr. Peale, I was wondering . . . do you know what it means to be 'born again'?"

Dr. Peale's face grew red and in an uncustomary show of anger, he shot back, "Yes, I do!" and concluded the meeting.

A week went by before Dr. Peale reinitiated the meeting with his director. "I'd like to finish the conversation you began some time ago," Dr. Peale began. "Your question upset me because you assumed that I did not know what it meant to be 'born again.'" The director, still wondering about the answer, listened as Dr. Peale explained: "I was brought up under the same teaching as you. I understand the need for salvation based on the cross of Christ. But it bothered me that evangelicals seemed to love the Bible and care little about people. So I determined that I wouldn't follow that course. I would love people more than the Bible. In retrospect, I acknowledge that in loving people, I've not always honored God's Word as I should have. However, you, evangelicals, have erred on the other side. You've loved the Bible and disregarded people. Maybe we have something to learn from each other."

Truth and love: One without the other just won't do. The two must always walk hand in hand.

But if it requires two people to speak the truth—"one to speak it and one to hear it"—perhaps for too long, preaching has contented itself in figuring what to say while ignoring where the listeners were.

Good communication, after all, is analogous to a map. In deciphering a map, you must first know, as is often noted, YOU ARE HERE in order to get where you want to be. Some preaching has relied solely on knowing where people need to end up without bothering to understand their present position.

I want to affirm my commitment to the expository preaching of God's Word and the need for all preachers to not create the message but uncover God's message from the text. Good biblical exegesis presumes the preacher will possess something to say.

More than ever before, the danger to the Christian faith is not that people reject Christ but that they reject a caricature of Christ.

Frederick Buechner articulates the task: "Take any English word, even the most commonplace, and try repeating it twenty times in a row— umbrella, let us say, umbrella, umbrella, umbrella—and by the time we have finished, umbrella will not be a word anymore. It will be a noise only, an absurdity, stripped of all meaning. And when we take even the greatest and most meaningful of words that the Christian faith has and repeat them over and over again for some two thousand years, much the same thing happens. . . . Sometimes the concepts of Christianity seem to be worn out and, as a result, we have a hard time paying attention to them. Familiarity may not breed contempt as much as it breeds inattention."[18]

At the very heart of preaching burns your desire to touch listeners at the core of their being, right? Your passion finds its origin in the heart of the Father and in the full knowledge that God does transform lives through His Word. The challenge for the biblical communicator moving into the postmodern era, then, is to present the message of Christ with freshness, relevance, and meaning to a generation of listeners who don't know what they're missing.

2 | Postmodernity: Animal, Vegetable, or Mineral?

Every day it seems we're served up greater portions of the postmodern mindset. But would you recognize the taste of postmodernity if you had one? Look at this *Time* magazine reviewer's description of the recently released film *Chasing Amy:* It's "a witty, trash talking, politically incorrect comedy on the theme Boy Meets Lesbian."[1]

A closer evaluation shows something more—a classic slice of postmodern thinking on display in all its splendor.

In an important scene Alyssa, a practicing lesbian, gives the viewing audience the benefit of her philosophic framework. She explains to her new boyfriend (yes, you're reading that right) how she began living as a lesbian: "I didn't just heed what I was taught, that a man and woman should be together, the natural way. I'm not with you because of what family, society, life tried to instill in me from day one. . . . It seemed stupid to cut oneself off from finding that [right] person, to immediately halve your options by eliminating the possibility of finding that one person within your own gender . . . that one person who complement[s] . . . so completely." Alyssa closes her admission with the reaffirmation, "I got here on my own terms."

Ladies and gentlemen, welcome to postmodern times—times, as Alyssa shows, where:

- The former sources for answers on how to conduct one's life—like family and society—are obsolete.

- Each person becomes his or her own authority in interpreting life and in determining what's the right path. "Do what's right in your own eyes," postmodernity seems to say.
- Complete openness to possibilities is applauded, and the attitude prevails that only stupidity or arrogance would cause one to eliminate options based on someone else's prescribed standard. Life is meant to be experienced, and the brave reach out to embrace life's many options. (In *Chasing Amy*, the implication is Alyssa is to be commended as courageous while the straight male character is portrayed as naive and sheltered for having acquiesced to his viewpoint without ample experimentation of alternative lifestyles.)
- Relationships are essential, and the pursuit of meaningful relationships is a worthy goal, perhaps even the highest goal.

The problem, though, in understanding postmodernism is defining the movement beyond features like these. Even the word "postmodern" is used with various meanings. It can be descriptive of a particular genre of literature, art, or architecture. Here, I'm using the term "postmodern" to refer to a movement in the history of ideas, since, as Os Guinness explains, "modernism as a set of ideas may well have collapsed and 'postmodern' may therefore be legitimate to describe the set of ideas that succeeds it."[2]

So here it's important to note that postmodernity, as a reactionary movement, resists being categorized. Some will try to define it, like English writer and theologian David Cook: "Postmodernism moves beyond the 'modern', scientifically based view of the world by blending a scepticism about technology, objectivity, absolutes and total explanations with a stress on image and appearance, personal interpretation, pleasure and the exploration of every spiritual and material perspective."[3] But postmodernism is better understood descriptively and by its features, rather than by definition.

What's Modern versus Postmodern?

Postmodernity's roots begin in modernity, or the Enlightenment. Christian thinker Thomas Oden maintains "that the modern age lasted exactly 200 years—from the fall of the Bastille in 1789 to the fall of the Berlin Wall in 1989."[4] Other scholars prefer an earlier date, beginning with Rene Descartes' famous statement, *cogito ergo sum* ("I think, therefore I am"), 1641, as the launch of modernity. For Descartes represents the point in time philosophically where rationalism takes the supreme position in the area of epistemology, the study of knowing.

"As the Enlightenment unfolded, Cartesian doubt gave way to scientific debunking mixed with a spirit of social creativity. The idea of progress, of constant betterment of the human condition, took on almost mythic force. . . . Doubt was what fueled scientific inquiry, but the product appeared to be certainty: Science, for many people in the modern era, merely replaced religion as the source of absolute truth."[5]

The Enlightenment grew to be a period of scientific certainty, human optimism, and the belief in inevitable progress toward a better world. Reason supplanted the role of faith. In modernity, faith and morality were labeled subjective truth and, therefore, were not suitable for discussion in the public arena. People no longer needed to cling to superstitions or even biblical revelation because now, through empirical study and scientific rationalism, one could conclusively determine what was true and real. This is evidenced in astronomer Marquise de Laplace's retort to Napoleon on why his five-volume work, *Celestial Mechanics*, failed to even mention God.

Laplace replied, "I have no need of that hypothesis."[6]

Consequently the Enlightenment movement shaped the thinking of Western civilization. The church found itself in mortal combat with the forces of secular humanism, which had abandoned God and the need for faith. People of the age began to believe in science and human reason instead, making science the new priesthood of the masses. In the process these tenets of modernity emerged:[7]

- True knowledge, that which corresponds to reality, exists as a certainty with reason being the sole arbiter of determining truth.
- The world was perceived on two levels: the objective, physical, and scientific realm (which was open to public debate) and the subjective, spiritual, and moral realm (which was a matter of personal conviction).
- The world was seen to exist in a cause and effect relationship, so that the things of the world could be understood through empirical evidence.
- Knowledge was inherently good, dealing with "facts," which were viewed as "neutral" and "value-free."
- Progress, meaning technology, scientific discovery, and economic advancement, was good and would eventually lead humanity to a better world and personal happiness.
- Humanity was basically good and using the powers of reason and ingenuity, people could solve all worldly problems.

- The individual was autonomous and society not only recognized the rights of the individual but was duty bound to serve those rights. (Previous to modernity, the individual was viewed as subservient to society.)

"It became the goal of the human intellectual quest to unlock the secrets of the universe," Stanley Grenz concludes, "in order to master nature for human benefit and create a better world."[8]

This spirit of human optimism and arrogance fueled humankind's entry into the twentieth century, when Grenz acknowledges the current postmodern shift began to murmur: "In the postmodern world people are no longer convinced that knowledge is inherently good. In eschewing the Enlightenment myth of inevitable progress, postmodernism replaces the optimism of the last century with a gnawing pessimism. . . . Members of the emerging generation are no longer confident that humanity will be able to solve the world's great problems or even that their economic situation will surpass that of their parents. They view life on earth as fragile and believe that the continued existence of humankind is dependent on a new attitude of cooperation rather than conquest."[9]

So where modernity was cocky, postmodernity is anxious. Where modernity had all the answers, postmodernity is full of questions; where modernity clung to certainty and truth, postmodernity views the world as relative and subjective. Postmodern people have not only abandoned ideology and truth but are likewise suspicious of those who claim to say "I know."

In the end, ten distinctives would emerge as the hallmarks of postmodern people:

1. They're reacting to modernity and all its tenets.
2. They reject objective truth.
3. They're skeptical and suspicious of authority.
4. They're like missing persons in search of a self and identity.
5. They've blurred morality and are into whatever's expedient.
6. They continue to search for the transcendent.
7. They're living in a media world unlike any other.
8. They'll engage in the knowing smirk.
9. They're on a quest for community.
10. They live in a very material world.

Reacting to Modernity

Essentially, postmodernity is a reaction to modernity. Or, as beloved preacher and theologian J. I. Packer says, "The only agreed upon element is that postmodernism is a negation of modernism."[10] A postmodern ethos could be summed up from the words of the rock group Talking Heads' song "Road to Nowhere": "Well we don't know where we're going and we don't know where we've been." To which, the postmodern generation can add, "and we don't *like* where we've been either."

Where modernity reveled in reason, science, and the human ability to overcome, postmodernity wallows in mysticism, relativism, and the incapacity to know with any certainty both what is true or the answers to life's great questions. Modernity once proudly boasted of changing the world and solving all human ills through technological advancement and human progress. Now that dream is seen to be an illusion. Technology and progress have not only failed to solve all human dilemmas but in the course of events have actually contributed to human suffering as evidenced in such cases as: the threat of nuclear annihilation, the destruction of the rainforests, cyber-pornography, global pollution, and the depletion of the ozone, to name just a few.

In the West, Martin Robinson writes, "We began to realise that the very technology which we had relied upon to bring us Utopia, was in fact in danger of destroying the whole earth."[11] The demise of modernity signals an awakening from the illusion of human progress.

In brief, postmodernism refers to a worldview, a way of perceiving the world, that is a backlash against the Enlightenment dream and dismisses any overarching set of ideas. Postmodernity is the worldview that says no worldview exists. The Enlightenment arrogance sought to provide answers to all questions. Postmodern people simply live in the quandary of not knowing and of potential meaninglessness. Look at the contrasts:

Modernity	Postmodernity
romantic view of life	absurd view of life
purpose	play
design	chance
hierarchy	anarchy
word	silence
a completed work	process
analysis from a distance	analysis through participation

Modernity	Postmodernity
creation/synthesis	deconstruction/antithesis
present	absence
centering	dispersal
semantics/words	rhetoric/presentation
depth	surface
narrative/*grande histoire*	antinarrative/*petite histoire*
metaphysics	irony
transcendence	immanence[12]

The difference in worldview can be witnessed even in the TV shows watched by the moderns versus the postmoderns. Previous generations grew up on *Father Knows Best, Ozzie and Harriet, The Dick Van Dyke Show,* and *The Brady Bunch,* each brimming with hope and goodness. This generation's leading TV families are *The Simpsons,* the Bundys of *Married with Children,* the Castanzas of *Seinfeld,* and the colorful children from *South Park,* all losers without a clue.

These shows in particular demonstrate the postmodern shift: The baby boomer of the seventies grew up with *Scooby Doo* cartoons, where each week the crew would tackle a mystery with all unexplained, supernatural phenomenon. The Scooby crew would greet every mystery with a plausible and rational explanation, and—bingo!—mystery solved in one half hour.

Today we have the *X-files,* where supernatural elements take place from week to week without a scientific or rational explanation. The *X-files* also reveals an underlying suspicion in our society with insiders, or those who really know what's going on, perpetually deceiving the public with elaborate conspiracies. Hence, its slogan, "The truth is out there."

Where *Scooby Doo* declared to one generation that life's unsolved mysteries were done with wires, *X-files* contends life's mysteries are beyond our reach, laden in conspiracies too elaborate to ever unravel. The different perspectives speak to the complexity of life as we enter the new millennium. The truth may be out there, but we will never know it, postmodernity says. The average Joe is forced to live as an agnostic, muddling through life with unresolved issues. Ambiguity remains constant to postmodernity.

Another example of how the postmodern worldview differs from modernity is seen in such movies as *Being John Malkovich,* where viewers discover a secret compartment that allows a person to actually crawl inside the head of actor John Malkovich. Remember, this isn't a science fiction film but supposedly a depiction of contemporary life with an unexplained quirk. The creators of the movie just ask the viewer to suspend belief without explanation or apology. It just happens—and reflects the dismissal of the assumption of cause and effect, or that everything has a rational explanation.

Postmodernity possesses a more open mind. One person's reality is equally legitimate to the next person's—and the progression is to embrace everyone's point of view.

Modernity's arrogance in certainty is countered by postmodernity's profound openness. The implication of this new openness shouldn't be lost in relation to biblical revelation. Our Christian conviction rests on the notion that "God is, and He is not silent." To this, postmodernity shrugs, "perhaps."

Rejecting Objective Truth

In light of the disillusionment with the Enlightenment, society is naturally skeptical. Since the postmodern movement rose out of the study of language that concluded that any talk of objective truth is purely illusion, one can never speak of knowing something objectively, or even state something is true because it corresponds to reality. Postmodernism, after all, maintains that a person can really only say, "according to my perception, this is true."

The Simpsons, always keen to reflect contemporary culture, satirizes this dilemma with truth in one opening monologue to a show: "Hello," a character greets viewers. "I'm Leonard Nimoy. The following tale of alien encounters is true, and by true I mean false. It's all lies, but they are entertaining lies and in the end, isn't that the real truth? The answer is . . . no."

Even Bart Simpson can't help but chuckle at a society that can no longer give meaning to truth—a society, by the way, that repeats popular ad slogans about the ambiguous like "Is it live or is it Memorex?" or "Maybe it's real, maybe it's Maybelline."

You see, postmodernism would argue that you can't divorce yourself from the interpretative process of knowing; therefore, your own perceptions, understandings, bias, and presuppositions will always taint your conclusions about what's true.

Walter Truett Anderson illustrates the various worldviews in the story of three home plate umpires in baseball. In explaining their philosophy of umpiring: "One says, 'There's balls and there's strikes and I call 'em the way they are.' Another responds, 'There's balls and there's strikes and I call 'em the way I see 'em.' The third says, 'There's balls and there's strikes, and they ain't nothin' until I call 'em.'"[13]

The first umpire represents the modernist in which objective truth exists and can be known. His calls correspond to the reality of what is. The other two umpires represent postmodernist positions, the second being mainstream and the third more radical—where truth is only a construct by the individual; in other words, truth is what we make it. Society is left with the relativism of each individual perception to formulate his or her own "truth."

So, to the question posed, "Is it live or is it Memorex?" the reply comes, "What's the difference?" Nothing can be truly known. Reality isn't about what's there but what each person perceives to be there.

"Postmodernism says the idea of a world of facts, or an objective world, is an illusion," concludes Martin Robinson. "Everything is subjective. So the relative pluralism that was present in modernity (with regard to values and morality) has now been extended to the whole of life. Everything is pluralistic now. All views are just as good as mine."[14]

Can you see where this is going regarding biblical preaching? In the postmodern world the authority of the Bible is brought into serious question. At best, the postmodern outlook places the Bible on equal footing with other sacred books like the Koran, the Vedas, the Talmud, and even less-respected writings. Likewise, even those who do accept the Bible as carrying unique authority might also say, "That's your interpretation, not mine!"

Remember when President Bill Clinton was asked in an interview about the compatibility of his Christian faith with his acceptance of homosexuality? He openly accepted the authority of the Bible, but disagreed that the Bible condemns homosexual practice as immoral. It was his way of remaining true to the Bible while arguing that this is only an interpretative difference.

That's the way of postmodern times: Truth is up for grabs.

Playing into this is the fact that the Enlightenment viewed the world on two levels. On one level there is the metaphysical world of values, morality, and faith. On the other level there is the empirical or physical world of science, reason, and mathematics. "Later generations teased out the implication that the objective world (of science and reason) was the real world," observes Martin Robinson, "and the subjective world (of faith and morality) was less important."[15] Or, as Friedrich Nietzsche projected, a conclusion was reached that the subjective world of values, morality, and God didn't even exist at all! Nietzsche argued this subjective world of God and faith represented categories of human origin and could—yea, should—be summarily dismissed. Human beings were then freed to live as they please, unfettered by the restraints of traditional concepts of good and evil, and right and wrong. Nietzsche took the first steps of dismissing all matters of faith and morality as irrelevant to life. So whereas Nietzsche said only the objective world mattered, now postmodernity declares only the subjective world actually remains.

Consequently the introduction of postmodernity has proved of some benefit to Christian faith. The Enlightenment sought to relegate matters of faith to the rear of the bus as either insignificant or nonexistent. Postmodernity returns value to faith and affirms the nurturing of our spiritual being as vital to humankind. Unfortunately, with the loss of truth, people will now seek faith without boundaries, categories, or definition. The old parameters of belief do not exist. As a result, people will be increasingly open to knowing God, but on their own terms.

Likewise, since reality is what one makes it, how will society as a whole handle issues of morality and justice? Who's to say someone is wrong or right? Whose moral standard will speak for all? How can people even speak of common decency anymore? Must the biblical communicator be left with the challenge of presenting Christ in the relativist context where truth, like beauty, is in the eye of the beholder?

Skeptics Suspecting Authority

Since all truth is relative, postmodernity is wary of anyone who claims to possess the truth. Walter Truett Anderson likens this to the lesson from *The Wizard of Oz*. "After a long quest for the great Oz, Dorothy and her friends reach his palace," Anderson says. "They are ushered into the throne room and finally into the Wizard's mighty presence. Lights flash, and a great voice thunders. Dorothy and friends are suitably terrified and impressed, until Dorothy's dog Toto pulls away the curtain to reveal that behind the awe-inspiring machinery is nothing but an ordinary human being. The wizard is seen at last."[16]

Today anyone claiming to possess extraordinary powers and insight is nothing more than an ordinary person either maliciously deceiving others or just playing games. As witnessed with the *X-files*, truth can be twisted and distorted to suit those who are in control.

Some of the French philosophers who pioneered the concepts of postmodernism—Foucault, Derrida, and Lyotard, for example—argued that truth is not an objective idea but a human construct, something that individuals create. As a result, truth and reason were no longer viewed as morally neutral. Truth is seen as a tool, perpetuated by those in control as a means of oppression and maintaining control of the underclasses; the most dangerous creatures are those claiming to know.

Even Christopher Columbus has fallen from a modern hero to postmodern villain. Richard Middleton and Brian Walsh cite the five hundred-year anniversary of the voyage of Christopher Columbus as a prime example of the oppressive constructions of truth. In the age of modernity, for hundreds of years Columbus was hailed as a hero for discovering America, the authors note. Maybe because history books were written through the eyes of conquering Westerners—those wishing to legitimize their conquests—the voyage of Columbus was deemed a triumphant liberation. Though it's been common knowledge that indigenous people already lived in America, Columbus still was honored for his triumphant breakthrough in opening up the new world. Today, Middleton and Walsh observe, "The native people of the Americas insist that 1992 marks the anniversary of 500 years not of glorious discovery but of cruelty, lies, oppression, genocide and the wanton rape of what was truly a paradise."[17]

The people who had no voice, the indigenous people of America, viewed the same event with a completely different interpretation. The truth according to postmodernity has a way of being told so that it benefits those in power. As a result, there's now a reversal. Modern heroes are postmodern villains and modern villains have become postmodern heroes with the likes of *Bonnie and Clyde, Ned Kelly,* and *Billy the Kid.* People who were once despised are now seen as rebels against an oppressive system.

Now, as the world moves into a postmodern age, the people who once had no voice—women, children, the homeless, and native peoples—all share an equal standing. Everyone (and not just those in charge) now has a right to be heard. Postmodernity rejects all worldviews because any one way of understanding the world will inevitably leave out someone, leading to marginalization and oppression. Tolerance becomes the balancing point to keep power equally distributed. The people of the twenty-first century have been conned too many times. When someone claims to know the truth, postmodernity asks, "What's your angle?"

For this reason, postmodernism has a built-in aversion to what is called a "metanarrative," or a "big story." The metanarrative is the all-consuming, all-encompassing overview that seeks to answer the big questions of human existence. Postmodernity carries two objections to the possibility of a metanarrative. One is epistemological. "If a narrative purports to be not simply a local story but the universal story of the world from *arche* to *telos,* a grand narrative encompassing world history from beginning to end, then such a narrative inevitably claims more than it can possibly know. . . . But if metanarratives are social constructions, then, like abstract ethical systems, they are simply particular moral visions dressed up in the guise of universality. . . . The result is that all kind of events and people end up being excluded from the way in which the story gets told. No metanarrative, it appears, is large enough and open enough genuinely to include the experiences and realities of all people."[18]

The second objection to metanarratives is ethical: "Metanarratives are inevitably oppressive and violent in their claims to 'totality.'"[19] In the end, injustice prevails and people eventually pay the price for allowing metanarratives to exist.

Once the grand stories are removed, the only thing that remains is the *petite histoire* or the "little story." Here relativism resurfaces. The only true understanding that anyone can ever speak of is what's been personally experienced. Building on the *petite histoire*, postmodernity rejects the concept of historical record. "History is only an attempt to impose order on past events, but since life has no meaning, you can't impose order. In the end, history can only be the story of the conquerors and it is not a reflection of what actually happened."[20] Hence, postmodernity has given birth to the "revisionist" view of history.

An interesting note here is the holocaust. Already, views are being put forward that the Jewish holocaust of World War 2 either did not take place or was embellished way beyond the recognized figures. What's most fascinating here is that so many actual survivors still exist, along with extensive documentation in film and artifacts. How can anyone refuse to believe the seemingly irrefutable evidence? This is a symptom of postmodern skepticism, the age of the conspiracy theory. "Do not believe what they tell you." (Whoever they happen to be.) What does this mean for the average preacher? People are willing to question a historical event of only half a century ago, because to do so suits their worldview. How much harder is it to speak convincingly about the resurrection of Christ, which took place two thousand years ago and will most likely clash with their existing worldview?

Postmodernity and personal interpretation are joined at the hip. This first became clear in the art world with the impressionist movement, in which artists depicted not necessarily an object or landscape but an impression of a moment in time. Later, abstract paintings like Wassily Kandinsky's *Black Lines,* finished in 1913, allows the viewer to determine the meaning. The emphasis moves from what's on the canvass to what's in the reader's mind.

The emergence of the music video in contemporary culture expresses this same thrust toward personal interpretation. Certain videos tell no coherent story but instead flash a collection of graphic images, leaving viewers with a vague impression.

In the end, each viewer must draw his or her own conclusions about the meaning. In the same way life is a series of disjointed events and random happenings in which the individual must draw his or her own conclusions based upon personal experiences. Significant to postmodern thinking, the authority to derive meaning lies in the hands of each individual; *authority is from within, not without.* In relation to preaching, postmodern people will tend to perceive the preacher as voicing a personal viewpoint. "That is *your* interpretation of the Bible," they will say. The Bible becomes like Kadinsky's *Black Lines*—one sees what one wants to see, with people responding more to an inner voice to authenticate the value of what's just been experienced.

When it comes to religious authority, many people used to view Christianity as having monopolized choice seats on the bus of Western society, while other world religions—particularly Buddhism, Hinduism, and Islam—had been bullied into sitting at the rear. But this is no longer the case. Today Christians are experiencing a backlash. "Christianity has had the floor long enough," many postmodern people are saying; the more Christians argue that the nation's heritage of belief rests in Jesus, the more resentment they create.

The general public seems to be clamoring for a new voice, for someone other than a Christian to speak; this new openness has given rise to alternative belief systems, cults, and what's being called "designer religion"—really old-fashioned syncretism, which mixes and matches the tenets and practices from numerous faiths. Indeed, the New Age movement, which mixes Christian and Eastern beliefs, is nothing more than a postmodern heresy.

So, while scientific rationalism has been dethroned, and before Christians have a chance to celebrate that fact, all these other belief systems have come waltzing in, each claiming all the rights and privileges afforded to the message of Christ.

The Defender of Faith . . . Any Faith

Christianity can no longer demand nor expect privileged status, but must wait its turn to be heard like all the other faiths. This new pluralism is witnessed in Charles, the Prince of Wales. The future King of England and head of the Anglican Church bears the title "Defender of the Faith." Charles has already spoken to this, preferring to alter the title to read "Defender of Faith." In his role as he sees it, he is not to promote one faith but all faiths.

You see, in a postmodern framework, the Christian faith stands as a valid option, a way, but not the way; in an open forum Christianity holds no special claim to be heard over competing beliefs.

Sound familiar? This mindset parallels that on Mars Hill in Acts 17. At the time, Christian belief was the new kid on the block, but the apostle Paul was given a fair hearing, "You are bringing some strange ideas to our ears, and we want to know what they mean" (Acts 17:20).

Now that the roles are reversed, we must come to grips with our present context. The church must understand that its aim cannot be to silence other beliefs but to uncover opportunities to present the message of Christ. In the eyes of postmodernity, the religious spotlight can no longer shine upon the Christian faith alone, and preachers of Christ's gospel must now be content to share the world stage with all the other players.

The New Hymn: "Give Me That One-World Religion"

As the world has developed into a global village, suspicion toward authority has deepened. One of the most influential books of our present age is Joseph Campbell's *The Power of Myth*, which argues that all religious faith evolved from myth and storytelling within cultures. Essentially, Campbell writes, each religious system becomes a construct based upon the perceptions of the people of that particular tribe. Each culture shares an intuitive understanding of God and contextualizes that understanding in stories. From the stories, each culture derives a system of beliefs, which is true for the members of that culture. The world has now become, you might say, smaller with all cultures being aware of one another and being asked to coexist side by side. Campbell argues that all beliefs are inherently the same, and none any better or worse than the others. Instead of despising the minor discrepancies and celebrating their distinctiveness, people everywhere are called to recognize the commonality of belief and be free to enjoy their faith in the various cultural expressions evidenced in the world today.

At Christmas, Everyone Gets the Same Gift

An example of this freedom is witnessed in the Christmas episode of the hit nineties TV series *Northern Exposure*. The show, which revolves around the exploits of the eccentric residents of the small Alaskan town Cicely, focused in this episode on one character's sense of loss for Christmas tradition. The character, a lapsed Catholic, wants to celebrate the baby Jesus in a manger.

Fortunately, the native Alaskans are conducting their own traditional festival, which involves the dramatic reenactment of their own god-child story from Eskimo folklore. The tale unfolds as the raven god is filled with compassion toward humanity because an evil chief has stolen the sun, subjecting the people to live in darkness. The raven appears on earth, assuming the form of a pine needle. As chance would have it, the daughter of the evil chief swallows the needle while bathing in the river and becomes pregnant.

As a baby, the raven could not be pacified. The evil chief tries everything to calm him, but finally, in exasperation, the evil chief hands over the sun to the god-child in order to placate him. Once in possession of the sun, the god-child transforms back into his true form of the raven and returns the sun to its rightful place so that darkness no longer covers the world.

The parallels of this story are unmistakable: a messiah, an incarnation, a virgin birth, a redemption—just like the Christian faith.

At the close of the episode, all the good citizens of Cicely can smile warmly, knowing each person is free to enjoy his or her own expression of faith, for one's faith is actually just a cultural expression of the same cosmic truth. In the words of the Anglican Dean of Perth, Western Australia, "There's no need to damn those who don't agree with us. God is the God of variety, not of uniformity. . . . God doesn't seem to be in favor of turning all Jews, Muslims, Hindus and so on, into Christians. Christian faith need not require the idea that it is the only way to God."[21]

Faith, asserts postmodernity, comes in a variety of wrappings but inside each is the same gift.

For Christians this should raise the issue of the uniqueness of Christ. Is He any different from the Savior in the other beliefs of the world? How has postmodernity shaped people's perception of Christ? Doesn't Jesus carry respect, not authority? People heed the words of Jesus, yet no differently from the respect given Gandhi, Martin Luther King Jr., or Bono of U2. How can biblical preaching engage people who do not tolerate authority?

"Duty, Honor, Loyalty . . . Nah, I'll Pass"

The same suspicion of authority also translates into a detest for institutions. This significance to the average church shouldn't be missed. In modernity, loyalty to an institution was a highly regarded quality. An office worker or athlete would spend an entire career with the same organization. Now, one is better off to be mercenary, a free agent hiring out one's service to the highest bidder. The person who endures mistreatment and unpleasantness out of loyalty is considered a sap.

As the Vietnam War indicated, people will no longer support their country in what's perceived to be an irresponsible action. Loyalty is perceived as a weakness, not a virtue; institutions, as witnessed on the *X-files*, are generally viewed as corrupt and self-serving, and the church does not escape this criticism. In fact, to many postmodern folks the church represents one of the largest and most self-serving institutions in the history of the world.

David Buttrick speaks to the mistrust: "This institutional self-preservation creates an atmosphere of doubt where people assume the Church is merely speaking out of something it has at stake. Postmodern people are skeptical of such hidden agendas."[22]

Likewise people are no longer going to tolerate local churches that fail to measure up in any of a number of ways. The church's perceived self-preoccupation will be interpreted as a failure of the Christian faith. As local churches fail to overcome these suspicions, people will simply walk away, and statistics on church attendance bear out this truth. People are no longer confined to denominational boundaries, geographical distances, or even theological constraints in finding a place of worship to fit them. They'll go where they feel comfortable; loyalty is definitely a thing of the past. With such long-held values diminished, it's clear that challenging people to self-denial and the cost of following Christ will prove a tricky exercise in the postmodern environment.

Living in the Missing Persons Era

Remember, postmodernity grew out of the deconstruction movement, which put forth that meaning in language was not objectively understood and that interpretation was highly subjective. In other words the same set of words can be construed validly into two different meanings by two different readers. As the concept of deconstruction was set in motion, the same principles began to be applied to "self."

"If there are no absolutes in the objective realm," observes Gene Edward Veith Jr., "neither can there be absolutes in the subjective realm. There can be no fixed identity, no sense of self, no unified human soul."[23]

The identity crisis flows, not only from others' changing perception of a person but also from the uncertainty of one's own self-perception. Kenneth Gergen probes this postmodern dilemma in his book *The Saturated Self*, concluding that no one really knows who he or she is; therefore, assume any identity.[24] A person, like the truth, is nothing more than a social construct that is constantly forming and being reconstructed to suit the situation at hand.[25]

Woody Allen's movie *Zelig* shows this with a title character who possesses a chameleon-like identity. Zelig adapts himself to his surrounding, so even when being interviewed by psychiatrists he takes on the mannerisms and speech of his examiners. Of course, the dilemma remains that Zelig does not exist as a person but only as a facade with nothing lasting underneath. Therefore, just as words have no real meaning, but are subject to the individual interpreter, a person has no real identity or meaning either.[26]

Is there any doubt as to why postmodern times are marked as an age of insecurity and anxiety?

In modernity, a person struggled to find meaning in a mechanized world, being dehumanized. In postmodern times, personhood is an illusion, and people are decentralized. Postmodernity compounded the already existing identity crisis brought on by modernity. By stressing the role of individual freedom, modernity began to weaken one's sense of identity through the breakdown of the family and other bonds.

Traditionally the family unit provided the place where a person could develop a keen sense of self. Now, Veith writes, "The exaggerated individualism that characterizes modernism has split families, with each parent seeking his or her own private identity with no regard for the children, who likewise are left on their own. Ironically, such extreme individual autonomy does not allow for the formation of a strong sense of identity, which is generally formed by nurturing solid families."[27] So in postmodernity the value of individual freedom continues unabated, sending society reeling even farther.

The irony is that as individualism grows, it comes at the expense of the individual who fails to perceive his or her sense of connectedness in the world. Postmodernity, when taken to its logical conclusion, can create a kind of solipsism in which the only world one can ever know is one's own private existence.

Likewise modern technology has seriously contributed to the breakdown and loss of self. Human existence is commonly cloaked in technological language. Postmodern writer Jean Baudrillard calls the human mind "a pure screen, a switching center for all the networks of influence."[28] Already a subculture of computer aficionados known as cyberpunks has emerged. He adds: "Their goal is to exist in their own electronic world of virtual reality, virtual sex, and virtual communities. They seek to achieve, in the words of one observer, 'the fusion of humans and machines.'"[29]

This issue comes up again in reference to the blurring of realities and loss of any category for distinctiveness. In this case the postmodern blurring obliterates the lines between human existence and non-human existence.

As a result of what Gergen calls the "decentered self," confusion reigns. "Without external standards (truth and morality) and without internal standards (a sense of self and dignity), there is only cynicism, panic, and 'free fall.'"[30]

For this reason, postmodern times favor short-term commitment. "Indeed, instead of long-term commitment, the postmodern self just moves onto the next game, to the next show, to the next relationship," comment Middleton and Walsh. "This is the nomadic self, on the road with the carnival."[31]

The key then is to keep one's options open. Sure, something may work for the time being but things change and a person needs to be able to swing with the times.

With the decentered self comes the plurality of choices and too many choices can produce stagnation. "A postmodern approach to choice in a pluralistic universe results in moral paralysis. In the end, no choices can be made—or at least no choices that really matter."[32]

A scene from the movie *Dead Poets' Society* offers a good reminder of the nature of this paralysis. The film's Professor Keating, played by Robin Williams, instructs his young charges to "discover your own walk." Marching in one circle in an outer courtyard, each teenage boy learns to express himself with his own stride. One of the boys, however, remains motionless. When questioned, he replies that his "walk" is in choosing to go nowhere. Without a center, all choices are virtually the same. To better one's self is no more worthy than snorting cocaine or lying on the couch watching *Jerry Springer* all day.

Postmodernity is a consumer age, where people will relish options. Plurality demands these options in which all choices share equal footing. Because there's no center, no clear target, there exists a need for a variety of possibilities on the parameter of life. We're all like Zelig. We have the freedom to become whoever we wish, yet without a certainty of knowing who we really are. Adrift at sea, every person will seek out something, some reference point to give life some meaning.

Managing the Blur of Morality

Everyone's had a moment when, looking around, it occurs "the world is changing and I am seeing it change," writes Peggy Noonan, a political journalist and former speechwriter for both Presidents Ronald Reagan and George Bush.

"This is for me the moment when the new America began," she tells. "I was at a graduation ceremony at a public high school in New Jersey. It was 1971 or 1972. One-by-one a stream of black-robed students walked across the stage and received their diplomas. A pretty girl with red hair, big under her graduation gown, walked up to receive hers. The auditorium stood and applauded. I looked at my sister, who sat beside me. 'She's going to have a baby,' she explained. The girl was eight months pregnant and had the courage to go through with her pregnancy and take her finals and finish school despite society's disapproval. But society wasn't disapproving. It was applauding. Applause is a right and generous response for a young girl with grit and heart. And yet, in the sound of that applause I heard a wall falling, a thousand-year wall, a wall of sanctions that said: We as a society do not approve of teenaged unwed motherhood because it is not good for the child, not good for the mother, and not good for us."

Noonan continues, "The old America had a more delicate sense of the difference between the general ('we disapprove') and the particular ('let's go help her'). We had the moral self-confidence to sustain the paradox, to sustain the distance between 'official' disapproval and 'unofficial' succor. . . . We don't so much anymore. For all our tolerance and talk we don't show much love to what used to be called girls in trouble. As we've gotten more open-minded we've gotten more closed-hearted."[33]

We're morally confused and insecure, Peggy Noonan concludes. We no longer know how to discern good from bad. Our new moral measuring stick may as well be "Do unto others what is expedient," because where we, as a society, once exuded moral self-confidence, we now seem more muddled in moral self-doubt. Good and right are merely social constructions; each individual is left to create a formulation of what's morally acceptable. It's as if twenty-first-century society protests, "Who's to say what's morally right for me?"

Consider the words of this woman: "I feel that I'm faithful to Christianity, but I've done some things that people around me, I guess, would consider immoral, sinful, and they still have trouble embracing the things I've done. In fact I don't think my mother visits me too much because I am living in a situation in which I am not married and stuff like that. But I don't share her views on that, and I know her views are rooted in her religion. But it doesn't work for me that way."[34]

In the Western world, modern people applied reason as a gauge to ethical behavior—and the Judeo-Christian ethic was accepted in principle, if not in conduct. But in a postmodern society multiple standards of morality may apply and situation ethics prevail. The same act may be deemed right or wrong depending upon the situation and motivation. Morality, like belief, becomes a matter not of principle but of "what works for me."

Morality Lesson 1: Love Yourself

The search for morality can incur a profound pragmatism—and pragmatism dismisses the search for what's true and right as well as what happened in the past and what may take place in the future. Pragmatism, in fact, simply settles for what works.

"The simple postmodernist answer is that since coherent representation and action are either repressive or illusionary (and therefore doomed to be self-dissolving or self-defeating), we should not even try to engage in some global project," summarizes David Harvey. "Pragmatism then becomes the only possible philosophy of action."[35]

History is shunned as irrelevant if not contrived. What worked for others in the past has little bearing on what will be of value to the person living in the twenty-first century. Choices become essentially amoral as no taboos exist anymore.

"We do not live in an immoral society—one in which right and wrong are clearly understood and wrong behavior is chosen," Tim Keller says. "We live in an amoral society—one in which 'right' and 'wrong' are categories with no universal meaning, and everyone 'does what is right in his or her own eyes.'"[36]

The morality of any decision, which might vary in view of the individual or situation, is secondary to the expediency of the moment. The police have coined a term, "theft of opportunity," in which law-abiding citizens commit acts of theft because they deem that they could not be caught or were unfazed because everyone else was doing it.

Morality Lesson 2: Do unto Others As You Wish

"Morality, like religion, is a matter of desire," according to Gene Edward Veith—and that desire takes precedence for postmoderns. "What I want and what I choose is not only true (for me) but right (for me)," Veith explains of the mindset. "That different people want and choose different things means that truth and morality are relative, but 'I have a right' to my desires. Conversely, 'no one has the right' to criticize my desires and my choices."[37]

Since each individual has the right to construct his or her own moral code, the single most detestable act is to impose one's own morality upon another individual. This principle of noninterference finds a familiar ring to *Star Trek* fans as the all-important "prime directive." The voyages of the *Enterprise* explore new worlds but the prime directive forbids them from tampering with another culture at all costs. No one can claim to be right or possess truth. Something is simply "true" for oneself. As Haddon Robinson illustrates, "If someone appears on the Jay Leno Show and says,

'I've been married to the same woman for forty-two years,' the audience will applaud. But if that same person were to continue, 'And I believe life-long monogamy is the biblical standard that God has for all married people,' they will boo him off the stage. The prevailing attitude of society is, 'If that's your ethic, fine. But don't impose it on us."[38] Do you see, in this context, how tolerance has become the highest virtue for postmoderns?

A carryover effect of postmodern ambiguity is a blurring of all lines and distinctions, including gender. One of the fashion statements of postmodernism is the androgynous look—deliberately choosing with clothes style and cut of hair to look neither definitely male nor female. Gloria Steinem, founder of *Ms.* magazine, asserts, "In sexuality, the assumption that a person must be either heterosexual or homosexual has begun to loosen up enough to honor both the ancient tradition of bisexuality and the new one of individuals who are transgender and cross what once seemed an immutable line."[39] Some men who have pursued an openly homosexual lifestyle are looking to reunite with a woman, acknowledging that they actually prefer the freedom of bisexuality, not being locked into just one category. Conceivably, with the postmodern infatuation with options, homosexuality could become a nonissue as the demand to recognize bisexuality for all people will become the norm.

Clearly, this moral ambiguity presents major difficulties to the legal system, which must define and enforce a code of behavior that will promote the best interest of society as a whole. In Australia, a national campaign was launched with the slogan, "Courtesy Pays." The campaigners understood full well that the only way to motivate people to be polite was to convince them it's in their personal best interests. An appeal to kindness as a virtue, for the sake of society? What's that? But being polite could pay dividends for you. No wonder the tensions grow between the rights of the individual and the rights of society in such issues as smoking, pornography, abortion, free speech, euthanasia, legalization of drug use, capital punishment, and homosexuality. What gives any one person or any one system of morality the right to dictate to another? Someone put it this way, "When you lose the law of God, you end up with a society of lawyers." Morally speaking, postmodernity teeters on the brink of anarchy.

Morality Lesson 3: Do unto Others . . . Oh, Whatever

Have you noticed this moral indifference? To postmoderns, some aspects of morality have become such nonissues, they're considered hardly worth discussing. In one *Time* article, one young girl attempts to dissuade another from sleeping with a boy for the first time and her friend reacts, "It's just sex."[40]

Any challenge to certain moral issues like sexual infidelity, recreational drug use, coarse language, or the accumulation of personal wealth can be met with, "So what's the big deal?" So preachers must not only point out the moral way but also establish why one should care about morality in the first place. Take, for instance, the story of Joe, the young Christian who abandons his newfound faith to pursue a married woman. Joe declares, "I know I'm doing something you think is wrong but I want to be happy, and that's that. Love is more important than your version of morality."[41] So postmodern people are more likely to be spontaneous in their decision making, often ignoring the consequences of their choices; they won't hesitate to make a choice inconsistent with a prescribed set of values. The Nike shoe company tapped into this when it targeted a generation X audience, and adopted the saying, "Just do it!"

Another reason postmodernity insists on options is that something may work for a while, then in time be discarded as obsolete. This is why people may prove reluctant to make long-term commitments. They want to keep their options open in case something better should come along or if the situation changes. "It's good now but I don't know what tomorrow will bring" is the attitude. Loyalty as a value? Not to this generation. On the contrary, the person who remains in an unhappy marriage out of allegiance or the sake of the children will be regarded as a coward for failing to grab hold of life.

With the pragmatism comes a resistance to being locked-in to any one way of thinking. This will be evidenced through a diversity of tastes in the areas of entertainment, art, music, role models, as well as religious beliefs. People will mix and match what suits them best at the present time.

The lack of any moral compass point is evidenced in an episode of the popular television show *Friends*. Monica, one of the friends, decides that she is tired of waiting to meet Mr. Right to start a family and opts to bear a child using a sperm bank donor. As she grapples with this decision, in the end, she decides against the move, not for any ethical reason or out of her concern in raising a fatherless child but because it was not right for her—her own feelings stood as the sole arbiter of the choice. Morality, values, ethics? What works for you?

Postmodernity and the Search for the Transcendent

G. K. Chesterton warned when people cease believing in God, it's not that they believe in nothing, but they'll believe in anything. With the loss of modernity's substructure, it doesn't leave much for anyone to hold onto because there are no external standards by which to ascertain what's good or right. As a result people begin to look inward. "[Postmodernists] are unwilling to allow the human intellect to serve as the sole determiner of what we should believe. Postmoderns look beyond reason to nonrational ways of knowing, conferring heightened status on the emotions and intuition,"[42] observes Grenz.

For the modernist the issue in cultivating a faith was credibility. So much of the debate surrounding Christianity centered on issues like the authority of Scripture, the "historical Jesus," and the "empty tomb of Christ." In postmodernity, a key issue of faith is desirability. The issue isn't so much whether it happened, which is unknowable from a twenty-first-century standpoint, but whether one views these beliefs as desirable. In other words, one chooses to believe something because one wishes it were true. Look at one of the fastest growing belief systems in the world: Mormonism. The Mormons understand that the average person is more influenced by a perception of good than the content of good doctrine. In 1998, the highest ranking Mormon official was asked to comment about a long-held tenet that essentially God shares the same substance as that of any human being. The offiicial simply replied, "We don't emphasize that anymore."

Excuse me, but what does that mean? That Mormons won't deny that tenet as wrong nor instruct it as right? Or that if you ignore something it will go away? The Mormons have cleverly understood that appearance means more than substance—it's the classic triumph of style over substance.

Veith comments on the growth of beliefs like Scientology: "Many people tremendously enjoy the aliens and galactic conflicts that are the staple of science fiction. Would it not be even better if these were real?"[43] Therefore, the issue of belief moves from one of credibility and even plausibility to simply what one would wish to be true. With the loss of any external measurement for gauging what is true, all that remains is the inner sense of what seems and feels comfortable to the listener. Is it any wonder then that the belief in a literal hell is in massive decline? The very thought of hell does not sit well with people—Christians or non-Christians.

The Quest for Wholeness: Use the Force, Luke

This inward look has produced a greater realization of the spiritual capacity of human beings. Likewise, it's cultivated a deeper sense of the mystic element of life too. Of course this is a backlash against modernity, which only recognized something as true if it could stand up under empirical and scientific examination. Postmodernity embraces a wider perspective of reality, taking into account the spiritual and intuitive aspects of human existence. As a result the New Age movement's grown, and along with it an embrace of the supernatural often expressed in an anti-intellectual manner with crystals, palm readings, star signs, psychics, and the like.

In keeping with the philosophy that all beliefs stem from a common ancestry, there's renewed interest in ancient, and even pagan, beliefs. The incorporation of these ancient beliefs into modern society seeks to recapture what technology and science have stripped from the contemporary world. God is no longer seen as removed from the natural world, but more a part of it as exemplified in the original *Star Wars* film. Remember in the final battle scene where, fighting against the dreaded Death Star, hero Luke Skywalker is instructed telepathically by Obi-Wan Ben Kenobi to "use the force," instead of the craft's aiming instrumentation. As a result the decisive blow hits the mark. The Death Star is destroyed and everyone rejoices that civilization is saved.

Postmodern people's reaction to modernity is much the same. The loss felt in modernity has resulted in a new search for the transcendent, anything beyond the empirical realm. The thinking is this: *Society has lost its soul. Somehow we need to "use the force."* That means preachers today must tap into the craving for reconnectedness of the spiritual and physical existences. *Preachers must help listeners regrasp the spiritual that is all around us* and restore a sense of wholeness.

It's Not Nice to Fool Mother Nature

The Enlightenment viewed nature as somewhat separate from humanity, a thing to be studied and even mastered. Martin Robinson observes, "In modernity you understand things by breaking them down into their constituent parts and studying them in the smallest detail. Now there is an intuitive recognition that life is holistic. Life has core and the core reality of life is spirit, not matter."[44]

However, postmodernity brings a sense of cosmic connectedness to life and the universe. Nature is no longer a thing to be scrutinized under the microscope of science but nature brings wisdom from which people can learn and in which people must coexist.

The movie *Jurassic Park* vaunts nature, who in her wisdom has chosen to eliminate dinosaurs. It is only the arrogance of the scientists who dare attempt to undo what nature has done. *Jurassic Park* stands as a contemporary Frankenstein, in which mere humans meddle in areas beyond their reach.

The postmodern view is to appreciate the wisdom as well as the beauty of nature. We hear and read a lot about the need for wholeness, as if modernists had become disjointed. "Wholeness also entails a consciousness of the indelible and delicate connection to what lies beyond ourselves, in which our personal existence is embedded and from which it is nurtured. The wider realm includes 'nature' (the ecosystem), of course."[45] Modernity almost succeeded in destroying the environment; postmodernity has given rise to the Green movement and environmentalists.

Our Mother Who Art in Nature, Hallowed Be Thy Name?

So many postmoderns worship nature as a sacred goddess; in the absence of anything greater, nature fills the void in the search for the transcendent, the "otherness" of life. A guy I met in a twelve-step program once remarked to me that his "higher power" upon which he would draw strength to overcome his alcohol dependency was the Indian Ocean. Nature is sacred and as a result, environmental issues rate high on the people's priority scale.

To illustrate the impact of the Green movement, I spoke to a room full of primary age children on the value of stillness. Stillness allows us to hear from God, I told them. I then posed, "What do you suppose God might want to say to you?" The responses were interesting: "Don't pollute." "Plant a tree." "Look after the animals." "Remember to recycle." Clearly, the environment was on the mind of God. In fact, to this generation, "sin" and "wrong" will most likely be interpreted as an offense against nature. Pollution is a sin against the God of nature. The implications of this mindset are far-reaching. Morality must allow for people to operate within what is natural for them. Take, for instance, an issue such as homosexuality. Postmodernity would view the state as a person's "nature." The sanctity of "nature" carries such force that people will offer ready approval to homosexual practice, in not wishing to violate nature. Nature, as opposed to any external moral system, must stand pre-eminent as that which directs life.

Livin' Large, Baby

In the postmodern search for the transcendent, people will be encouraged to experience as much of life as possible or, as generation Xers say, to go about "livin' large," getting as much out of life as you can. Only the brave push the boundaries; the weak resign themselves to constructs that someone else produced. The avenues to more life could well take the form of experimentation with drug use, a counterculture existence, extreme sports, or sexual encounters of all kinds.

The closest many postmodern people will ever come to a transcendent, supernatural experience is through sexual encounters or recreational drugs. "Take Joie, for example. At age 20, she's into tattoos and all-night rave parties, and one day hopes to hold a political office. Upon meeting her, she purrs with a smile, 'I mean, honestly, have you ever met anyone as cool as me in your entire life?'"[46]

Joie's livin' large, experiencing as much of life as she can; all of this relates back to the loss of "self," and the idea that each person is only a social construct. As Walter Truett Anderson explains, "In the [sixties], when drug use came out of the closet and became a part of the public reality of Western civilization, it was commonly believed that the psychedelics (such as LSD) enabled the user to 'drop out' of socially constructed reality and to 'tune in' to a cosmic reality beyond culture; with the right drugs, you would find the Real World, and the True Self."[47]

Today, the "true self" exists in a state of flux and can be shaped by external forces, drug use being no better or worse than the Bible. Postmodern thinking concludes there's no "real" world, no alternative reality, and no true self; there's only what one makes of reality. Therefore, if one chooses to use mind-altering chemicals, fine. That's merely one option to the social construct of self. As Anderson sadly concludes, "We will have to come to terms, as we stagger into the postmodern era, with the hard-to-avoid evidence that there are many different realities, and different ways of experiencing them, and that people seem to want to keep exploring them."[48] So get ready. "Just say no" will inevitably return the response, "But why not?"

Keep in mind postmodernity's search for what is beyond. For many people today, the only readily acceptable answer to the search is found in the forces of nature. For others, the search will involve a delving into mysticism, the occult, ancient Celtic beliefs, witchcraft, as well as crystals, tarot cards, astrology, and chanting. The search will take some people into drugs and sexual exploits. The Christian community may react in a combination of outrage and fear, instead of recognizing these seekers as confused and lost individuals groping for meaning.

The apostle John writes, "There is no fear in love" (1 John 4:18). Will churches in postmodern times respond in fear or with compassion as people search in all the wrong places? Will preachers have a voice to be heard in their pursuit of something greater than themselves?

It's a Media-Mad World

The provocative movie *Jesus of Montreal* tells the story of a modern-day actor who portrays Jesus in an avant-garde, outdoor Passion Play. The actor portraying Jesus gradually takes on a Christlike persona, fulfilling a messianic role in his real life in contemporary Canada.

The makers of the film thought carefully about each scene. When it came time to re-create Christ driving the money changers from the temple, the present-day Jesus trashes a filming set and throws the network executives out of the television studio. Is it so surprising that the television studio serves as the modern equivalent to the temple, the contemporary house of worship?

Without a doubt, comments Gene Edward Veith, the media remains the single most influential force of the twenty-first century: "A major force in the shaping of the postmodern mind has been the impact of contemporary technology. The product of rationalism, the electronic media may well make rationalism impossible."[49]

Consider it a trade of Gutenberg for Spielberg, because in the modern world the printed word ruled. In fact, *Time* magazine named Gutenberg the "person of the last Millennium" for inventing the printing press, and paving the way for the Enlightenment—a movement of ideas grounded in the written word.

In the same way, the advent of television ushered in the postmodern age. When *Life* magazine asked "Who's Top Boomer?" in a survey to find the baby boomer generation's fifty most influential people, notably, the list was dominated by television and movie personalities, sporting heroes, and pop stars. Only one writer cracked the top 50—best-selling author Stephen King came in at number 30. Oprah Winfrey was the highest-rated woman, coming in ahead of Roseanne Barr (number 10) and Madonna (number 14). Somewhat inexplicably, Bill Gates landed at number 7 behind Steven Jobs of Apple computer fame at number 2; perhaps even more bizarre was the inclusion of John Belushi (number 12), who died of a self-induced drug overdose ("Man, I've modeled my life on *Animal House*"). The top vote-getter was the master image-maker and storyteller, Steven Spielberg.[50]

As a result of the deconstruction movement, the force of the written word was diminished. Words carried no true meaning. Enter the image. Images leave the viewer, not with carefully crafted ideas and precepts but with impressions. Images function to allow the viewer to construct one's own interpretation. Hence, television both suits and helped to create the postmodern ethos.

In addition, the twenty-first century is undeniably the information age, whereas, modernity flourished on the back of the industrial age. In his book *Amusing Ourselves to Death*,[51] Neil Postman argues that the world has moved from a print culture to a media culture. Media now dominates the way in which people think and discuss ideas publicly.

Veith summarizes Postman's position: "Reading a 300-page book demands sequential thinking, active mental engagement, and a sustained attention span. Reading also encourages a sense of self—one reads in private, alone with oneself and with one's thoughts. Watching television, on the other hand, presents information rapidly and with minimal effort on the part of the viewer, who becomes part of a communal mass mind. Visual images are presented, rapid-fire, with little sense of the context or connection."[52]

Once again, the music video exemplifies the barrage of powerful images in a nonsequential order without context and clear meaning. Television allows the viewer to absorb data without strain in an indiscriminate manner.

Postmodern times, however, tend to confuse truth and entertainment. "Film and video can now render the wildest fantasies and make them seem realistic. Real events, by the same token, are fictionalized. It's little wonder that the TV generation has a hard time distinguishing between truth and fiction."[53]

Social commentator Bill Moyers made this point in the BBC documentary *Primetime President*. In his interview with advertising writer Barbara Lippert, she observed: "The problem . . . is that there is no distinction between advertising and everything else. . . . Everything's blurred. . . . When you see everything is marketed and designed and positioned, then you begin to wonder, what is reality?"

Communications professor Kathleen Jamieson suggested to Moyers: "Television has privileged visual argument, and as a result it's created a whole new grammar. Now politicians don't have to argue the old way, with evidence . . . they telegraph with pictures. When juxtaposed, pictures can create things that didn't actually happen in the real world."

Moyers sums up the impact of the TV image with this story: "The other night, after the presidential campaign debate, David Brinkley asked his colleague Peter Jennings, who had been one of the questioners, for a reaction to the debate, and Peter said, 'It's very hard for me to react, I didn't see it on television.' Now, here was a man who was participating in the reality . . . yet he couldn't react to it because he hadn't seen it on television. What does that say about reality?"[54]

Postmodernity blurs the lines between commercial and product, actual event and fiction, and news and entertainment. Postmodernity has even named television programs that present factual information in an amusing and lightweight fashion: "infotainment." It's all part of an underlying belief: You create your reality; I'll create mine.

Television and movies further blur the lines of reality in simulating life and creating an alternative reality on screen.

In another area of blurred lines, the futuristic classic movie *Blade Runner* depicts a world where "replicants" inhabit society as synthetic humans, or androids, created in a laboratory. Replicants coexist with people and are virtually indistinguishable from those born and raised by humans. The movie raises the moral dilemma: Who is to say that an artificial being is any less real than a human being? Many people would suggest the same concerning the world one creates on a television or movie screen or in a "virtual reality" computer-operated game. Who is to say that this "reality" is any less real, since what people call reality is merely a social construct anyway?

Several movies on home video, like *Who Framed Roger Rabbit?* and *Space Jam* (starring basketball player Michael Jordan and Bugs Bunny), showcase human actors alongside cartoon characters, as if the animated character were real. This is an indication of the blurring of what's real and what's artificial.

As the title of Walter Truett Anderson's work on postmodernity suggests, "Reality isn't what it used to be."

Meanwhile, Jean Baudrillard in *Simulations* argues that the present age is one of simulated reality, the real and artificial are inseparable, and in the end there's no need to attempt to distinguish between the two. Joey Horstman comments, "Perhaps Jean Baudrillard is closer to the truth after all when he characterizes ours as the age of simulation. For just as shopping malls simulate the great outdoors, replacing sun and trees with fluorescent lights and green plastic plants, we simulate danger with amusement park rides, friends or enemies with talk-radio hosts, rebellion with torn jeans and black boots, sex with lewd phone conversations, revolution with improved fabric softeners, and freedom with the newest panty liner. We simulate real life by eliminating risk and commitment, end up mistaking what is real for what is only artificial."[55]

The world of the television screen and cyberspace no longer replicates reality, but creates its own.

Facing the Knowing Smirk

The character Scott Evil, son of arch-villain, Dr. Evil, represents the postmodern generation in the sixties spy spoof *Austin Powers, International Man of Mystery*. In a scene surrounded by his henchmen, Dr. Evil laments, "As you know, every diabolical scheme that I've hatched has been thwarted by Austin Powers. Why is that?" Scott, the clued-in son, states what every viewer knows perfectly well, "Because you never kill him when you get the chance and you're a big dope." Scott Evil is way ahead of the contest; he's a classic example of the knowing smirk.

That smirk is ever present in the popular or "pop" culture that postmodernity has cozied up to increasingly. Pop culture represents popular influences that transcend geographical and cultural boundaries.

"Modernists exalted art above the reach of ordinary people," Veith explains. "Artists were an elite priesthood; only highly trained specialists or others in the know had any idea what they were trying to do. Postmodernists, on the other hand, in line with their radical political ideas, reject the institutional elitism of the high culture. . . . They mock the conventions of the art world and openly (though sometimes ironically) embrace the pop culture, consumerism, and kitsch."[56]

In the Renaissance period, art was viewed as a serious means of reflecting reality and expressing important truths. Now art forms become a means of expressing the loss of truth, fragmentation and isolation, and the lack of real meaning. The precursors of postmodern art were individuals like Picasso and Duchamp with the Dada movement, which by the way, comes from the French word for "rocking horse"— and it was chosen as the name of their movement, incidently, by opening a dictionary and blindly dropping a finger upon any word in a random encounter.

Later, others like Jackson Pollock created paintings using swinging buckets and creeping earthworms to symbolize the randomness of life. These artists questioned the presuppositions of their times. They viewed life as meaningless and reflected this outlook in their art. Art in the postmodern times continues as social commentary affirming that rationality and causality are not all they're cracked up to be.

Stocking Culturally Damaged Goods

Postmodern culture has learned not to take itself too seriously. "*Spy* magazine reports that camp is on the rise: 'This is the era of the permanent smirk, the knowing chuckle, of jokey ambivalence as a way of life. This is the Irony Epidemic,'"[57] according to Walter Anderson. The traditional values of modernity are met with jest.

Take, for instance, the song "Love and Marriage." Written in the fifties and performed by ol' blue eyes, Frank Sinatra himself, the song's lyrics celebrate how "love and marriage, they go together like a horse and carriage." Yet, in the nineties, the song was used as the theme for *Married with Children* and has now become an anthem to marriages gone wrong—a mocking parody that suggests love and marriage are damaged goods.

In some ways elements of the Christian faith fall into the same category. After countless western movies, could we ever ask anyone to sing "Bringing in the Sheaves" or "Shall We Gather at the River?" with a straight face? The people of the twenty-first century through TV and movies carry with them a high degree of cultural awareness, even regarding the Christian culture, so that the use of cliches and jargon will more than likely merit a chuckle or a yawn. For preaching, Christian cliches are anathema.

The Ironic versus the Heroic

Postmodernity is the age not of the heroic but of the ironic. It's an age when the antihero rules with such icons as Kurt Cobain, Cartman from *South Park*, Bart Simpson, Dennis Rodman, Beavis and Butthead, and Madonna. We exalt those who throw aside convention; since life has no objective meaning, this is perceived as one cosmic joke with no punch line. So, Andy Warhol paints the Campbell soup can or produces a film of a steady camera merely observing someone sleeping for hours and calls it "art." It's an art that does not seek to disguise its irreverence for what past generations held dear and precious.

A group of young people may enjoy something like *Speed Racer, The Brady Bunch,* or *Leave It to Beaver,* but they are laughing at it, not with it. As a result, timely expressions as in Robert Mapplethorpe's exhibit *Pulp Fiction* and the Andy Warhol collection reflect a culture that no longer believes in the values and norms of modernity. Postmodernity possesses little life of its own but feeds off the remains of modernity's dying carcass.

Retro: When the Future Dries Up

In relation to fashion and music, "retro" is bringing back in style a taste from the past. They thrive on the reinventing of former conventions, the psychedelic look of the sixties, the disco chic of the seventies, and the new wave of the eighties, and in each case, the trend was linked with music.

Examine the hit movies of the '90s: *The Avengers, Lost in Space, Maverick, The Fugitive, Mission Impossible,* and *The Brady Bunch.* Do these carry a familiar ring? They're all based on television shows of the fifties, sixties, and seventies.

As has been alluded to, the problem of postmodernity is a void of answers or new ideas; postmodernity is a buzzard with nothing but the bones of the past upon which to feed. The rock group, U2, sings, "When the future dries up, we re-invent the past."[58]

Such is the lot of postmodern times. All hope, all meaning, all ideas have dried up and all that remains is to do over what has been done before. All the retro and nostalgia allows people to relive the good ol' days when society had values but existed in a state of naivete or self-delusion as depicted in the movie *Pleasantville*. Anderson observes, "Entertainment, fashion, marketing, and the popular arts are full of camp, much of which boils down to young people enjoying things their parents and grandparents enjoyed—Humphrey Bogart movies, swing, tap dancing, drive-ins, Hawaiian shirts—while doing so in a way that makes it clear to one and all that they are just kidding."[59]

Postmodernity uses art and fashion to signify that there's no deeper meaning, only the now, the immediate. Veith comments, "A society devoted to instant gratification, conditioned by the immediacy of its information media and by its lack of moral restraints on immediate pleasure, will demand instant gratification in its arts and entertainment. . . . People who have no beliefs lack a sense of personal identity and an inner life. They are thus, in every sense of the term, superficial."[60]

This retro movement of reviving the past in a contemporary expression applies to history as well. History is viewed as nothing more than a style. By contemporarizing the various fads, the postmodern society claims the trends as its own. In the same way, Veith observes, "revisionist historians reinterpret past events according to contemporary concerns, seeing history through the lens of feminism, multiculturalism, and post-Marxist politics. Instead of recreating the mindset of the time, contemporary renditions present the past as a mirror of our own times."[61]

Examples of this revisionist outlook of history on a popular level abound in movies such as *The Right Stuff, Braveheart,* and the notorious *JFK*. A classic example of revisionist history on film is *Rambo*, which retells the Vietnam war story the way Americans would have liked it to happen. *Rambo* creates the notion that defeat came because bureaucrats handcuffed fighting men like John Rambo, preventing them from doing what they do best. In the movie, John Rambo, the renegade, accomplishes what the entire U.S. military was unable to do: win the war.

Another example is *Robin Hood, Prince of Thieves*. The movie presents, as Veith describes it, "the medieval outlaw as suffering post-traumatic stress syndrome from the Crusades. Accompanied by his merry band of multicultural homeless victims, he and the feminist Maid Marian oppose the Sheriff of Nottingham's multinational corporation and save Sherwood Forest's environment."[62] Postmodernity has a way of embracing the past and re-creating it into its present understanding of the world. And why not? After all, history is only what we make it out to be. Much of the Christian faith is tied to conventionality and the quaint surroundings of modernity. Carson contends, "the harsh reality is that most Americans, including most of those in our churches, have been so shaped by the popular culture that no thoughtful preacher can afford to ignore the impact."[63] One task of the biblical communicator will be just getting people to take the Bible seriously again.

Questing for Community

The Enlightenment exalted the status of the individual to new heights, then the Reformation brought stirrings of the rise of the individual. In reform thinking, the onus moved from belonging to the Church, the corporate body, to each individual's responsibility to believe and accept Christ on a personal level. With the translation of the Bible into the languages of the people, each person bore the priestly honor of reading and studying God's Word for himself or herself. Postmodernity hasn't jettisoned the value of the individual; however, a deep longing for community has begun to surface.

Television viewing is becoming more a social event. Like a night at the movies, generation Xers commonly gather in one apartment around television sets to watch sitcoms like *Friends,* a primetime hit in the ratings about six attractive, twenty-something men and women. These shows are really about relationships, Iliffe observes: "The authenticity of relationships and the integrity of community hold a powerful attraction for a new generation of young people struggling to find something lasting in today's throwaway culture—something precious in the midst of a society that feeds on trash and greed."[64] As the singer/songwriter Sting declares in one of his award-winning tunes, "You could say I've lost my belief in science. You could say I've lost my faith in the Holy Church. But if I ever lose my faith in you, there'd be nothing left for me to lose." You see, in an age of meaninglessness, there's not much for people to cling to. As people search for what's transcendent, most will encounter the meaning in and through relationships.

Also contributing toward the pursuit of community is technology's development, according to John Nesbitt's forecasts in his best-seller *Megatrends*. He called the phenomenon "high tech/high touch,"[65] explaining that increased use of technology would lead people to seek more human touch. Generation X represents the group most immersed into computers and technological gadgetry. The effect is an increased desire to be more attached to nature but in a similar fashion, a craving for meaningful relationships.

The second contributing factor not to be missed is the breakdown of the nuclear family. "While baby boomers value success and achievement, baby busters value belonging and acceptance. . . . That desire for acceptance and belonging stems from the loneliness and alienation of splintered family attachments."[66]

For many generation Xers, simply being together and talking about life helps them know that they're not alone in their common struggles and longings. According to Veith: "The combination of social changes, technological developments, and postmodernist ideology has undermined the very principle of a unified national culture and has driven individuals to find their identities in subcultures."[67] Subcultures represent pockets of people finding acceptance and security through the formation of communities, a place to belong.

Consequently the process, or how things are done, becomes increasingly important because the bottom line alone matters less. Working carefully and constructively in relationships to achieve a goal will mean that accomplishing a task may take even longer. Crass task orientation at the expense of relationships will be met with stiff opposition. This attention to process affects preaching as well as how the church functions. Communication must be more than the dissemination of ideas or obtaining a predetermined response from the listener such as coming forward or raising their hand in commitment.

Since relationships rate foremost, authenticity and trust act as vital ingredients in relating well. "Unlike the sixties and seventies, when there was a crisis of skepticism among young people, today there is a crisis of suspicion," observes Jim Ingram, director at L'Abri, speaking from his encounters with today's youth. "That means the first step we take is to establish a relationship of trust with young people who have been hurt and let down. We take time to get to know the person. . . . We can only overcome this deeply held suspicion if we can first prove that we can be trusted."[68]

Postmodernity comes with a generation that has grown up in broken homes, been lied to by politicians, and deceived by church and community leaders. The church makes bold claims but rarely delivers on its own message of love, reconciliation, and compassion.

"The struggle," comments Roof, "is to get beyond the facade, the external shell of religion, to its 'embodiment,' or the link between spirituality and responsibility."[69] Yet, that will be a challenge as this is a generation without heroes. Today's listeners don't believe in much anymore, and nothing is more distasteful than empty ritual divorced from everyday living.

The people of postmodernity will warm to more participatory events and activities. Educationally speaking, they'll want to be actively involved in the learning process. For instance, while baby boomers were more consumed with downloading information and data, generation Xers want to interact with what's being said and see the way something works in everyday life. Boomers are the products of TV screens and busters are the product of computer screens. All of these come with profound implications to the church and how Christians will undertake to do ministry in the days ahead.

Living in the Material World

In the film *Apollo 13*, technology fails. Three marooned American astronauts must now rely on their human know-how to get themselves back to earth, preventing a cold death in space. With a crippled spacecraft, human ingenuity must find the way home.

Postmodernity presents the same dilemma: Technological advances will not get us home, so we are left to our own devices to find a way. David Cook sums up the postmodern spirit as follows: "Gone are the optimism and confident expectation that everything will get better, and that disease and human failings will be overcome. In its place we have a disillusion with all that is modern and a search for another framework of life. There is a loss of certainty, and in its place there are a skepticism and cynicism about life, each other and the future."[70]

Many postmodern people no longer look to the future or for a grand design; what remains is the here and now. Postmodernity purports that words, literature, history, and art contain no real meaning. "Scratch to get beneath the surface," postmodernity tells you, "but you'll discover there's nothing there—no depth, no substance. Life is superficial and appearance counts for everything. You need not take anything seriously because everything's merely froth and bubble."

Yet, postmodernity adds, "People are like an onion. Peel away the layers and you'll find something concrete. You'll discover that all anybody consists of is a multitude of layers." It's in this framework that postmodernists live and move and have their being, which raises the question, "What is left of life?"

The pop group Wang Chung suggests in one song, "On the edge of oblivion and all the world is Babylon and all the love and everyone's a ship of fools sailing on. So everybody have fun tonight."

The film *Trainspotting* echoes this as it chronicles the lives of streetwise heroin addicts in Great Britain. A Christian youth worker would later comment, "The advertising for *Trainspotting* uses the phrase, 'Laughing in the dark,' reflecting the attitude of enjoying the moment despite the ultimate meaninglessness of life."[71]

Some will seek a higher meaning, while others will opt for a self-help path, but for many, the answer will simply be good times. The ancient philosophy of hedonism grew out of a belief that this earthly existence was all life offered.

Cook speaks for the generation Xers of postmodernity: "We want to have fun. We want the good things in life and we want them here and now. Our needs are at the centre of our existence."[72]

In postmodernity, the ride of life is headed down a dead-end road, so one might as well sit back and enjoy the scenery. Cook adds: "So the only reality is the perpetual present. The only world is today—now. Time is just a series of 'now' events that have no order or meaning. They are essentially chaotic."[73]

The movie *Pulp Fiction* embodies this sense of the meaningless, featuring a web of plotlines, in which the viewer is introduced to a collection of seedy and despicable characters with little trace of moral evaluation of them or their actions. In a scene cleverly designed to capture one of the largest laughs of the movie, an accidental gunshot in a moving vehicle blows the head off of an unsuspecting backseat passenger. Life contains no lessons, no morals, no redemptive acts, just random violence often cast in a humorous light. Picking up the existentialist chord, postmodernity proclaims that life is an absurd, cosmic joke, so one can despair or laugh at our predicament.

Postmodernity could easily have produced a society so full of despair that people merely rolled over and conceded that life is not worth living. The rise in teen suicide in the Western world testifies to this sentiment. However, for the most part, generation Xers are keen to experience life and live life to the full. One need only observe the booming entertainment, electronic games, and sporting industries to see how hard people are willing to work at their play.

Bill Cosby lampoons this pursuit of pleasure in a stand-up comedy act about a good time on the weekend. Cosby acts out the person who announces to his family on Friday night, "I'm going out to have a good time . . . because I deserve it."

This good time translates into drinking so much alcohol that he ends up vomiting into the toilet or as Cosby describes, "placing one's head where one's rear should be." Cosby is quick to remind the audience that this is all done in the name of a good time. The pursuit of pleasure is not always a pleasurable experience, nor a satisfying one, but people keep trying all the same.

Accompanying pleasure-seeking in a relativistic society is the need for options. A consumer culture demands variety and gets it, for after all, people become bored and the customer is always right. For example, the nineties have witnessed the explosion of extreme sports onto the cultural scene; activities of previous generations like cycling, skiing, mountain climbing, and skating are deemed passé and too pedestrian for today's youth. The "adrenaline junkies" are constantly seeking the bigger rush. With this pursuit come new experiences such as snowboarding, mountain biking, base jumping, bungee jumping, and sky surfing.

This propensity toward variety has resulted in shorter attention spans as the TV remote control has become a standard operating fixture in most homes. And another result: If you don't like what you're watching, there are fifty other cable channels to choose from; if you don't like what's on any channel, you can play Nintendo. When Nintendo bores you, then you can always catch the latest video release. In a postmodern society, you see, boredom may be deemed the greatest of all sins.

The Pepsi generation is not alone in seeking variety. Parents of the X-generation will be wanting more out of life as well. As the boomers turn fifty, retirement communities will no longer consist of shuffleboard, lawn bowls, and card tables. The demand must be met for jogging tracks, workout gyms, and a plethora of sporting pleasures. The retirement village as we have traditionally understood it will be changed dramatically and will not look back. The proliferation of four-wheel-drive vehicles, affectionately known as "yuppie assault vehicles," will continue as a trend. The typical owners of these vehicles are profiled as overworked professionals with little discretionary time. They, however, see the purchase of these vehicles as shrewd because, in their thinking, "We may want to go camping or do some off-road driving." The likelihood of which is slim, but the consumer contents himself in knowing, "I'm keeping my options open. It's there if I want it."

Who Says Money Can't Buy Happiness

The search for meaning will also drive people down the materialistic trail. The lavish spending of the eighties created a significant reaction against the crassness of materialism in the nineties. However, it didn't extinguish the postmodern drive for things. With renewed interest in the environment and relationships, materialism took a knock, but that's far from a deathblow.

We're more aware now of the pitfalls of materialism, but somehow feel that contributing to the Greenies keeps our pursuit of new toys in perspective. David Cook writes that even though today's youth are environmentally and spiritually more conscious, "Generation X seems at one level genuinely and thoroughly materialistic [wanting] things and the pleasure and experiences that things bring. . . . What once would have been regarded as luxuries (entertainment systems, computer games) are now viewed as necessities of life."[74]

So those of us living in postmodern times seem to want it both ways, and we don't want to sacrifice one thing for another. If life is about "livin' large," postmoderns believe, the best way to go about it is with money and freedom from any responsibilities of employment. Australia's lottery campaign has picked up on this idea with the question, "What ya goin' to do when you win lotto?" The great dream of traveling the world, fine cars, fancy restaurants, basically "livin' large," is dangled like a carrot before millions of willing participants each day.

"The modern economy saw people as producers," Veith declares. "The postmodern economy sees them as consumers. The American economy is now 'market-driven,' which means not only that companies must have up-to-the-minute information about their customers, but that they must aggressively advertise what they sell."[75]

Again, it's worth remembering that a fallout of the consumer age is people have grown cynical of always being targeted for a sale, and this cynicism extends to the church. Postmodern people view their time as a commodity, and a precious one, so the very thought of "wasting" a Sunday morning with little or no take-home value is repugnant.

Like it or not, this is our culture. God calls Christians to speak into this culture His thoughts and His message. As biblical communicators, your task is not a simple one—it's to bring God's truth to bear upon a people who are searching for, yet uncertain of, truth and falsehood; of people open, but skeptical, and livin' large while running on empty.

3 | Rules for Engagement

Four principles will make the difference in the effectiveness of your preaching in our postmodern climate: Not engaging listeners at the expense of the message, knowing that good communication takes two—and time, your degree of risk to get involved with those you're speaking to, and how you address the world in which your listeners live. Each of these things deserves a closer look.

Don't Engage at the Expense of the Message

International speaker Ravi Zacharias declares, "Every generation will try to get [preachers] to change the message. . . . We are called to be faithful to our calling in the Word."[1] The Bible is clear on this: "Preach the Word; be prepared in season and out of season; correct, rebuke and encourage with great patience and careful instruction" (2 Tim. 4:2).

Or as Ian Pitt-Watson rightly states: Make the "what" of your preaching more important than the "how."[2]

In examining the how of preaching in a postmodern climate, and seeking to maintain both the authority and integrity of God's Word, three dangers become clear. The first is preachers could lose confidence in God's Word or, with only a Bible in hand, feel overwhelmed by postmodernity's tidal-wave-like force. The second: Preachers might stoop to a type of reduced perspective that shrinks God and His truth to accommodate listeners. Third: Preachers might adapt an essentially pragmatic approach.

Where does that fear behind the first danger come from? Well, the struggle to address biblical issues can be daunting when people no longer remember the questions. It makes you appreciate what the apostle Paul must have felt in writing to the ruling city of the known world, "I am not ashamed of the gospel of Christ because it is the power of God for the salvation of everyone who believes" (Rom. 1:16).

Regarding the second danger, if the preacher relinquishes the reliance upon the supernatural presence of the living Word, no cultural insight can fill that void. Either God has spoken and still speaks to the hearts of people or preachers are to be pitied above all.

"People are driven from the Church not so much by stern truth that makes them uneasy," George Buttrick once said, "as by weak nothings that make them contemptuous."[3]

Duane Litfin is quick to underscore that need for integrity: "We are not talking about 'pulling punches' or shading the truth so as to make it palatable. Such practices can be a subtle form of lying to an audience and are unethical."[4]

The tension remains in knowing what's culturally expendable and what's biblically nonnegotiable. For instance, some churches now conduct worship services on days other than Sunday. Is a particular day for worship cultural baggage or does the fact that early Christians met for worship on the day of Christ's resurrection make it nonnegotiable?

Inevitably every preacher will be required to proclaim godly truths that are counterculture, principles that run against the grain of general society. But that, remember, was the nature of following Christ. You cannot lessen the demands of authentic discipleship, nor should you avoid simplifying the Christian life into ten easy steps, or twisting the promises of God into Jesus' plan for health and happiness. Distortions of God's message, for whatever reason, are a disservice to the Lord; genuine concern for biblical integrity and one's listeners will demand that they come to understand God's truth and calling in all its complexity and fullness.

The preacher's third danger of falling into pragmatism is serious. When you know the right switches to flip, you may be tempted to preach in order to garner a response. But just because something works doesn't make it right or biblical. A preacher may completely mishandle a text, close with a heart-wrenching story of a boy and his dog, and have people repenting up and down the aisles.

That's why when we speak of effective preaching, this is not to say the preaching necessarily works or gets results. Effectiveness must be understood in terms of bringing the listener to a clear appreciation of the biblical message.

Steve Brown puts it this way, "I don't think we need to change our material. We're not market-driven in the sense that we find out whatever they need and then provide it. That's from the pit of hell and smells of smoke. We listen to the pain of the world and then go to God's Word and say, 'Does it speak to this pain?' If it does—it just does, it really does."[5]

Our knowledge of the listeners, their bias and predisposition to and against certain ideas, becomes a means, not a substitute, to leading them to a full comprehension of all God is and what He intends for their lives.

Many pastors and laypeople still carry misconceptions about what is meant by "expository preaching." John Stott affirms this: "All true Christian preaching is expository preaching. If by an 'expository' sermon is meant a verse-by-verse explanation of a lengthy passage of Scripture . . . this would be a misuse of the word. . . . It refers to the content of the sermon (biblical truth) rather than the style (a running commentary). To expound Scripture is to bring out of the text what is there and expose it to view. . . . Whether it is long or short, our responsibility as expositors is to open it up in such a way that it speaks its message clearly, plainly, accurately, relevantly, without addition, subtraction or falsification."[6]

So, as Stott distinguishes, the content is biblical and style will vary. The content, however, remains grounded in careful exegesis of God's Word. With that always in mind, seek the most effective approaches of bringing the postmodern heart, mind, and soul to God.

Communication Takes Two—and Time

Since preaching involves a divine encounter, the fallacy might be drawn that basic communication principles somehow need not apply. Just return to Bible-based preaching, some preachers might argue in a call for less attention to communication skills and techniques. These folks are kind of Christian Luddites who want to get back to the basics.

Granted, the Bible is the required text but the proper preaching of God's all-important message should likewise maintain excellence in communication. Donald Smith defines the aim of communication as "to gain access to the mind through the gate of understanding," and he acknowledges "the Holy Spirit brings a response that [the human communicator] can never produce by artful communication." But that doesn't mean you shouldn't try to communicate more skillfully, he says: "The best we can do is strive to give understanding. We can give the message so that there will be clarity in hearing. When we have helped someone comprehend the message, the Holy Spirit makes the mysterious inner link."[7]

By the same token, communication skill alone is not the clincher in speaking to postmodern people. In his book *Why Don't People Listen?* Hugh Mackay cautions against what he calls the injection myth, or treating messages rather like drugs that act on other people's minds. The injection myth, he says, "assumes that messages have inherent power. In order to be effective communicators—the theory goes—we first have to craft our messages as carefully as we can, so as to maximize our impact on the listener."[8]

If the message is well presented, why don't people hear it?

"People are not blank slates on which we write our messages," Mackay says. "People are a pulsating bundle of attitudes, values, prejudices, experience, feelings, thoughts, sensations and aspirations. They are active, not passive, even when they are listening."[9]

Our message is not a drug injected into the listener to somehow overpower him or her. In Mark 4, Jesus likened the gospel to seed spread over a wide area—whether it grew or not depended on the receptiveness of the soil or the human heart.

For this reason, theologian and author Calvin Miller discovered: "The more you know about your audience, the greater are your chances of achieving your persuasive goals. Over and over during the research and preparation phases of your speech you should ask the question, 'Who is my audience?'"[10]

So you must know the One from whom the message comes, you must know the message, and you must know the ones to whom the message will go.

Ask yourself before delivering a message: "Do the words and ideas here have relevance and meaning?"

Edward de Bono explains the difference. "A toilet sign at an airport may have meaning but no relevance if you do not happen to need to go to the toilet. If you need to go to the toilet, the sign has both meaning and relevance. If you were in Japan or Greece and could not even read the lettering, the sign would have relevance but no meaning. So you would never know how relevant it was."[11]

For many postmodern listeners the message of the Bible has no meaning, and they don't understand it. For others the message of the Bible has no relevance and bears no importance. Many listeners feel as if the Bible has nothing substantial to say to people living in our time; for some the message of the Bible has neither meaning nor relevance. The role of the preacher is to supply both meaning and relevance to people who initially do not understand the message nor perceive its need. Preaching must consist of both aspects, meaning and relevance. In addressing postmodern listeners, to assume the meaning or relevance of what is about to be preached represents a costly error in judgment.

The apostle Paul wrote, "I have become all things to all men so that by all possible means I might save some" (1 Cor. 9:22).

Duane Litfin elaborates on the value of adapting the message to the listener, "We are instead emphasizing the need to take advantage of all the elements within any given speaking situation so that your audience, to the greatest extent possible, will be able to comprehend and willing to act upon your ideas. You can achieve this by (1) understanding your audience, who they are, how they think and feel, what their perceived and unperceived needs are; and then (2) relating your ideas to them in such a way that they can see your meaning and its relevance to them."[12]

Look at the model of communication in the story of Nathan and King David (2 Samuel 12). Granted, Nathan holds the role of prophet, but David was the king, a warrior king, the king who had taken another man's wife and eliminated the husband. Imagine you're Nathan. It's easy to arrive at the various scenarios that could have resulted from this confrontation with David. The majority of these scenarios end up with you—Nathan—dead. As king, David could have lashed out at Nathan, or ignored a stern rebuke and hardened his heart even more.

Nathan, however, takes the proud king off guard, by stealth. Nathan returns David to his humble beginnings as a shepherd boy. He unfolds the story of the poor man, possessing nothing but a little ewe lamb he had bought and raised (2 Sam. 12:3), adding the tender touch that the lamb slept in his arms. The message captured the heart of the fierce warrior-king as he recalled his own boyhood experiences.

As David listens intently, readers can imagine the veins in David's neck beginning to bulge. By the time Nathan reaches the closing injustice where the little ewe lamb is callously taken away, David shouts in anger, "As surely as the Lord lives, the man who did this deserves to die!" (2 Sam. 12:5).

Then, Nathan utters the immortal words, "You are the man!" (2 Sam. 12:7).

In the story of the lamb, in knowing David's background, Nathan was able to pierce through David's defenses so that God's Spirit might convict him and bring him to the point of repentance: "I have sinned against the Lord" (12:13). The same story might not have touched a different man, but it was perfectly tailored for David, the shepherd boy turned king. David was both the poor man and the rich man in the story. He viewed himself as the poor man at first. By the conclusion, he knew he stood before God as the callous, rich man. It helps to know one's audience so that the message can penetrate the walls of self-deception and self-denial. See how knowing one's listener makes you a more effective communicator for God?

Communication Means More than Issuing Words

George Hunter III asserts that today's mass audiences "doubt the intelligence, relevance, and credibility of the church and its advocates."[13] This is a polite way of saying, "people don't think much of preachers." Part of the problem may be that preachers often don't think much of their listeners either. How long can we continue to address questions that our listeners are not asking? And will we maintain an approach that suggests to them, "You don't live in the same world that I do"?

The communication task is more than the mere use of words. Communication is the reception of words and perceptions by the listener on a cognitive, intuitive, and emotional level. The message received has more to do with the tone of a speaker's voice, the gestures, and facial expressions than the words chosen.[14]

Aristotle spoke of the *logos*, the words, the *ethos*, the motive of the speaker, and the *pathos*, the emotional appeal to the audience. Each of these elements plays a key role in the communication process. For modern listeners, preaching was the age of the *logos*, the word. For twenty-first-century listeners, preaching must value the *ethos* and *pathos* as well, both the message's perception and feel.

Calvin Miller highlights the necessity of these three ingredients, stating, "If the speaker's ethos is corrupt, then the *logos* will be self-seeking and the *pathos* of the audience will render them feeling tricked or deceived. If the speaker's ethos is sterling but the *logos* is not well developed, the *pathos* will be rendered suspect. If any portion of the Aristotelian triad is weak or incorrect, the communique will be spoiled."[15]

Unfortunately, many sermons may be delivered with careful theological correctness in word, but then a non-Christian expression in tone. In fact too often preaching has reflected a harsh and critical spirit. People may assume from the speaker's demeanor that the preacher does not like them much and conversely, that God does not care for them much either. "Much of what passes as 'prophetic' preaching is actually just anger cloaked in a sermon" laments Haddon Robinson. "It's simply another way of telling the world to get lost."[16]

Tony Campolo tells the story from his own boyhood experience of attending a revival meeting, when the tent meeting was in its heyday. The stern evangelist vividly described the fiery torments of hell that awaited the unrepentant sinner. Closing his message, the speaker pointed a bony finger to his audience and pronounced, "If you leave this place without knowing Jesus and cross the street outside and get hit by a car, you will go straight to hell."

Campolo recalls, "The message did not make me want to know Jesus but it did make me look both ways when I crossed the street."

Inadvertently the wrong message was communicated. The message of grace and redemption was heard as a message of judgment and condemnation. Which message are we about—grace or condemnation? Remember, the "how" of what is said can make a difference as to whether the "what" is received.

Risk Involvement

Engaging with the listener presupposes two factors: the speaker's interest in and understanding of the listener's world. The proper motivation for ministry remains Christ's love—that is, the love of Christ experienced in the speaker and the love of Christ for those being served. For Paul writes, "Christ's love compels us" (2 Cor. 5:14).

"Any hope for involvement must start with the attitude of the preacher," suggest Ralph and Gregg Lewis in *Inductive Preaching.* "He or she has to want involvement. But that desire must grow directly out of care felt for the people. No one cares how much we know until he knows how much we care."[17]

This returns us to the speaker's *ethos.*

The other presupposition to engaging the listener entails understanding the world. Donald Smith encourages preachers: "Study the audience, learn their needs, interests, and ways of expressing their concerns; then rephrase the message to capitalize on their susceptibilities—after all, the message is so important that they must be made to listen."[18]

Since in preaching both the meaning and relevance have to be supplied, capturing and maintaining interest can be a difficult task. In reality, the sermon creates a clash of cultures: the culture of Christ with its norms and values and the postmodern culture with its own norms and values.

For the logos of the Christian message to connect with the contemporary listener, the preacher must first enter the listener's sphere of postmodern understanding.

Steven Covey, in his best-selling book *The Seven Habits of Highly Effective People,* relates the necessity of seeing life through the eyes of another:

I remember a mini-paradigm shift I experienced one Sunday morning on a subway in New York. People were sitting quietly—some reading newspapers, some lost in thought, some resting with their eyes closed. It was a calm, peaceful scene.

Then, suddenly, a man and his children entered the subway car. The children were so loud and rambunctious that instantly the whole climate changed. They sat down next to me and their father closed his eyes, apparently oblivious to the situation. The children were yelling back and forth, throwing things, even grabbing people's papers. It was very disturbing. And yet, the man sitting next to me did nothing.

It was difficult not to feel irritated. I could not believe that he could be so insensitive as to let his children run wild like that and do nothing about it, taking no responsibility at all. It was easy to see that everyone else on the subway felt irritated, too.

So, finally, with what I felt was unusual patience and restraint, I turned to him and said, "Sir, your children are really disturbing a lot of people, I wonder if you couldn't control them a little more?"

The man lifted his gaze as if to come to a consciousness of the situation for the first time and said softly, "Oh, you're right. I guess I should do something about it. We just came from the hospital where their mother died about an hour ago. I don't know what to think, and I guess they don't know how to handle it either."

Can you imagine what I felt at that moment? My paradigm shifted. Suddenly, I saw things differently, and because I saw things differently I thought differently, I felt differently, I behaved differently. My irritation vanished. I didn't have to worry about controlling my attitude or my behavior; my heart was filled with the man's pain. Feelings of sympathy and compassion flowed freely.

"Your wife just died? Oh, I'm so sorry! Can you tell me about it? What can I do to help?"

Everything changed in an instant.[19]

Before one can begin to bring meaning and relevance to the listener, the preacher must gain entry into his or her sphere of understanding. This speaks of the incarnational ministry of Christ, who first entered our realm so that we might enter His realm.

Listeners become involved as they sense the speaker's involvement in their lives. This addresses the ethos, the attitude of the speaker as perceived by the listener, which weighs heavily in the postmodern perception. Some preachers might resent the fact that the message of Christ could be evaluated upon the merits of the messenger, and not upon the worth of the message itself. However, the Bible has not shied away from the reality that the Christian message can be either vindicated or dismissed based on the behavior of those heralding the message.

What was it Jesus said? "A new commandment I give you: Love one another. As I have loved you, so you must love one another. By this all men will know that you are my disciples if you love one another" (John

13:34–35). In a similar way, Jesus prayed, "May [Christians] be brought to complete unity to let the world know that you sent me and have loved them even as you have loved me" (John 17:23).

In a postmodern context, where authority is suspect and people mistrust those in power, what may make the difference as to whether one listens or tunes out is the perceived attitude of the preacher. "Does the speaker care about me?" or "Can I trust what I am about to hear?"

The information age of postmodernity is also the advertisement age, a time in which people have become accustomed to being lied to and deceived. How can we disarm these fears and apprehensions?

"Let people know you have nothing to gain personally from influencing them," Tom Nash says, cautioning against a sales approach to the gospel. "[Then people] will be more likely to believe you."[20]

For this reason the twenty-first century may signal a decline in the effectiveness of itinerant preaching in which the speaker is an unknown quantity and lacks a preexisting basis of trust upon which to speak. The issue of trust will be the unexpressed reality in the minds of those who fill the seats.

On the other hand, when the speaker demonstrates an understanding of contemporary concerns and issues as well as the pressures to reject a biblical worldview, listeners will sense a personal interest. Listeners today will have their antenna up, looking for the speaker's personal agenda or angle. Is the speaker's desire to wield influence or chalk up another notch on the response list? When compassion and mercy flow from the messenger, people may walk away having listened and be unwilling to embrace the message and yet still maintain an openness because they perceived genuine concern.

The trustworthiness of the message may well be measured by the trustworthiness of the one delivering the message. Mackay explains, "Before other people will be prepared to level with us (let alone make themselves vulnerable by revealing too much about themselves) we must show ourselves willing to level with them."[21]

Ralph and Gregg Lewis agree: "Meaningful ministry requires more than risking our sermons. It means risking ourselves. It means placing ourselves in the pew with our people, admitting our humanness to ourselves and to them, and preaching with the conviction that we all are 'workers together with God.' That personal risk is the price of involvement; the preacher becomes vulnerable."[22]

If people perceive the preacher as lording it over them or as somehow speaking down to them from an exalted position, this will be an obstacle to the message.

Since personal involvement means removing obstacles that might prevent communication, we should consider carefully elements in preaching like the layout of the platform, pulpit, lighting, and congregational seating. For instance, large pulpits might look beautiful to the eye, but may be communicating an aloofness and distance between the preacher and the people.

Be aware of physical appearance, too. Does your attire obstruct or help communication? Pointing with an outstretched index finger is commonly understood to be the gesture of a superior person to an inferior one, so why do that? Why not seek to remove the obstacles that block communication?

To illustrate this, the pastor John Wood, the father of best-selling author Catherine Marshall, went calling upon a new member of his congregation at the man's place of work. When the pastor extended his hand in greeting, the man apologetically replied, "Can't shake hands with you, reverend. My hands are too grimy."

With that the pastor reached down and rubbed his own hands in the coal dust and then offered his blackened hand to the worker, asking, "How about it now?"[23]

Risking involvement is part of the communication process and it means being willing to enter the listener's world and open up your own.

Address Where You Live

Why do people get bored and lose attention to talk? Could it be the listener was never engaged from the outset?

"The interest [of a listener] may lie in the word 'interest,'" writes Edward de Bono. "What makes something interesting? The answer is extremely valuable because if you are making films or designing TV programmes or publishing books you need to know what your viewers and readers are going to find interesting."[24]

Sermons can fail to garner any interest because people frankly may not be interested in the Bible and can't see why they should be. Well then, what is on the mind of people living in our day? What is of value and interest to them?

The listener gets involved when the preacher addresses an area of human need. In sermon preparation this can mean addressing an area of unresolved conflict within the listener that is a common and universal need. Consider Abraham Maslow's hierarchy of human needs, in order of importance:

1. Physical needs of food, health, and survival
2. Safety needs of personal security

3. Love needs of belonging to a group
4. Esteem needs of being respected and appreciated
5. The need for self-actualization to fulfill one's potential.[25]

Calvin Miller argues that there are six basic questions that every generation raises: "What is the purpose of life? What am I doing here? How did I come to be? Where will I end up? How can I be happy, or happier, at least? What does it mean to be human?"[26]

Ravi Zacharias adds, "Life's difficulties make the questioner more reachable. God often enters our lives through brokenness to show that we're not as autonomous as we think."[27] Through connecting areas of human brokenness and apparent need to the biblical passage, the preacher draws the listener to become involved in what's said.

So have human needs changed in the postmodern shift? It's not so much that the needs have changed but how people perceived them. A classic example is Menninger's *Whatever Happened to Sin?* The problem of sin didn't disappear but how people perceived the problem changed.

Dealing with the biblical concept of sin may be one of the greatest challenges to twenty-first-century preaching. In the current cultural climate, sin and guilt are no longer an issue or have been recalibrated beyond any scriptural recognition. So a message might begin with the assumption that people want release from their guilt.

However, the problem has moved, now becoming "How can I feel good about myself?" which is not to be confused with any condition of forgiveness. This shift from sin to self-image reflects a move, not just in society but in the church.

We have replaced a fundamentally theological perspective with a psychological approach to life and the world. Sadly, much of what passes as biblical preaching is nothing more than pop psychology wrapped in poor exegesis. As preachers, are we asking, "How can I help my listeners to think more biblically about their lives?" "How can I cultivate a theological understanding of their world when they have grown accustomed to thinking in psychological terms?"

Preachers should be asking, "How does the shift from modernity to a postmodern world affect a person's perception of Christianity?" For those schooled in modernity, the issue surrounding the Christian faith was, "Is it true?"

As a result, many preachers and apologists sought to address the intellectual inquiries of the listener. In postmodernity, the question of truth is not dismissed entirely but people no longer understand "reality" as an act of reason alone. Therefore, in connecting with the needs of the listener one should be aware that within postmodernity, the "heart," or intuitive and emotional response evoked within the listener, is oftentimes a more powerful and fruitful avenue than the "head," which is a more cognitive and rational approach. Addressing the needs of the listener will involve more than taking an intellectual approach to issues. It also means touching the emotional and intuitive areas.

Again, this brings back the injection myth of communication. Many critics of preaching to human need argue that biblical truth is like medicine. People don't need to be convinced of the medicine's effectiveness; they simply need to consume it and allow it to work.

However, I would argue that the communication of God's Word is more complicated than that. Preaching that consistently connects with the listeners does so by uncovering the area of human need within a passage of Scripture and then speaking in a way that compels the listener to hear what the Bible says.

Some critics have argued that preaching to the need of the individual reduces the Scriptures to self-help material and turns God into the great "need-meeter" in the sky. Some would say that the preacher who speaks this way merely fosters a crass, human self-centeredness. This, of course, might be true if one both begins and ends with meeting human needs. Consider the ministry of Jesus. Could not this same criticism be leveled at Jesus Himself who said, "Come to me, all you who are weary and burdened and I will give you rest" (Matt. 11:28)?

Connecting through a human need as the starting point of one's sermon is only the first half of the process. Yet, in order for communication to commence at all, there must be some level of commonality. Something must click within the heart and mind of the listener to say, "This is worthy of attention." Far too often, sermons begin at the point of the text, at a point of meaning for the preacher like, "Let's see what Paul has to say in Colossians 2 for us." The assumption that the speaker makes is that people care what is in Colossians 2 or that even godly people in the maelstrom of life have arrived on Sunday in a frame of mind prepared to listen to Colossians 2.

Michael Hostetler, in his excellent work on sermon introductions, writes, "If a sermon fails to engage the listeners in their need and to relate to their sins and failures, their fears and hopes, it is both a homiletical and a pastoral failure."[28] Biblical preaching needs to recognize the current needs and issues from the listeners' perspective in order to move them to God's perspective.

Preaching may also draw upon life experiences common to the speaker and listener, Hostetler adds: "Most sermons should begin with the life experience of the listener. I call this 'the secular' derived from the Latin word *saeculum*, which means 'age' or 'time.' . . . It suggests the experience of life in the world, day-by-day, week-by-week. It is this temporal life that makes an effective contact point for the sermon introduction and provides the best way to grab attention and establish rele-vancy."[29] He further states his case, "preaching today must prove the Bible's relevancy, not presume it. That is why secular references at the start of a sermon are much more likely to relate to the audience."[30]

Life experiences provide a means of establishing both interest and relevance. One must imagine two spheres that represent the life of the listener and the life of the speaker. In leading off an address with a story from ancient history, the speaker is beginning at a point outside both spheres.

To speak of one's own passion for rock collecting may well touch deeply within the speaker's sphere but remains outside the sphere of the average listener. If a preacher were to relate an experience of being stood up for a date in high school, just about everyone listening would iden-tify on some level. Listeners then hang onto the speaker's words because they, too, have felt the sting of personal rejection. The preacher then moves the listeners from their own world to the biblical world, with a bridge phrase like, "The passage we're examining this morning addresses how we can break the heart of God. . . ." People have been moved from indifference to identification.

On the use of story Mackay says, "The key word here is 'identifica-tion'. When we find ourselves identifying with a person in a news item, or a character in a film, a play or a novel, we are drawn into the story in a way which doesn't happen if we remain mere spectators to it."[31]

Paul, in Acts 17, began his address on Mars Hill by referring to the altar to the unknown god. Paul's starting point targeted both the unre-solved need arising from a polytheistic system that inevitably left some gods out and the life experience of the listener who immediately iden-tified with the custom of ritual prayer to satisfy the many deities.

Postmodernity has leveled all authorities. Assumptions are critical, since it's difficult to build upon a foundation that doesn't exist in the mind of the listener; never forget listeners won't readily accept as a given that the Bible or any other source is true or valid for their life.

Consequently, life experiences form an intuitive basis in attempting to understand what is real and what is not. In other words, because all authorities are tainted and subjective, all that remains is the look inward. If the preacher can connect with a real life experience of the listener, this will validate to the individual that what he or she is about to hear possesses a ring of truth.

Educator and theologian Roberta Hestenes affirms this in adult learn-ing. "As adults grow, they learn to trust their own judgment and expe-rience more and more, and they test what they hear from others against their own sampling of reality," she explains. "If what the teacher says is not validated by their experience, they will not take the teacher's message seriously."[32]

In time, hopefully, the listener will be moved from that framework of self-reliance to a scripturally based foundation where the Bible is taken as true on face value. But few contemporary listeners begin at this point of trust either as converts of Christ or as Sunday worship attenders. So if the biblical communicator insists upon beginning from the authority of God's Word and not the experience of the listener, many listeners won't make a meaningful connection from the Bible to their lives. People only process information that they can apply immediately. A fallout of living in the information age is that people need to be shown that what they're about to hear will directly affect their lives, or they'll tune out. Hestenes states, "Probably no more than 10 percent of adults genuinely want to learn for learning's sake, to know the Bible simply in order to know the Bible (as a child might do in Sunday School). . . . Most adults want information they can use now. They want connections to everyday life. . . . Most of my teaching is essentially Bible-centered. But I try to find those crucial links between the Bible and real-world living."[33]

Preachers in the past may have imparted the meaning, or what is said, and left the listener to establish relevance, or what difference the information makes. This formula just doesn't wash anymore. People living in the information age will want to know the why of belief before knowing what to believe.

Another reason why establishing an early connection with the listener is vital to the communication process is because of what Hugh Mackay calls "the principle of reinforcement."

"Communication comes easily when a message supports what the other person already believes," Mackay warns. "But perhaps it is not so easy to appreciate that when you attack someone's cage (a person's way of seeing) you are just as likely to produce the reinforcement effect as if you had agreed with them. When we are attacked, we defend. In the process of defending our existing point of view, we actually reinforce it. It is one of the greatest frustrations of the communication process that if you attack someone else's point of view, the most likely outcome is that you will reinforce the very view you wanted to change."[34]

The direct, frontal assault on someone's position may be the simplest approach, but it rarely achieves the desired outcome. Those who advocate "Just tell it like it is" from the Bible may be only reinforcing the listener's already held perceptions.

Preaching has, at times, suffered because it was viewed as a one-way exercise of getting the message out to people. In fact, too many preachers, in their eagerness to present the wonderful truth gleaned from the text, have taken their message, backed up, and dumped it upon listeners like a cement mixer releasing its payload.

To connect today, however, a preacher involves listeners in the learning. Preachers show more of their own process in going through the Word to uncover those gleaned truths. Preachers must think of their listeners as the math teacher who says, "Let me see your work." Creative delivery enables the listeners to discover the truth for themselves as opposed to having ideas dropped in their lap. Creative processes such as an inductive structure of one's sermon, the use of story and narrative, dialogical forms of speaking will be elaborated further in this work.

People today get bored when not involved, and won't listen when they fail to see the meaning or importance of the message. In fact, they'll go a step farther and tune out when the message fails to connect with their interest. Preachers must think carefully as to how the material will be presented in order to create interest and involve the listener effectively in the communication process. Understanding postmodern people and their struggles is merely a prerequisite to connecting with them. It's about creating an atmosphere of trust, vulnerability, and commonality from which people might hear what God's Spirit would say to them.

4 | Challenging Listeners

The Mormon two-year missionary internship, which requires door-to-door confrontations, is one of the least effective means of outreach for the church of the Latter Day Saints. So why do the Mormons continue what's well documented as ineffective?

The answer lies in the statistics that show how after these missionaries have suffered daily abuse for their beliefs over a two-year period, there's every likelihood the candidates will remain Mormons for life. The more opposition people encounter, in other words, the more entrenched they can become in their own belief systems.

It's the same with postmodern listeners. Confrontational preaching, for example, doesn't have to be adversarial in approach. Directly assaulting a person's belief system or behaviors can only place that person on the defensive and strengthen the very beliefs you're attempting to dislodge.

But there are other ways to confront and effectively challenge both postmodern beliefs and biblical unbelief.

Become More Relational

In reference to the Mormon missionary who knocks on your door, you would do better to establish a friendly dialogue rather than a harangue. A gentle rapport will lead to authentic communication.

In dealing with the seemingly irreligious or misguided, an inherent strength in postmodern times is the belief that every person's perception is valid. With this belief comes an openness to explore and investigate the worldview of others.

One reason the Christian worldview is so highly criticized in a postmodern context lies in the apparent Christian unwillingness to coexist with any other viewpoint. Christians are then perceived to be threatened and incapable of dealing with a person's refusal to embrace our way of thinking. *Our inability to dialogue creates problems.*

"Creating identification means taking the postmodern world seriously and addressing it from a collaborative rather than an adversarial stance," suggests Craig Loscalzo. "A postmodern world demands a pulpit willing to be a viable conversation partner."[1]

For preachers to become "viable conversation partners" entails both a demonstration of understanding and listening to postmodern people. Preaching becomes less about the dissemination of ideas and more about relating to listeners with stories and life experiences.

Postmodernity, after all, is wired for exploring new frontiers. How can you communicate in a way that will draw the twenty-first-century listener to accompany all of us as Christians down the path of discovering the Bible's viewpoint?

Likewise, the relational aspect of preaching will be reflected in a deeper sensitivity and respect to the listeners. What preachers perceive to be an issue of belief may well end up being an issue of trust. Before people ask, "What have you to say?" they may ask, "Why should I even listen to you?"

Internationally known preacher Ravi Zacharias modeled this sensitivity during an exchange at the University of Thailand:

> I was speaking to the issues of existentialism, Marxism, pantheism, and Christianity, when a Muslim stood up and said, "You have just insulted your God by mentioning Karl Marx and Jean Paul Sartre in the same sentence in which you mentioned Christ." I could feel the irritation welling up inside me.
>
> I wanted to retort, "I have done nowhere near what the Muslim world has done in stripping Christ of his deity." Instead I paused, took a drink of water, and said, "I deeply appreciate your sensitivity. I know where you are coming from. But don't forget you also used all three names in the sentence as you raised the question for me. Did you mean to equate them by naming the three of them?"
>
> "No," he said.
>
> I replied, "Neither did I. Mentioning two names in the same sentence is hardly suggesting they are equal. But I want to commend you for your sensitivity because in many cultures we have lost reverence for the name of God."[2]

The natural inclination would be to deflate such a critic, but Zacharias was able to turn it around to compliment him; in return he gained a better, more open hearing that day from the students. Zacharias sums up the need for respect this way, "Nothing is as offensive as answers perceived to be mere words, uncaring of a human situation."[3] The privilege of speaking God's truth into someone else's life will not be granted. It should be earned.

Tune in to the Secular

The very word "secular" is that which is "not religious." It's no longer enough just to know one's Bible. Preaching must demonstrate a working understanding of the issues, concerns, and the interaction of people's daily lives, helping the listeners to interpret their world from a biblical standpoint.

Look at the apostle Paul's approach on Mars Hill in Acts 17. The apostle evidences some prior inquiry into the nature of the Epicurean and Stoic philosophies, which disregarded any belief in an afterlife.

The preacher in the twenty-first century will be one-part theologian, one-part sociologist, one-part evangelist, and one-part mystic—a person who genuinely encounters God.

It's a shame when fellow preachers write off even the attempt to engage our culture and state, "Why bother?" It's deemed a waste to peruse contemporary influences like Marianne Williamson's *Return to Love,* Joseph Campbell's *The Power of Myth,* Jonathan Demme's film *Philadelphia,* or to tune in to the *Oprah* show. Yet, these are the thought-shapers of our society.

For me, the isolationist approach is analogous to my role as father to my two children. If I as a parent fail to instruct them about sex, drugs, and the other issues they're sure to face, someone else will; if I don't pass on my values, someone else will pass on theirs.

At times biblical preaching has been reluctant to speak directly to the grittier matters of life. At one point I decided to speak frankly to our young people about sexual matters from a biblical perspective. I was well aware that I was walking a thin line because most people prefer their sermons to be G rather than PG 13 or worse.

An elderly man in his eighties approached me afterward and I braced myself for a verbal blast. In a low voice he gruffed, "When I was a young man, we never heard messages like that in church." Then after a pause, he added, "But we needed to."

In response to that same message, a young woman who had experienced the ordeal of raising a fatherless child later approached me to say, "If I had heard that message eleven years ago, my life might have been entirely different."

I came away from that experience affirmed that those of us in preaching can hide away from the messy issues or we can tackle them head-on in order to direct our listeners to where God would have them.

Since postmodern people live by sound bites of information on a large number of subjects, they'll expect (and demand) that you be widely informed as well. In order to avoid a knowing smirk and the derision that accompanies it, today's preaching needs to demonstrate a scope of understanding and interact critically in the areas of sociology, psychology, current events, and pop culture. If the preaching task is to help people develop a Christian worldview, it's no longer enough simply to know the Bible.

Many people presume the Bible is irrelevant to contemporary society; the preacher has to convince otherwise. Consider the preaching of Jesus. As Alister McGrath observes, "Jesus' preaching thus begins where people are—in the everyday world of rural Galilee. He told stories that reflected the world of his audience. . . . Yet the familiarity of this world is disturbed by unexpected twists in the story."[4]

Those unexpected twists were the confronting element to the way people commonly believed. Again and again, in the sermon on the mount, Jesus declares, "You have heard, but I tell you. . . ." Jesus met his listeners in their world but then proceeded to lead them to the reality of His Father's world.

The issue, then, concerning preaching is that not only has the climate changed but the questions and presuppositions of the listeners have altered too. "Thinking carefully about the relevant characteristics of the audience enables you to discover the problems you will face," Duane Litfin writes, "and [to discover] the possible advantages you can utilize to communicate effectively."[5]

The danger for today's preacher is one of answering the questions that no one's asking anymore. Christian scholar and apologist Alister McGrath declares, "There is an obligation to strive for the presentation of the Christian faith in terms and modes of expression that make its challenge intelligible and related to the peculiar quality of reality in which [people] live."[6]

To reach people where they live with the gospel, one needs to know the right address. Take, for example, the issue of guilt. Previous generations struggled with the knowledge of personal wrongs and failures. Forty years ago people visited ministers seeking absolution and to gain restraint from their impulses. The present mood can be captured in the bumper sticker SCREW GUILT. At one time guilt may have been identified as an inner gauge of personal accountability—a signal of something gone wrong. Now guilt is merely a nuisance, a faint noise in the engine courtesy of a previous owner. Guilt problem? Just ignore it.

Today's listeners may possess some sense of personal sin, that is, "I've done bad things." Yet postmodern people generally lack a sense of sin—sin with a big "I" in it, a deep sense of inadequacy standing in the presence of a Holy God who dismisses any claim of self-sufficiency. Therefore, as one considers a message built on "the answer to guilt," expect the response, "What's the question?"

For example, instead of assuming people understand personal guilt, I might begin a sermon on the topic by speaking about a secular and nonmoral issue: the breakdown of my car: "My Subaru conked out while I was driving for a reason. I had failed to properly interpret the warning signs the car was sending. . . . " You see, then I introduce guilt as a divine warning sign provided by our manufacturer, God. With theological issues like guilt, I don't presume a biblical foundation but instead seek to foster an understanding—I first broach a secular idea that can then be tied to the theological concept.

Be More Apologetic

What I mean by "more apologetic" is that Sunday sermons cannot assume or presume too much about their listeners' Christian worldview.

"Much of current sermonizing sins in that it takes for granted everyone still knows all that needs to be known to live a godly life," comments Calvin Miller. "Don't assume that people know and accept faith or any aspect thereof. Rather, supply convincing argument as to why faith is more reasonable than doubt."[7]

Some sermons will continue to speak to the converted, the insiders, and will fail to engage both the unchurched and those churchgoers who remain postmodern in their thinking. These will likely become churches of the status quo and may soon be congregations that find themselves in survival mode struggling to find anyone to listen.

The local pastor ministering in the twenty-first century would do well to adopt a style of preaching with a more apologetic tone every Sunday, not just on special outreach occasions. Loscalzo states, "The preacher's ideal role resides in giving meaning. Apologetic preaching helps people grasp the world theologically, to bring theological meaning and understanding to their lives. . . . Apologetic preaching equips Christians, intellectually and spiritually, to intelligently present and defend the Christian faith. It gives people the means to address questions of theodicy, sin, and salvation in Christ, which, when misunderstood, become obstacles to faith."[8]

To further clarify what is meant by "apologetic preaching," I am suggesting biblical preaching that grapples with doubts, unpacks Christian assumptions, and contemplates the unbelief of the skeptic. Calvin Miller in his appeal to preach to increasingly secular audiences states, "The church . . . has become so interiorized that it only 'reads its own mail' and only 'speaks its own interests to the people of Zion.' Marketplace preaching is a call to get outside the walls and find out once again what people are talking about and what their interests and needs really are. . . . The church must speak to the interests of the marketplace if it is to hold its attention."[9]

Most ministers would be amazed at the prevalence of the postmodern framework in the average Bible-believing church pew. If preachers only knew. Pastors everywhere need to consider a more apologetic approach, a meaning-giving approach, as postmodern society grows increasingly skeptical and the church grows steadily insular.

Preaching to today's listeners will require a working knowledge of the common ground of postmodern belief and unbelief. With the postmodern shift comes new openness to areas of Christian faith such as human spirituality, the existence of the supernatural, and a search for the transcendent. Postmodernity claims to dismiss meaning and rational thinking; however, this inconsistency can be exposed. For example, Ravi Zacharias refers to the Wexner Center for the Performing Arts on Ohio State University campus, which is said to be the first "deconstructionist building." Zacharias states, "Puzzlement only intensifies when you enter the building, for inside you encounter stairways that go nowhere, pillars that hang from the ceiling without touching the floor, and angled surfaces configured to create a sense of vertigo. The architect, we are duly informed, designed this building to reflect life itself—senseless and incoherent—and the 'capriciousness of the rules that organize the built world.' When the rationale was explained to me, I had just one question: Did he do the same with the foundation?"[10]

Ravi Zacharias reveals both the duplicity of postmodernity and the means by which one can begin to engage postmodern listeners: by exposing the assumptions, beliefs, and rationale upon which postmodernity rests. His conclusion, "The point of engagement must come through common ground that even the postmodernist assumes in disbelieving something."[11]

On the surface, postmodernity questions everything, but in reality, all belief or disbelief rests upon something. The preacher's task is to understand the common ground of belief and unbelief in order to engage the postmodern listener effectively.

For example, using a situation from my own life: My wife serves as an airline hostess as well as my partner in ministry. One day in the plane's galley, a colleague of hers sounded off without warning. "The problem with you Christians is you judge everything," this woman said. She failed to appreciate that she too makes judgments, that she, too, discerns right from wrong. But if my wife were to spit in a passenger's face without any provocation, would this critic deem the act as acceptable? Of course not. She does possess concepts of right and wrong. The rub comes as she lacks the insight into her own moral framework. The problem is not in whether to make judgments but to uncover from where she derives her standard for making those choices. So by being more apologetic, I mean unpack ideas and expose the framework of people's thinking.

Apologetic preaching applies even amid the faithful, too. Even church-goers are no longer content to receive "just the facts" style of preaching. Listeners require more than a directive of what to do. They want the "why" and the "how" as well. An example of this is found in the book *When Men Think Private Thoughts*. Gordon MacDonald passes along a letter from a young man in the congregation in response to Gordon's upcoming talk on sexuality. "I don't want to be offensive, but if you're going to raise the subject, and I'm glad you are, can I please suggest that the last thing we need to hear is one more talk on purity . . . what we aren't supposed to be and what we shouldn't be doing." The letter continues, "[We] don't need to be persuaded . . . if only [we] were sure what sexual purity really means and if, in fact, it's possible to live up to it. And most of us don't feel that we are."[12]

This young man echoes the frustration of seeking to live a God-honoring life with little or no assistance from years of church attendance. I would argue that many Christians feel this way on a myriad of subjects such as managing one's finances, balancing of priorities, controlling sexual desires, and godly decision making.

As a parting word for apologetic preaching, we must realize that people will often reject God's message for personal rather than intellectual reasons. Frankly, it's just easier not to believe in God. Paul Vitz, a professor of psychology at New York University, confides about his own spiritual journey: "As some of you know, after a rather weak, wishy-washy Christian upbringing, I became an atheist in college in the 1950s and remained so throughout graduate school. . . . I am an adult convert or, more technically, a reconvert to Christianity who came back to the faith, much to his surprise, in my late thirties in the very secular environment of academic psychology in New York City." Vitz bravely confesses, "In the list of superficial, but nevertheless, strong irrational pressures to become an atheist, I must list simple personal convenience. The fact is that it is quite inconvenient to be a serious believer in today's powerful secular and neo-pagan world. I would have had to give up many pleasures and a good deal of time."[13]

The crunch of unbelief will occur in various shapes and sizes, and embracing God and His Word can be more a matter of the will than the mind. John Stott observes: "I remember a young man coming to see me when he had just left school and begun work in London. He had given up going to church, he said, because he could not say the Creed without being a hypocrite. He no longer believed it. When he had finished his explanations, I said, 'If I were to answer your problems to your complete intellectual satisfaction, would you be willing to alter your manner of life?' He smiled slightly and blushed. His real problem was not intellectual but moral."[14]

Brennan Manning observes, "The difference between faith as 'belief in something that may or may not exist' and faith as 'trusting in God' is enormous. The first is a matter of the head, the second a matter of the heart. The first can leave us unchanged, the second intrinsically brings change."[15] This change, however, may be the very element people fear most.

Encourage Accountability

With the preaching game in most churches, people have learned how to play and win. You know the game: If the pastor should stumble upon something that strikes a certain note of conviction, don't sweat it. The following Sunday the pastor will move on to address an entirely new topic and what brought about conviction won't be heard again for a while. Isn't it interesting how pastors and churches can function in this manner year after year, where most businesses wouldn't survive this approach? In a business, after all, once a problem area is identified, effective management focuses on remedying it.

Every preacher secretly relishes the story of the pastor who delivered the identical message on "loving one another" three Sundays in a row. After the third time, an irate parishioner prodded, "When are you going to preach something different?"

The reply came, "When this fellowship starts putting into practice this message, you can have a new one."

Granted, "accountability" was the buzzword of the nineties, but with good reason. Much of what passes for ministry is just wishful thinking. We hope that something is going to stick somehow.

The preaching task needs to work off more than a liturgical calendar or Bible themes. I know I want my preaching to reflect a three-point strategy:

- Balance the preaching of the biblical text, alternating Gospel narratives and New Testament Epistles with the Old Testament literature and the Psalms.
- Develop the community of faith with direction and values for the overall fellowship. (Ask, for example: If the leadership could pinpoint one area for corporate growth over a given year, what would it be?)
- Consider each churchgoer's spiritual development. Try to imagine the strength of a congregation that had worked in these three areas over a ten-year period. Without a strategic plan in place, from Sunday-to-Sunday it can be one step forward and two steps back with a congregation that never seems to get anywhere.

Likewise, much of today's preaching can lack purpose. People hear a message without being directed to act in any measurable, practical, or tangible way. Biblical preaching must set not only a standard to live up to but a target to hit. Preaching should move the listeners beyond a sense of feeling uncomfortable or guilty to a point of decisive action. For many folks your message will be their only serious interaction with God for the week. So what are you providing? Thoughtful preaching will always provide the listener with an answer to the question: "How can I respond in either thought or action to what I've heard?" The preaching that offers the listener nothing can expect nothing in return.

Then, to get serious about assisting people in growth, some form of feedback is required each week. Give your listeners every opportunity to let them show that they take this stuff seriously as well. Preaching that makes a difference will direct the listeners to a clear, practical, and focused response for each message.

So biblical preaching to twenty-first-century listeners entails communicating on a relational, secular, and apologetic level with accountability and purpose. Tim Keller, who pastors a congregation in New York City, affirms this approach. "This is a critical and difficult balance for the Christian preacher," he says. "Every message and point must demonstrate relevance or the listener will mentally 'channel surf.' But once you have drawn in people with the amazing relevance and practical wisdom of the gospel, you must confront them with the most pragmatic issue of all—the claim of Christ to be absolute Lord of life."[16]

5 | Obstacles

While the postmodern shift will open some doors, it's already closed others. For instance, to postmoderns the Bible is no longer accepted as the authoritative Word of God, Jesus appears fascinating but not the unique Savior, the attitude "whatever" rules and so there's little belief in an absolute truth, there's little acceptance of a master plan for the universe and our lives, and most people today no longer believe in future judgment.

But before getting discouraged, you can investigate each of these five areas of particular difficulty due to the change in sociological climate.

Preaching to the Biblically Clueless

Every preacher begins work recognizing that the Bible stands as the basis of authority for all; the proclamation of the divinely inspired message from God is foundational to any ministry.

However, what exists in the speaker's mind and in the listener's may not be the same thing. Remember, the postmodern movement originated in debate over the use of language and interpretation; in the fifties through the seventies the inerrancy debate raged in what was labeled "The Battle for the Bible."

But the battleground has shifted. The real issue is not one of an inerrant text, as much as having any authoritative text at all. The issue is no longer about what is in the text or what the original author intended but about what is in the interpretation of the text as understood by the present-day reader.

"The postmodern mistrust of words and texts will put new pressure on the field of hermeneutics, particularly at the professional theological level. There are already some theological teachers (and there are bound to be more) who will swallow the deconstructionist line—where any objective truth, history or meaning is emptied from the text, the meaning becoming a matter of what readers construct for themselves."[1]

The biblical communicator who succumbs to this hermeneutic relinquishes speaking for God. When we lose divine revelation, all that remains is human speculation and uncertainty.

These suspicions about language, which are subtle but persuasive, represent significant obstacles for communication. Alister McGrath argues for a more tactical approach in our use of the Bible, *allowing the listener to reserve judgment upon the Bible in order to give the biblical message a hearing.* "No Christian will wish to abandon a passionate commitment to the truth," he writes. "Nevertheless, the postmodern situation demands that Christian truth claims be, for purely tactical reasons, relegated to the background temporarily, in order to commend the claims of Christianity on grounds more acceptable within the postmodern worldview."[2]

In other words, McGrath says: *A priori* acceptance, or presumption of the authority, of God's Word need not be the starting or focal point in a postmodern era that views texts as relative and authority as oppressive.

In the book *Letters from a Skeptic*, author and theologian Gregory Boyd dialogues with his unbelieving father over the issue of the authority of Scripture. Boyd challenges his father to examine the Gospels and the claims of Christ, not as "God's Word" but as one would examine any historical document. "Dad, I'm not asking you to accept on 'blind faith' that they are God's Word," the son pleads. "Forget about that altogether for right now. I'm simply saying, look at them as you would any ancient document. Apply to them the same criteria historians apply to other ancient documents when they research history. My contention is that, when the Gospels are treated in this critical-historical way, they fare very well and can be trusted to tell a good deal about the person of Jesus Christ, enough, in fact, to know that God was present in Him and working through Him in a most significant way."[3]

Boyd recognizes that the key issue is trust. People in a postmodern context are unprepared to trust something without first being able to examine and probe its reliability.

So when evangelicals insist that the Bible must be accepted as authoritative before the book can even be read, postmoderns feel pressured to make a hugh leap of faith—and they won't do it. The focus of the biblical communicator must shift from asking, "How do I protect the Bible from people viewing it as just another book?" to a more strategic issue, "How can I get them to examine the Bible to see if it is true?"

We Can Get Our Hackles Up or Get Our Message Out

Our sense of protectiveness actually addresses the bigger issue of how we handle the sacred. Many elements of the faith that we consider sacred and above reproach are viewed as fragile and unable to withstand scrutiny by those who do not believe.

Take, for example, the movie *The Last Temptation of Christ*. Many Christians deemed the movie blasphemy, an agenda to undermine biblical faith; some evangelical leaders even wanted to purchase the movie only to destroy it so that no one would ever see it. But the general public couldn't understand the outrage. Director Martin Scorsese—who was raised with a Catholic education—was attempting (albeit from a flawed understanding) to grapple with the dual nature of Christ. How could Jesus be both God and man? This seemed probing to many folks, an honest attempt to tackle, head-on, a perplexing theological issue.

Granted, the film gives an unbiblical understanding to Christ, but instead of an angry and defensive reaction, evangelical Christians could have seized the opportunity to dialogue about a biblical concept of who Jesus is and what He came to accomplish among us. Imagine the possibility of asking an unchurched person to view the movie and then, over a coffee, discuss it. This could well be the only time in years a person might have a serious discussion about the person and nature of Jesus. Some folks might still maintain that a vocal defense is necessary in order to increase the belief in the deity of Christ within the fabric of society. But I've got news: that belief is already gone. You can strive to preserve what is already lost or you can seek to rebuild a clear understanding of Christ.

By the same token, postmodern listeners perceive the hands-off approach to issues like the person of Jesus, the authority of the Bible, and the moral absolutes of God's Word as not allowing honest examination of the claims. That gives the impression that biblical claims are brittle and untenable, only embraced by the unthinking or naive individual; this is interpreted as a weak faith and insecurity over it. So obviously the need for reverence remains, but the view of what's sacred must be balanced so as not to extinguish opportunities of genuine inquiry and dialogue.

Let Them Taste and See That God's Word Is Good

A tactical approach doesn't prevent preachers from handling the Bible with confidence and expounding the Scriptures as authoritative. It just means remembering that in the postmodern listener's mind, the authority of the Bible remains up for grabs. It will develop in time.

Bill Hybels adds to this approach, "Over time, I want gradually to increase respect for Scripture, so that some day they won't have to ask all the why questions but will be able to say to themselves, 'Because it's in the Bible; that's why.' "[4] Our task involves helping others grow to appreciate the Bible and one way is by demonstrating our confidence in the Scripture and why we subscribe to its truthfulness.

This brings up several related aspects in handling God's Word in postmodern times. For one, allow the listener to experience firsthand the beauty and wisdom of God's written truth. People today are generally ignorant of what the Bible actually says. They think they know the biblical message based on slogans, quick summaries, and sound bites, but they don't. They are biblically clueless. The key rests in coaxing the listener to accompany the preacher on a journey, to sample that first taste of the Scripture's goodness.

George Hunter III reminds us: "Some church leaders have a university professor friend who 'lost his faith,' and these leaders now imagine that all secular people are philosophically sophisticated geniuses who have read Christian literature from Augustine to Zwingli and rejected the Christian case *in toto* on rational grounds. But the vast majority of secular people are not epistemologically sophisticated; most are naive, superficial, gullible people who may fall for anything."[5]

Is the Christian message being rejected because they've heard too much or too little? If we as preachers are committed to the process of allowing our listeners to search, then people need to be given reassurances, both verbally and nonverbally, that they can suspend judgment on belief while being free to investigate the Bible for themselves.

Preachers might be astonished at the responsiveness to such an offer in our climate. It's not that postmodern listeners are unhappy for the preacher to believe. On the contrary, the people of postmodernity admire men and women of strong conviction such as Mother Teresa, Gandhi, Martin Luther King Jr., and even Billy Graham, although they may not agree with their convictions.

What postmodern listeners don't want is for the preacher to demand that they believe, at least not without adequate time and consideration to weigh and evaluate what's communicated. Using the often expressed metaphor of fishing, do you try to land the catch on the very first nibble?

"The effort to know the truth involves struggle, groping, feeling one's way," Lesslie Newbigin contends. "It is true that there are also moments of sudden illumination, but these come only to those who have accepted the discipline of patient groping, of trying out different possibilities, of sustained reflection."[6]

The role of preachers must be defined as more than laying out God's truth but also in assisting the listener's struggle to find the truth for his or herself. Ask yourself: Am I a facilitator of the patient groping for truth? Do I permit people to grapple with the weight of God's Word? If my preaching is perceived to be uninteresting and uninvolving to the listener, how will people ever begin to develop an appreciation for God's message?

I recall a conversation I had with an unchurched man in his thirties living in my hometown of Perth, Western Australia. I'd asked him, "Do you ever attend church?"

He replied, "Not really."

"Do you ever wonder about spiritual matters?"

"Well, yes, who doesn't?"

I framed the next logical approach, "If you have questions about spiritual matters, don't you feel that the church could address some of those issues?"

His response was interesting: "The church is for those who already believe, not for people like me."

Now where do you suppose he got an idea like that?

Most likely, from us. People harbor the misconception there's no room for doubt and questioning in the church. Until we as biblical communicators and believing communities grant people the permission to test the teaching before belief, they will stay away in droves. We must learn to present God's truth unashamedly while allowing people the freedom to investigate.

"I've been surprised to learn you really can challenge unchurched people as much as you would anybody else," Bill Hybels concedes, "as long as at the moment of truth you give them absolute freedom of choice."[7]

One practical thing that's important, then, is for the preacher to be mindful of the biblical assumptions carried into the pulpit with any given message. The preacher may know with confidence that something is true, and may simply accept the idea at face value. However, those assumptions should be unpacked from time to time, so the listener can understand the framework too.

That is, *allow the listener to see the process by which you arrived at the conclusions of faith.* Let people know that you too wrestled with your faith before coming to a place of conviction.

One way of surfacing these presuppositions is by framing them in the form of questions:

Why is it necessary for Jesus to be human?
Why couldn't God just dismiss sin?
How does the cross make sense?
Isn't it true that Jesus never claimed to be God?
What do I mean when I speak of "sin"?
What does the Bible mean by "salvation"?

If the speaker goes too far into the message without explaining key concepts or addressing the underlying issues, people will tune out. Breaking down the assumptions puts the biblical concepts into digestible bites for untrained listeners.

Elizabeth Achtemeier pinpoints four questions for the biblical text from the standpoint of the pew:

1. "What would my people doubt to be true in this text?" If listeners hear something read or stated that conflicts with their accepted view of reality without any explanation, listeners will conclude that you don't live in the same world as they do.
2. "What do my people need to know or be reminded of in this text?"
3. "With what inner feelings, longings, thoughts, and desires of my people does this text connect?" Questions two and three force the speaker to think about where the text touches the lives of listeners.
4. "If this text is true, what kind of world do we live in?"[8] In taking time to address underlying ideas of the text, the preacher gives listeners the information they need to process ideas on their own rather than accept ideas blindly; this conveys a respect for listeners who might not share a Christian worldview.

The listener's trust in the message can be further instilled by the preacher's authenticity. When people are uncertain as to what to believe, all they have to go on is what they have before them. In the case of preaching, it's the Bible and the preacher.

For this reason, Haddon Robinson advises, "If listeners know you love and identify with them, they will let you say strong things. Most people are just asking that you be aware of them and not write them off."[9]

Delivered in a spirit of gentleness and humility, the incarnational role in ministry will surface again and again in dealing with the postmodern ethos. For people to learn to trust the Bible and Christ, they may need first to learn to trust the preacher and God's people.

In the same way, we can lend confidence in God's message to the listener by our willingness to address the hard questions that arise out of human doubt and skepticism. We communicate to our listeners that we are undaunted in facing such questions and as a result, we then empower the listener to ask these same questions without being condemned for it.

Dogmatism: The Postmodern Kiss of Death

The preacher should be wary of the appearance of narrow dogmatism, which communicates that all of life is black or white. Leaving no room for any option or discernment will be viewed as oppressive and anti-intellectual.

In a scene from the classic TV show *All in the Family*, the lovable bigot, Archie Bunker, is explaining to Mike, his son-in-law, the proper way in which to put on his socks and shoes. Mike prefers to don his gear sock-shoe then sock-shoe. Archie attempts to convince him that it is better to do both socks first, then add the shoes to your feet. You see, for Archie Bunker, there was a right way and wrong way for everything, including putting on your socks and shoes. His was a black and white world, and I remind you that for ministry purposes Archie Bunker is not a good role model.

In handling the Bible for postmodern listeners one significant change required in these shifting times is limiting the number of ideas introduced in any one message and to avoid making unsubstantiated claims. At first glance this appears silly. You may think: *What do you mean by limiting the number of ideas.*

Well, forty years ago news anchor Walter Cronkite used to sign off his broadcasts, "And that's the way it is." Likewise, forty years ago, the preacher would bombard the listener with a litany of factual information and statements concerning the nature of God as if to announce, "And that's the way it is."

As I've reflected upon the peaching to which I grew up listening, much of it made assumptions about the listener's biblical knowledge and spiritual interest. As a result the Bible was taught like a lecturer delivering a textbook. Many of the ideas were just thrown out with the presumption that the listener wanted to hear the Bible and would accept these statements.

Today I find that approach to preaching acts to confuse listeners and reinforces to the seeker the message: "I've come to the wrong place because he's speaking with someone else in mind." The concept of limiting the number of ideas in a sermon simply means that in the time that's given, I'm better off presenting fewer biblical ideas and giving more time to develop each thought carefully. Preachers wishing to make propositional statements—such as "God loves you and has a wonderful plan for your life"—should be prepared to take the time to back up the claim in a way that allows people to perceive the truthfulness of the statement. Too many sermons still take the shotgun approach of discharging a buckshot blast of ideas in the hope of hitting something instead of the rifle approach in which careful aim is given in order to hit to the prescribed target. Today, people in the pew are simply reluctant to accept statements from the pulpit without first exploring the idea and examining why it's true.

In fact, *Regeneration Quarterly* magazine cites an abandonment of dogmatism as one of the top five characteristics that generation Xers seek in a church.[10] This could be expected from a generation raised on relativism and broken relationships.

Tom Nash adds, "When we turn to revealed truth, God's Word, we have the right to be more dogmatic, but even here we must be careful because our understanding or interpretation of Scripture is not necessarily the correct one."[11]

To put it bluntly, postmodernity despises the arrogance of infallibility. Preachers can counter the perception of dogmatism with five approaches:

1. Choose carefully and strategically what to say. Not every point should carry the same weight as in "I'll go to the cross for this." Be mindful not to allow salvation by faith to take an equal footing with the prohibition to attend R-rated movies. Know what's critical for the moment, and what's secondary.
2. Learn to speak in a positive manner about what the Christian faith is, and not what it's not. If people perceive a preacher's taking a cheap shot at other people, other denominations, or even other religions, the faith becomes suspect as petty and mean-spirited. Learn to affirm the truth without resorting to an attacking style that may appear vindictive and create a sympathy backlash.
3. Openly acknowledge that amid the categories of right and wrong, Christians do face a world of gray, where not all of life's answers are cut and dry. Oversimplifying life's issues will only increase the postmodern skepticism.
4. Admit to your own struggles and allow your listeners to see that you know you haven't arrived yet. Even in preaching, we're all traveling the same road, the journey of faith in Christ.

5. Don't go looking for a fight. When you argue a minor point, people will lose sight of the main point you wish to convey. Ravi Zacharias declares: "In addressing skeptics, the biggest trap is getting sidetracked into symptomatic issues. The most volatile of these, of course, are sexuality and abortion."[12]

Sadly, some biblical communicators needlessly alienate their listeners and place them on the defensive. While with some tact and wisdom, one can avoid the trapping of being seen as dogmatic and still remain faithful in the presentation of God's Word. The goal, of course, is to build a growing appreciation in the listener's heart for the beauty and strength of God's Word. Many will not accept the Bible as authoritative initially. Yet in time, our listeners will hopefully come to embrace God's Word even as we do. Remember, in speaking to your listeners, you cannot presume authority but you can endeavor to establish authority over time.

Deal with the Exclusive Uniqueness of Christ

Since all belief systems are social constructs differing in cultural form, postmodern thought possesses two leading features: inclusiveness and openness.

The religions of the world may appear diverse on the surface but postmodernity reminds us that underneath all beliefs are the same at their core. No one belief system stands above the other, or, as Don Carson puts it, in postmodernity "no religion has the right to pronounce itself true and others false."[13]

For this reason, Ross Clifford, the principal of Morling Theological College in Sydney, boldly made inquiries at a New Age event called The Mind, Body, Spirit Festival in Darling Harbour, if the Baptists could have their own stall at the pavilion called The Community of Hope.

Organizers' initial response was, "You can't be a part of this."

"Why not?" Clifford pressed. "All roads lead to Rome and I'm one of them. How can you possibly exclude me?"

Sure enough, the Baptists were in—after all, the postmodern value of inclusiveness must be upheld.

In a similar way, postmodernity values openness to new possibilities. Modernity functioned with an arrogance that declared certainty of truth and falsehood. Certain positions were immediately ruled out as irrational and impossible. Postmodernity tends to view the world in which anything is possible and nothing should be dismissed categorically.

For this reason, when Jesus stated, "I am the resurrection," modernity took aim at the concept of "resurrection," because dead people coming back to life is outside of the realm of scientific understanding.

Postmodernity views the universe as a large place that is far too unpredictable and is therefore untroubled by the possibility of a resurrection. (Granted, the unique nature of Christ's resurrection would still present problems.) The postmodern concern gives attention to the words, "I am." How can Jesus claim to be the sole possessor of power over death? Therefore, a major point of tension within postmodernity for Christians is not the supernatural claims per se but the exclusive claims of Christ.

To believe in Christ, to hope in Christ, to love in Christ's name—these are all well and good virtues. For Christians to insist that all must believe, hope, and love in Christ is totally unacceptable. To the postmodern mind, the exclusiveness of Christianity represents a remnant of Western colonialism and Enlightenment arrogance and therefore must be rejected. Exclusive claims of truth end up in the museum next to the flat earth model of the world. We know better now.

The Elastic Jesus: Stretch to Fit All Sizes

In the coming years, a pluralist worldview will impose an enormous amount of pressure upon Christians and ministers alike to concede that Jesus Christ is merely a way to God and not the way.

A slightly different slant acknowledges that eventually all will be saved through Christ, but in the meantime other belief systems are valid systems to direct people to Christ in the same way the Law tutored the Jewish people toward Christ. The assertion then goes that while other religions contain truth, the Bible contains all truth. So in the twenty-first century, the future battle line of biblical faith will be drawn in maintaining Christ as the sole mediator between God and humanity without bowing to pluralistic pressure to embrace other belief systems.

Once again, this kind of pressure reiterates the call for meaning-giving messages with both consistency and regularity. Reaffirmation of the key tenets of Christian belief such as the uniqueness of Christ isn't only for the unchurched but for the believer as well.

Defending the exclusiveness of Christ will require more than just reciting John 14:6, "I am the way, the truth and the life." It will mean demonstrating that Christ embodies God's message as opposed to being a mere messenger. The good news as recorded in 1 Corinthians 15 is not an idea but a person: crucified, buried, and risen again.

Put simply, *the Bible is not about what to believe but in whom one will trust.* That makes our message simple: Salvation is found in a personal encounter with Christ.

Preaching the person of Christ in postmodern culture can be simple and difficult at the same time. On one side, people today have a striking admiration for Jesus, and are both compelled and attracted to the records of Christ as found in the Gospels. In fact, the curiosity surrounding Jesus seems boundless these days—made-for-TV movies show interpretations of his life, scholars' discussion of Jesus in history are brought into primetime discussion.

On the other hand, to Jesus' question, "Who do people say that I am?" people tend to see the Christ as divinely inspired or possessing greatness but not as equal to God.

"Christ is so divorced from the historical Jesus," observes Don Carson, "that the terms can be given almost any content one wishes."[14]

"Probably no other generation subscribes to so many differing conceptions of Jesus Christ," adds Wade Roof's team of researchers. "Traditional Christian views of Jesus, as God's Son and Savior, have weakened: 46 percent of church dropouts say they think of Jesus as a great teacher or in some other way, but not as Savior."[15]

The paradoxical outlook about Christ indicates postmodern people tend to see in Jesus what they want.

Roof again observes: "Those who hold a more modern, as opposed to a traditional conception of self, also tend to think of Jesus more as a liberator and challenger, rather than in the conventional way as a shepherd; they are more impressed with Jesus' compassion and forgiveness than with the healing and miracles that he performed."[16] Take advantage of the admiration and interest that twenty-first-century listeners have in Christ, yet recognize the need to move the audience farther in understanding that Jesus is more than possibly imagined.

Add One Jesus, Subtract All Others

When preaching Christ, be mindful that the mathematics of faith involves subtraction as well as addition. Postmodernity is characterized by rabid syncretism that encourages individuals to pick and choose beliefs. Since matters of faith constitute private truth, one can believe anything or nothing, mix and match elements from the various systems of belief without any apparent difficulty.

"Greater attention to spiritual quest, an expanded number of religious options, and a consumer culture have all contributed to 'multi-layered' styles of belief and practice," Roof comments. "With a syncretism and eclecticism made possible by so many alternatives, boomers continue to recognize the 'merits of borrowing' from other traditions and figures."[17]

The end result is people in a postmodern culture will gladly embrace aspects of Jesus and view Him as one of many gods.

The mixing of pagan beliefs along with the self-revealing, creator God, however, finds steady rebuke throughout both the Old and New Testament. In reference to pagan idols, the God of the Bible is contrasted as the "living God" (Acts 14:15). A biblical faith must renounce all allegiance to other gods, as 1 Thessalonians 1:9 states: "You turned to God from idols to serve a living and true God."

There exists no precedent to suggest that God approves of idol worship as a secondary means to approaching Him. The Bible is clear on who Christ is and equally clear on the futility of false gods and idols.

Jesus Christ Himself spoke of true worshipers, those who worship in spirit and in truth. "Know that the LORD is God" shouts the psalmist (Ps. 100:3).

Casual readers may fail to understand that the second of the ten commandments, "You shall not make for yourself an idol," is a prohibition against worshiping the living God for less than who He is. The preaching task regarding Christ, then, is to bring people to the full recognition, making them into true worshipers.

Still, at some point the people of postmodernity must count the cost of following Christ. In this way, living in postmodernity parallels the experience of the early church under Roman rule. "The reason the Christians were killed [by the Romans] was because they were rebels," observed Francis Schaeffer. "First, we can say that they worshiped Jesus as God and they worshiped the infinite, personal God only. The Caesars would not tolerate this worshiping of the one God only. It was counted as treason. . . . If they had worshiped Jesus and Caesar, they would have gone unharmed, but they rejected all forms of syncretism. . . . They allowed no mixture: All other gods were seen as false gods."[18]

Like the Christians then, today's Christians must risk being alienated, ostracized, or even tortured in order to maintain the biblical standard that "there is no other name under heaven that has been given among men, by which we must be saved" (Acts 4:12 NASB).

Pluralism Isn't All It's Cracked Up to Be

"It is said that baby busters do not want to be lectured," Don Carson says. "They expect to be entertained. . . . As a result, they can live with all sorts of logical inconsistencies and be totally unaware of them."[19]

For the biblical communicator, those postmodern inconsistencies pose a direct challenge. Ravi Zacharias writes "that truth by definition will always be exclusive. . . . The issue, then, is not whether the belief system you espouse—monotheistic, atheistic, pantheistic, or otherwise—is exclusive. The issue is whether the answers to the four basic questions of life pertaining to origin, meaning, morality, and destiny with the context of each of these worldviews meet the tests of truth."[20]

In determining the veracity of an idea, then, inclusiveness does not serve as much of a guide. Postmodern listeners, in fact, assume inclusiveness is the unity of core beliefs—or that all religious systems are basically the same.

How many people can honestly claim to have investigated the tenets of belief in the major religions? Most are functioning under a blind assumption of unity. People would like to believe or accept by faith that all religions are basically the same.

Kathryn Tanner challenges religious pluralism by arguing, "Pluralist generalizations about what all religions have in common conflict with genuine dialogue, in that they prejudge its results. Commonalities, which should be established in and through a process of dialogue, are constructed ahead of time by pluralists to serve as presuppositions of dialogue. Pluralists therefore close themselves to what people of other religions might have to say about their account of these commonalities. . . . The pluralists' insistence on commonalities as a condition of dialogue shows an unwillingness to recognize the depth and degree of diversity among religions, or the positive importance of them."[21]

In pluralism the assumptions of inclusiveness are comforting notions because they remove the personal responsibility of an individual having to choose. Yet endless openness produces a stagnation; it works to remind listeners that the essential messages of world beliefs—the core teachings of who God is and what it means to be saved—are not inherently the same.

Preaching should direct people to weigh a belief system on its own merit based on personal investigation as opposed to the postmodern axiom that they are all the same. In the words of the prophet Elijah, "If the LORD is God, follow him; but if Baal is God, follow him" (1 Kings 18:21).

Following the model of the early church, you can draw attention to the merits of knowing Christ.

"I find it ironic," Michael Green comments, "that people object to the proclamation of the Christian gospel these days because so many other faiths jostle on the doorstep of our global village. What's new? The variety of faiths in antiquity was even greater than it is today. And the early Christians, making as they did ultimate claims for Jesus, met the problem of other faiths head-on from the very outset. Their approach was interesting. . . . They did not denounce other faiths. They simply proclaimed Jesus with all the power and persuasiveness at their disposal."[22]

Some people refer to this as "the Jesus factor." Whatever you call it, the point is the uniqueness of the Christian faith is grounded in the uniqueness of Christ.

Remember: Seeing Was Believing

The personal testimony of Christ's followers who were prepared to die testifying that Christ was the unique and risen Son of God will carry weight for postmodern people. Everybody has his or her own perception of reality, but how many people are prepared to die for it?

The early church was. Charles Colson draws a parallel from Christ's resurrection to the Watergate cover-up that eventually toppled Nixon's administration. "What does this twentieth-century fiasco tell us about the first century?" Colson asks. "One of the most common arguments against Christianity is a conspiracy theory. Critics often try to explain the empty tomb by saying the disciples lied—that they stole Jesus' body and conspired together to pretend He had risen. The apostles then managed to recruit more than five hundred other people to lie for them as well, to say they saw Jesus after He rose from the dead. But how plausible is this theory? To support it, you'd have to be ready to believe that over the next fifty years the apostles were willing to be ostracized, beaten, persecuted, and (all but one of them) suffer a martyr's death—without ever renouncing their conviction that they had seen Jesus bodily resurrected. Does anyone really think they could have maintained a lie all that time? No, someone would have cracked, just as we did so easily in Watergate. There would have been some kind of smoking-gun evidence or a deathbed confession. But these men had come face-to-face with the living God. They could not deny what they had seen. The fact is that people will give their lives for what they believe is true, but they will never give their lives for what they know is a lie."[23]

The eyewitness followers of Christ were willing to die for their perception of Christ as the true Savior. By today's measurement, to dare to live for Christ may mean as much.

The Jesus Most Never Knew

The uniqueness of Jesus presents an obstacle, but is also a powerful strength in preaching to postmodern listeners. Examining the distinctiveness of Christ, the question that every preacher should probe is, "How much do these people really know about the person of Jesus?"

Philip Yancey's best-selling book *The Jesus I Never Knew*[24] is a testimony to the fact that even those brought up in a Christian home can harbor a caricature of Jesus.

So, since postmodernity cherishes a fondness for Christ, preachers would do well to explore the richness of the Gospel accounts, giving ample study to the life of Christ on a regular basis.

"When one reads the Gospels rapidly, one after the other, again and again, one cannot but be struck by the towering figure of Jesus," Carson encourages. "Though they reflect the churches' convictions, the Gospels are not about the churches' convictions: They are about Jesus Christ. His excellence, uniqueness, authority, compassion, love, wisdom, holiness—all shine through passage after passage."[25]

Statistically, 46 percent of church dropouts have abandoned the evangelical position concerning Christ, but that leaves 54 percent of dropouts who remain open to Jesus as the unique Son of God.

Much of what is known of Christ fails to make proper sense if Jesus stands as just another teacher. For instance, in Mark 4, the disciples fear for their lives when caught in a storm upon Lake Galilee and Christ calms the wind and waves by the authority of his own command.

But we need fear preaching the person of Jesus. R. C. Sproul writes, "What is significant about this story in Scripture is the disciples' fear increased after the threat of the storm was removed. The storm made them afraid. Jesus' action to still the tempest made them more afraid. In the power of Christ they met something more frightening than they ever met in nature. . . . We wonder what Freud would have said about that. Why would men invent a God whose holiness was more terrifying than the forces of nature that provoked them to invent a god in the first place? We can understand men inventing an unholy god, a god who brought only comfort. But why a god more scary than the earthquake, flood, or disease?" Sproul continues, "They cried out, 'What manner of man is this, that even the wind and the sea obey him?' The question was, 'What manner of man is this?' They were asking a question of kind. They were looking for a category to put Jesus in, a type that they were familiar with. . . . The disciples could find no category adequate to capture the person of Jesus. . . . He was *sui generis*—in a class by Himself."[26]

Consider delivering a series of messages on the life of Christ without resolving the tension of which Sproul speaks: "What manner of man is this?" Instead, allow the listeners to grapple in their own hearts and minds concerning the nature of Christ. Even though postmoderns see nature as the supreme force, will they arrive at the Truth the Bible presents: Christ as the Lord of nature, above the natural world, even death?

"Indeed," James Sire writes, "the Gospels taken in their entirety present a coherent picture of a coherent person. The Jesus we see before his death is even coherent with the most amazing event of all: the resurrection."[27]

This would both capture listener interest and give time for each person to draw his or her own conclusion to the question, "Who is Jesus?"

David Cook in writing about Paul on Mars Hill argues, "He used the beliefs people were familiar with and showed that in Christ there was a better, fuller understanding of God."[28]

The person of Christ serves as a rich tapestry, embodying a number of the traits deeply admired in postmodern times. Preach a series on the person of Christ highlighting his compassion, integrity, serenity, and passion. To quote the booming African-American preacher E. V. Hill, "Preach Jesus! He's preachable."

The "Whatever" Age

One of the key issues confronting biblical communicators in the postmodern age remains the tension between objective truth and subjective truth. How will preachers deal with the issue of truth?

On the one hand, the preacher could be carried in the postmodern shift to espouse the view that, indeed, all truth is subjective and all truth relative. The danger arises that Christianity becomes legitimate only as an individual, personal preference, "it works for me."

On the other hand, the preacher might be seen as caught up in the trappings of modernity by insisting upon a certainty that the Bible fails to offer. Some would argue that evangelicals end up defending the necessity of objective truth needlessly.

Homiletician Craig Loscalzo relates the humorous cartoon that demonstrates the postmodern preaching dilemma. A minister displays a "Worship Attendance Chart" that reflects diminishing numbers at a staggering rate of decline. One of his parishioners advises him, "I'm no expert . . . but perhaps you shouldn't close each sermon with 'But then again, what do I know?'"[29]

"What our world is waiting for, and what the church seems reluctant to offer, is not more incessant talk about objective truth," Philip Kenneson says, "but an embodied witness that clearly demonstrates why anyone should care about any of this in the first place."[30]

The fact that most people today can't pick out Christians from non-Christians is bad enough, but if they could, what makes us "pick-outable" probably is relatively incidental to the gospel. Isn't this worse? And doesn't it suggest that critics are right in refusing to accept what we Christians say we believe but which our lives make a lie?[31]

Our verbal claims to real truth can be easily undermined by the inability of our lives to collaborate the message. How will biblical communicators, then, handle the message of truth?

Clearly, without the conviction of any objective knowing, the entire nature of divine revelation is cast into meaninglessness and preaching becomes another religious exercise of humanity reaching to God. Whereas, essential to the Christian message is that God reveals who He is to us.

Restoring the Ought to Action

Once subjectivism takes hold of truth, morality, then, becomes susceptible to the same line of argumentation as being entirely relative. James Sire demonstrates the necessity of truth in founding a morality of right and wrong:

> If all there is, is matter and what it does, then all there is, is, is. There can be no ought. . . . For example, in human action what is? Tender care for children is; child abuse is. Love and respect between persons are; hatred and fury are. Defense of the helpless is; violence and rape are. There is no need to go on. The world of human action is filled with both the commendable and the despicable. That is, we think that some actions are commendable and others despicable. And we have no trouble acting as if the commendable is right and the despicable wrong. But are they really? How can these actions actually be right or wrong? Only if there is a difference between is and ought. But how can there be a difference between is and ought in a world that just is? . . . If there is to be such a difference, it will have to be because some things in the world do not conform to something outside the world by which they are measured. There will have to be an existent moral realm or, better, an existent personal Being who in and of himself stands as the repository of goodness. Otherwise, . . . the words commendable and despicable, right and wrong, become only labels for emotional reactions (what any I commends or despises) or terms hiding suppressed desires (what any I is deluded into thinking it has chosen) or yearnings for personal power (what any I wants or doesn't want) or the choice (agonized or flippant, thoughtful or brash) of each I who by its own will creates the good by deciding or acting or both.[32]

Absolute relativism, then, throws any moral conduct and any moral oughtness into chaos.

Back on the God Standard

Ronald Nash points out the inherent flaws of pluralism: "Truth is a function of geography, that is, where people happen to have been born. This idea, carried to its logical implications, would make Nazism, cannibalism, infanticide, and witchcraft true because they would all be a result of geographic and cultural conditioning. . . . [Pluralism] also implies that beliefs can be true and false at the same time, true for people conditioned in one way and false for others."[33]

In that case, no one group or individual could ever be justified in condemning the conduct and position of another people group. It's surprising how few people haven't fully wrestled with the need for objective standards of truth and right.

In contrast to relativism, the moral code for Christians isn't arbitrary but based in the righteous character of God. Good is a reflection of God's holy character. Evil is that which runs contrary to God's person.

God is wired in such a way that He can never coexist with unrighteousness; made in His image, our morality is bound up in the creator God, who is wholly righteous, not a person's opinion, tradition, or any cultural bias.

Think of this holiness of God as no different from other characters' makeup. For instance, my friend J. can't stand sesame seeds—he can't eat them or even eat food cooked with sesame seed oil. It's not that he dislikes the taste, but when sesame seeds enter his system he gets an allergic reaction so violent he turns blue and his respiratory system shuts down. In J.'s case, sesame seeds and his body are completely and utterly incompatible. The two cannot coexist together. So it is with God and evil.

Belief That Is Caught, Not Taught

However, as important as objective truth is to the Christian faith, Philip Kenneson makes a valid point in stating that in postmodern times, what people hear will be drowned out by what they see in the lives of Christians.

People today are weary of words. Again, the focus moves from the credibility of the faith, that something is deemed true intellectually speaking, to the plausibility of the faith, that something is experienced as true in the way we live. This is where people of postmodernity live and this emphasis cannot be understated.

As a result ministry that lacks grace, compassion, and a sincere interest in affirming people will overshadow the words of the message. Lesslie Newbigin affirms, "Our use of the Bible is analogous to our use of language. We indwell it rather than looking at it from outside. But for this to happen it is clear that this 'indwelling' must mean being part of the community whose life is shaped by the story which the Bible tells."[34]

If a Christian wishes to speak the truth, then the truth must be seen in that person's life. It's easy to understand the repulsive nature of truth claims boldly proclaimed to listeners who are seemingly disregarded by the ones making such pronouncements.

To guard against intellectual arrogance, Christian communicators can remember that in reality, all Christians live as practicing atheists from time to time, including the preacher. Yes, even preachers can be fallible interpreters of the infallible Word.

"We believe in order to understand," Newbigin reminds us, "and at every stage we may be wrong. There is no guarantee against error. All our knowing is a personal commitment in which we have no external guarantee that we cannot be mistaken. . . . All knowing is the knowing of a fallible human subject who may be wrong but who can only know more by personally committing himself to what he already knows."[35]

The preacher who demonstrates humility with regard to his or her own subjective foibles as human interpreter offers a reassuring message to those suspicious of demagoguery.

"The vehemence of the debate over controversial issues—such as language about God, the inerrancy of Scripture, abortion, creation and evolution, the role of women in leadership, ordination of homosexuals, and others—too often breeds arrogant certainty," comments Donald McCullough. "Instead of an enriching exchange leading to greater discernment, we have shouting matches that shut off dialogue and fragment the Christian community. One must ask: Who is being served in all this—God or the god-of-my-understanding?"[36]

People who might have once accepted this proposition from the pulpit freely will now need to see that the preacher has grappled with the full implications of the issue while communicating in ways that invite dialogue and feedback. Truth claims cannot be used to coerce people into God's kingdom; people will have to be led by humility and gentleness.

God's Truth: Your Foundation or Battering Ram?

The preacher can confidently proclaim God's Word but should be aware that the twenty-first-century listener is not likely to be wooed or convinced with propositional "truth claims."

In the same way, imagine a husband in a struggling marriage telling his wife, "The Bible says that I am the head of the family and you are to submit yourself to my leadership."

Does that make everything better?

The wife may well turn around and reply, "I don't care because I refuse to listen to a jerk."

By demanding respect and authority, he will not gain it. Respect must be earned. He must first persuade her that as a loving husband, he is worthy of being followed. A marriage like good communication involves two parties.

Prominent pastor Ed Dobson comments, "In an earlier generation, it was enough for a preacher to announce the truth, and the congregation would ratify it. Today, such pronouncements are met with resistance. Today, I have to persuade people, even in the church, of the gospel and its implications. I must respect the right of an audience to make up its own mind. Today's listeners can feel at a gut level the difference between persuading and pronouncing. They react severely to preaching that doesn't respect their freedom to make up their own minds."[37]

The preacher cannot attempt to command a response by making a pronouncement about the way things ought to be. Preaching involves winning over the listener to respond. This means, among other approaches, using story.

"Story isn't a flight from reality," comments screenwriter Robert McKee, "but a vehicle that carries us on a search for reality, our best effort to make sense out of the anarchy of existence."[38]

Within every message, it's necessary to continually shift from the biblical world to the contemporary one, and the latter can provide fresh air to Bible ideas. In fact, an idea can come to life when seen in the context of how normal, everyday people have experienced this truth.

A properly used illustration, after all, can open the aperture of listeners' perspectives, helping them see beyond the confines of their own limited world to recognize a wider vista than previously imagined. For this reason, preachers should refrain from making declarative statements about God, humanity, and salvation unless they're prepared to demonstrate some validity, something tangible.

Newbigin observes, "The alternative to subjectivity is not an illusory claim to objectivity, but the willingness to publish and to test."[39]

In other words, the listener says, "Let me understand this and see how it works before I accept this as right."

So the preaching exercise becomes like a journey. As well-trained guides, preachers know the way. They've traveled the path many times before. But for listeners the experience of the uncharted journey is a wondrous adventure; as the trail unfolds preachers will want to see that when listeners arrive at the proper destinations that they were the discoverers.

You see, the mere statement of a truth as black and white elicits the response, "I agree [or disagree] with that."While a carefully worded presentation of an idea may allow the listener to suspend immediate judgment, "For now, it sits right with me [or it doesn't]."

For this reason "evangelical apologetics must attend to both reason and rhetoric, with as much emphasis on the latter as the former in order to make reason relevant and help people see the truth," state Timothy Phillips and Dennis Okholm.[40]

They're suggesting that reason alone (or claims of truth) cannot act as a battering ram upon society, but instead must be integrated with rhetoric (or an effective use of words) in order to help people comprehend and embrace the truth.

Alister McGrath declares, "When it comes to the big things of life, like believing in the Christian faith or believing in democracy, we live on the basis of probability, not certainty. . . . Christian faith is a risk because it cannot be proven."[41]

Since postmodern listeners are skeptical about truth, and the credibility of the faith—and people won't be bullied into accepting truth—the good preacher will attend to both the reasonableness of the Christian faith, as well as the plausibility.

Handling Resistance to the Master Plan

Postmodern times come with suspicions about authority and objective truth. These two suspicions are accompanied by a disdain for metanarratives or the grand scheme of things—the master plan that gives meaning and resolution to the issues of human existence.

To the postmodern mind each of these three aspects of modernity has been a tool for exploitation and manipulation by the powers that be. Postmodernity rejects all worldviews as its worldview. The twenty-first century holds that the world is too complex for any one belief system to apply to the numerous people groups around the globe. Therefore, a metanarrative is viewed as one group's attempt to impose its system onto others. So what does this mean to the Christian preacher of the gospel? Isn't the good news of Christ the epitome of the metanarrative? Maybe, but today terms like "missionary" and "evangelist" have become dirty words because they represent the imposition of one set of cultural ideas upon another.

In postmodernity, having no answers to life is preferable to an oppressive ideology. Postmodernity prefers to live in despair than be fooled into accepting a lie that ultimately seeks to enslave people for self-serving purposes. In other words, better hopeless than foolish. The rejection of the metanarrative is a symptom of the cynicism of our times.

The issue surrounding the metanarrative and preaching can come down to the speaker's ethos. Twenty-first-century listeners fear biblical communicators' motives and will question promotion of any particular worldview. Through humility, love, and patience, though, preachers can take measures to dispel the concern of people who have witnessed atrocities and deception in the name of truth and the name of God.

Good News for the Weak

Even though the biblical telling of the gospel resembles a classic exploitative metanarrative, the message itself exhibits pronounced features that run contrary to postmodern expectations, such as metanarrative elitism.

For example, Christ reached out to the marginalized people of His day and challenged the institutional forces of the religious hierarchy and Roman oppression. Yet, Christ did not dismiss the people of the establishment such as the Pharisees, soldiers, public officials, and tax-collectors. Consequently, Christ came and ultimately died, not to represent any one class of people but as the Gospels show, to embrace both those at the center and in the margins.

"This radical embrace was vivid testimony to his trust in the Creator of both center and margins, a Creator who is able to bring life even out of death," write Middleton and Walsh. "The person of Jesus, and especially his death on a cross, thus becomes in the New Testament a symbol of the counter-ideological intent of the biblical metanarrative and the paradigm or model of ethical human action, even in the face of massive injustice."[42]

The appeal to postmodernity from a Christological standpoint is not one mighty triumph but as Paul later writes, "God chose the foolish things of the world to shame the wise; God chose the weak things of the world to shame the strong" (1 Cor. 1:27). Clearly, the humility and suffering of Christ counters some of the metanarrative rhetoric of postmodernity.

Good News in Every Language

The global nature of the biblical story is wholly inclusive, pertaining not just to one people group but to all peoples. Even though the claims of Christ as Savior and Lord are exclusive, the scope of the message remains universal. "By the time we reach the New Testament it thus becomes crystal clear that the story the Scriptures tell is fundamentally the story of all creation. It is thus our story, no matter who we are, capable of speaking to us even in the midst of a postmodern crisis."[43]

The obvious inconsistency in postmodernity is the rejection of any worldview as a worldview. In other words, postmodernity states, "The only acceptable worldview is our own."

Hence, the rejection of the metanarrative actually violates the postmodern ethos of marginalizing those who hold to an alternative worldview. Postmodern thinkers defend their position on the grounds that it is inclusive, attempting to embrace all. Christianity can argue the same viewpoint. The gospel is not a metanarrative, an ideology imposed on people, but an intranarrative, a reality exposed in one people and one person—Christ, the redeemer to all the peoples of the world.

The Bible does not begin with the call of Abraham but with the creation of time and all humanity. In the end, the gospel remains scandalous: one people, one person, one place, one faith. Postmodernity may gasp at the proclamation of the good news in Christ but biblical communicators must be prepared to bear the ridicule on this point.

Good News for the Weary

The Christ message can represent clarity and stability in a culture adrift without an anchor. Many evangelical leaders are optimistic in the collapse of the metanarrative.

"When all metanarratives are breaking down, a vacuum of meaning develops. That is fertile ground for the Gospel,"[44] writes Peter Corney. For the person who has tried various options of life and found them wanting, who is weary of endless openness and possibilities, the Christian message provides a resolution. Middleton and Walsh note: "[The Christian message] is the story of the unswerving narrative intent of the Author of creation to liberate his creatures from their bondage, untangling the dead-end plots of their stories by incorporating them into his grand design, through what Jesus has done."[45]

Consequently, it's essential that the preacher not fall into the trap of being wishy-washy with a watered-down message. People who have tired of uncertainty will be seeking straight answers.

"People want to believe you have taken your own advice and while you've not arrived, you're on the way," observes Haddon Robinson. "Likewise, people want to listen to somebody who knows what the struggle is, but who has taken the Bible's message seriously."[46]

James Iliffe concurs that even young people today are skeptical about their skepticism. "I discovered that Generation Xers from all points of the globe were battling the same questions as I was," Iliffe says. "Although we were all tainted by the cynicism of our post-modern age, we hadn't really swallowed the relativism pitch—we were all still looking to find Christ, God, true truth."[47]

So the one thing a biblical communicator cannot fail to do is deliver the punch line of the gospel.

Danny Harrell, a pastor to generation X at Park Street Church in Boston, adds that postmodern people have high expectations beyond the punch line too: "Since they have been burned by so many broken promises, they're not into fads. Rather, they want to know the bottom line. They prefer honesty over politeness."[48]

Like the apostle Paul, the preacher must stand before postmodernity and proclaim, "I am not ashamed of the gospel of Christ for it is the power of God for salvation to everyone who believes" (Rom. 1:16).

Good News with a Personal Touch

An indirect, but effective, approach in tackling metanarrative criticism is to use the "petite narrative," meaning each person's own story. Remember, this is largely because of the postmodern mentality of legitimizing each person's view of reality.

"The basic postmodern attitude toward belief is that a belief that fits a person is fine for that person," state Timothy Phillips and Dennis Okholm. "No story is more privileged than another. This openness to the validity of the personal story of each person means that—at least in theory—anyone should be able to have [his or] her own story and should be free to tell it."[49]

A good technique, then, is to clothe the biblical passage in your messages with the testimonies of real people who lend plausibility to the stories from their own life experiences.

For those who view this as a compromising alternative, Michael Green observes that one man's own testimony played a significant role in the spread of the gospel in the early church accounts.[50]

An account of the apostle Paul's own conversion appears no less than three times in the Book of Acts. "Postmodernists will be open to hearing the stories of other persons because these stories give purpose and shape to social existence," Green explains. "Because the postmodernist diminishes the role of the author and the importance of the individual, the spiritual autobiography and personal testimony can exalt God and not the person. Postmodern people are not antireligious but anti-ecclesiastical; therefore, they may be open to the spiritual autobiography and personal testimony."[51]

Evangelist Leighton Ford picks up the effectiveness of the personal testimony in the book *The Power of Story*.[52] The Christian faith, presented as a set of facts without an effectual change to one's life and relationships, will be deemed of little or no value, Ford writes. But a person's story acts as a starting point to engage the listener with the transforming work of Christ.

Just as didactic preaching served modernity well, emphasizing New Testament Epistles, narrative preaching will resonate with postmodern listeners. Narrative preaching, as well as first person narratives in which the preacher takes on the role of the Bible character, attempts to communicate the biblical story while maintaining the story form.

In narrative, you see, a sermon is heard more like a personal account than a lecture. The account doesn't presume to advance the full scope of understanding regarding a particular theological issue but presents one vantage point, showing God's involvement in the everyday life of individuals.

Robert McKee, a leading movie scriptwriter, provides the following advice to budding film writers—and preachers could benefit from it too: "The famous axiom 'show, don't tell' is key. Never force words into a character's mouth to tell the audience about the world, history, or a person. Rather show honest, natural scenes in which human beings talk and behave in honest, natural ways. . . . In other words, dramatize exposition."[53]

It's in the honest struggle that people will relate. Remember, sermons can become like *Rocky* pictures, if the inevitable victory becomes boring and predictable. So to best intrigue and inform, invite listeners along as you investigate the spiritual journey of Bible characters.

A cautionary note: If you overstate first what takes place in trusting Christ, postmodern people may conclude, "Jesus did not work for me." And if the gospel comes packaged as a quick fix for all that ails, a metanarrative cure-all, the message just won't wash.

Besides the gospel message doesn't promise that if a person comes to Jesus, all problems will go away. The biblical communicator cannot deny that the gospel message is an all-encompassing design of God to redeem a lost world. One can, however, clarify that unlike human schemes, the gospel doesn't serve the rich and powerful or personal self-interest. By the same token, it doesn't exclude any part of humanity, as Christ died as a representative of all people. The changed lives in Christ will continue to cause postmodern listeners to either sit up and take notice or shrug their shoulders and walk away.

The Ultimate Hot Potato

More provocative than money or sex, there's possibly no stickier issue today than the subject of hell. After all, trend watchers indicate an increasing disbelief in the existence of hell across the board for Christians and non-Christians alike. So how can biblical communicators even mention hell and still be taken seriously?

"Nobody other than a small minority of fundamentalists believed in its existence, and nobody even appeared to be much interested in the subject," observes Walter Truett Anderson. "It had been quietly fading away for a long time, apparently—along with Calvinism and other visions of a stern and punitive God."[54]

However, Leon Morris wonders: "Why does anyone believe in hell in these enlightened days? Because Jesus plainly taught its existence; he spoke more often about hell than he did about heaven. We cannot get around the fact.... He said plainly that some people will spend eternity in hell.... He spoke plainly about . . . damnation as well as about salvation."[55]

So you can hardly ignore hell while extolling heaven. The two eternal destinies are linked; to dismiss the teaching on one naturally leads to the abandonment of the other. But if anything is gained from a reading of prophets like Jeremiah, it's learning that we need more preaching on the coming judgment with discernment. As Jeremiah faced, the unpopularity of the message is insufficient reason to remain silent. However, the twenty-first-century need for caution in preaching about hell is not for fear of offending listeners but for fear of confusing them.

Make Disciples, Not Just Followers

The Bible speaks unapologetically about hell's existence, yet will hell serve as a motivation to love and embrace God? If I promise my children to give them chocolate in exchange for attending Sunday school, all that I may be promoting is their deeper love for sweets, not God. If you push condemnation improperly, in your messages, you may end up promoting the wrong result.

In generations past, people maintained ties with the church in order to gain absolution as death approached and escape judgment. However, preaching that focuses on release from condemnation misses the bigger purposes of God. Remember, this is a generation that will not be coerced into belief; Christ followers aren't escaping something as much as they are embracing someone.

Preachers must be aware that the looming issue to the postmodern mind is, "What kind of God are you describing to me? Is your God good?"

As people are made aware that God is not only good, but He's absolutely holy, then they can begin to comprehend the justice of God. Preaching on judgment without an understanding of the kindness of God, however, may lead to a twisted conception—God as petty and punitive.

Preaching to people's fear doesn't work either. Listen to 1 John 4: "God is love. Whoever lives in love lives in God, and God in him. In this way, love is made complete among us so that we will have confidence on the day of judgment, because in this world we are like him. There is no fear in love. But perfect love drives out fear, because fear has to do with punishment. The one who fears is not made perfect in love" (1 John 4:16–18). Doesn't the message seem clear that the gospel is about removing fear through love, resulting in confidence at the judgment? Is fear a worthy motivation to drive people to God? In a postmodern context, fear of reprisal will not produce the quality of discipleship that embraces a full walk with God. Rather, fear can become an unhealthy basis for a relationship.

Ravi Zacharias relates the story of Joseph Stalin and the use of fear. "On one occasion, . . . Stalin called for a live chicken and proceeded to use it to make an unforgettable point before some of his henchmen. Forcefully clutching the chicken in one hand, with the other he began to systematically pluck out its feathers. As the chicken struggled in vain to escape, he continued with the painful denuding until the bird was completely stripped. 'Now you watch,' Stalin said as he placed the chicken on the floor and walked away with some bread crumbs in his hand. Incredibly, the fear-crazed chicken hobbled toward him and clung to the legs of his trousers. Stalin threw a handful of grain to the bird, and as it began to follow him around the room. . . . 'This is the way to rule the people. Did you see how that chicken followed me for food, even though I had caused it such torture? People are like that chicken. If you inflict inordinate pain on them they will follow you for food for the rest of their lives.'"[56]

Followership and discipleship are not the same thing. If people respond to the gospel out of fear, followership may be all one can expect. As people come to know God for who He is, a proper reverence will grow out of an understanding of God's character, His majesty, holiness, and power (Prov. 1:7).

The God Who Is There and Is Not a Jerk

Postmodern listeners come with preconceived notions of God and the Bible. This becomes an example of the axiom "a little knowledge is dangerous." People have a little understanding of the Christian faith, enough for them to ask questions concerning Christianity like, "How can there be a good God with so much evil in the world?" or "What about the person who has never heard about Jesus?"

If you look closely at these questions, the real query being raised is, "Is the God of the Bible fair and compassionate?"

Isn't it sensible, then, when issues of God's fairness arise in the postmodern mind, to attempt to deal with the greater issue of "What is the God of the Bible really like?" Postmodernity, after all, requires a big picture. When addressing the question of "Who is God?" modernity chose to break God down into manageable pieces, so generally the message is a discourse on God's attributes: omniscience, omnipotence, immutability, and the like.

Postmodernity falls in the similar trap of dissecting God by asking, "Who is God to *me?*"

The danger arises that one's concept of God becomes much like the Indian proverb of the elephant and the blind men. What is known is determined solely by the part one is holding at the time. The blind man grasping the tail comments that the elephant is like a snake. The one touching the ear believes the elephant to be like a fan. Both are true statements yet incomplete in and of themselves.

The twenty-first century suffers from an incomplete and inadequate view of God. Postmodernity is more comfortable with tribal deities and small gods who can be identified with and related to.

Yet ours is a big God. Due to the cold analysis of modernity and the subjective fragmentation of postmodernity, the largeness of our God remains an on-going theological theme for twenty-first-century listeners. That means biblical communicators must learn to speak about God in more than sound bites and superficial jargon.

Everything in Moderation

In addressing the coming judgment, preachers must remember twenty-first-century listeners need to see the big picture surrounding the need for justice. Straight from a page out of Jesus' ministry: The Master offers compassion and grace to the wayward, but reserves his harshest indictments for the religious leaders who obstinately refuse to acknowledge a divine outworking even though miraculous deeds are taking place right in front of their faces.

The justice of God, after all, flows out of His holiness. Yet out of the holiness of God likewise flows the provision of the cross. The logic of the cross becomes evident when the cross itself is seen as the appropriate entry point in seeking to understand the true character of God—

because at the heart of God's dealing with humanity lies justice, a just ending that brings hope.

A beautiful picture of this for me was when I attended a screening of the movie *Hurricane*, the life story of Rubin "Hurricane" Carter. I was captivated by the story, which is about Carter's plight—enduring seventeen years behind bars in a New Jersey correctional facility for crimes of murder that he didn't commit.

An African-American teenager named Lesra and three Canadian "do-gooders," in an enormous act of selflessness, decide to devote themselves to seeing Rubin Carter free once again.

The great line from the movie is, "Hate put me in here and love is going to bust me out."

After hearing new evidence obtained by Lesra, a judge overturns the conviction and declares Hurricane free to go.

As I watched the story unfold, tears streamed down my cheeks and I wasn't alone. Other theatergoers were moved too. The fact is people are overwhelmed at the beauty of justice. I believe people innately crave a just ending; they want to see justice served in this life and the next.

But postmodernity struggles with justice because of a lost sense of the transcendence of God. Without a wholly other God, all that's left is a world of imperfection and compromise. We are forced to live our lives on a sliding scale of wrong. That is to say, "sin, like everything else, in moderation never hurt anyone."

This is why people commonly equate staying out of prison as the measuring point of goodness. "Sure," some folks tend to assess, "I've messed up but I'm not bad like the people in prison." They conclude, much like our present-day justice system, that some people deserve punishment for "big" wrongs, while "little" wrongs can go unpunished. Further, most people cannot reconcile the idea of hell and justice.

The point of confusion lies *not in people's disdain for justice but in their failure to appreciate the absolute and holy character of God.* So the struggle for listeners is not that they cannot comprehend hell, as much as that in this age of relativity they cannot comprehend complete and utter holiness. Once listeners perceive God's holiness as Isaiah did in his vision (Isaiah 6), any claim concerning their own goodness vanishes and the gospel can sink in.

The Weeping Prophet Revisited

Now this doesn't mean preachers should avoid talking of hell, or touching upon it lightly. Postmodern people need to be informed and challenged regarding their eternal destiny. But to speak of hell and judgment in a glib fashion can undermine the redemptive purposes of God, turning people away from Him.

Dr. George Murray, an evangelist, tells the story of his trip to L'Abri, the Swiss chalet run by Francis and Edith Schaeffer years ago for spiritual seekers. One of their conversations after dinner was typically deep and theological, Murray recalled. Then someone asked Dr. Schaeffer: "What will happen to all those who have never heard of Christ?"

Dr. Schaeffer didn't give an intellectual, deep, profound answer. He simply bowed his head and wept.[57]

Jesus himself agonized over the people of his day, crying, "O Jerusalem, Jerusalem, you who kill the prophets and stone those sent to you, how often I have longed to gather your children together, as a hen gathers her chicks under her wings, but you were unwilling" (Matt. 23:37).

Biblical preaching needs to link the biblical admonition of coming judgment to the heavenly Father's loving concern as well as our own.

The Immediate Effects

Just as love is what will win people, the flip side of love—fear, as a motivation—is not only biblically inadequate, it's just not very effective either. "Secular people are conscious of doubt more than guilt," writes George Hunter III. "People who feel guilty are more likely to go to a therapist for freedom from the feeling than to a priest for absoluion . . . the profound sense of personal guilt has almost disappeared."[58]

The key to postmodern listeners then is to remember that *doubt precedes guilt*, meaning listeners' questions take precedence over their sense of wrong.

A recent article called "How to Raise Drug-Free Kids" even argued that scare tactics prove an inadequate inducement to keep kids off drugs (and drug abuse is an obvious consequence of a generation that insists upon instant gratification). Instead, the article urged, "Keep advice in the here and now. Talking to adolescents about long-term health risks doesn't have much effect. [Rather, appeal to what] teenagers are concerned with—looking good to their peers. Point out that cigarette smoking causes bad breath and could give them yellow fingers, or that if they drink, they might become ill and throw up in front of their friends."[59]

The best strategy, then, is not a focus on future consequences but more on immediate effects. A recent poll confirms this postmodern mindset. Fifty percent of leading athletes, surveyed in July 1998, indicated they would use performance-enhancing drugs, even with the knowledge that the drugs would kill them after five years, if they could be assured a top place in their sporting field.

The lesson is simple: We in the preaching field would do well to speak to the here and now about a life found in Christ's love that is so strong nothing, not even death, can separate.

A Lesson in Pigeons

Some people still would like preachers to get tough with listeners concerning judgment, and it's not unreasonable to suggest that an understanding of judgment could be seen in the light of a fuller comprehension of God and the cross of Christ. But preaching fear and judgment indiscriminately to twenty-first-century listeners poses three risks: A poor excuse to love God, an inadequate perception on the person of God, and an insufficient motive to act.

A friend in sales once gave the analogy that persuasion is like feeding pigeons. Once there was a man who wanted nothing more in life than to feed pigeons in the park. On his first approach, the man was so excited and eager, he rushed out into the park waving the bread crumbs and shouting, "Look what I've got for you!"

Of course, the pigeons were frightened and flew away.

On his second approach, the man hid crouched in the bushes and when one of the pigeons turned away, he sprang out of hiding and grabbed the bird, proceeding to stuff the bread into the pigeon's beak, declaring, "This is what you need! It's good for you!"

On his third approach, the man calmly took a seat on the park bench and began scattering bread crumbs around the ground. After a short while, the pigeons began to realize that the man meant no harm and that the bread was indeed good to eat. From that point, the man could feed the pigeons to his heart's content.

Preaching involves this type of wisdom, and an appreciation that in our zeal to reach people we can too easily frighten and intimidate our listeners. Yet our yearning is to speak the truth, challenging listeners in a manner that neither makes light of their condition nor compromises the testimony of God's Word. Remember the words of Jesus on sending out the twelve? The advice means more now than ever: "Be as shrewd as snakes and as innocent as doves" (Matt. 10:16).

6 | Inroads

One of the errors of modernity was reducing individuals to the level of mechanized creatures. Consequently, spiritual awakening became a hallmark of the new era known as post-modernity.

The *Newsweek* cover story, "The Search for the Sacred," affirms the awakening. "Detached from the sacred, culture has become a human construct we labor to create. But the yearning for a sacred dimension to life is far from extinct."[1]

"If spirituality as a term was abandoned in the 1960s," Martin Marty observes, "clearly it reemerged in the 1980s and 1990s. . . . Spirituality has been restored to its rightful place, in the way people think, talk, act, and live."[2]

These days, people will talk openly about the human "soul" and, conversely, about an inner sense that something is lost. One female baby boomer confesses, "Something is missing. You turn around and you go, 'Is this it? I have a nice husband, I have a nice house, I was just about to finish graduate school, . . . and there are things that are missing.' I didn't have stimulation. I didn't have the motivation. And I guess when you mention faith, I guess that's what was gone."[3] Something is missing or, as modernity came to understand, "There's a ghost in the machine."

Spirituality Is Hot, Religion Is Not

To the church's detriment, modernity's influence pushed Christian faith out of the public arena. The Enlightenment argued that there's a public world of science and reason, and a private world of belief and values; the church bought into this. Faith then became "a heart religion," divorced from the real, empirical world, observes Alan Roxburgh. God was not seen to be actively involved in the real world except in a private, subjective encounter within the believer. It's like the classic hymn "He Lives" says, "You ask me how I know He lives, He lives within my heart."

No wonder, Roxburgh muses, that as postmodern people seek meaning in their lives or symbols of empowerment, they don't turn to the church: People seek "experience that will reconnect [them] with the spiritual foundations of life, while many churches have been moving in quite a different direction."[4]

Many churches appear far too cerebral and removed from the real world, offering only a "head trip." The spirituality that will attract the postmodern person must be tangible and integrated into everyday life. It involves declaring a faith that's not a refuge from the real world but rather confronts this time and place. A private belief without any meaningful expression in day to day living will only reaffirm a hollowness that postmodern people despise.

Belief without Boundaries

While spirituality is provoking keen interest among postmoderns, their quest for experiences lack theological and traditional religious boundaries. Faith and spirituality, after all—along with everything else for postmoderns—are subjective in nature and therefore can't be critiqued in a reasonable fashion. What's the point, then, to academic discussion where there can be no right or wrong?

Further, postmodernity doesn't discern the difference between faith and superstition. In fact much of what passes as spirituality falls far short of the biblical model, allowing superstition to fit with the postmodern ethos of disliking constraints.

"Astrology is a nice, user-friendly belief system," observes Walter Truett Anderson. "It doesn't ask much of you, and it explains any number of things: It tells you why you are the way you are, why your friends are the way they are (isn't that just like a Scorpio?), and why the things that are happening today are happening today."[5]

In A Generation of Seekers, Roof explains, "There are currents flowing that act across the great spiritual divide. The new values [of baby boomers] emphasize self-fulfillment and self-growth, inner spiritual discovery and exploration. A greater sense of self, appreciation of the body, of gender and spirituality, of reaching out to others, and of letting go are all themes that find common expression."[6]

Roof identifies three ambiguities of the present generation of people. One, they search for spiritual values but do not wish to have any constraints imposed upon them. For many idols are preferable to the Christian worldview. As David Wells explains, "Why do people choose the substitute over God himself? Probably the most important reason is that it obviates accountability to God. We can meet idols on our own terms because they are our own creations. They are safe, predictable, and controllable; they are, in Jeremiah's colorful language, the 'scarecrows in a cucumber field' (Jer. 10:5). They are portable and completely under the user's control. They offer nothing like the threat of a God who thunders from Sinai and whose providence in this world so often appears to us to be incomprehensible and dangerous. . . . [People] need face only themselves. That is the appeal of idolatry."[7]

Two, they wish to cultivate belief but are distrustful of leaders and institutions.

Three, they crave community yet stress personal fulfillment in their lives.[8]

This is the generation that wants it all and on their own terms. It's the Burger King society when it comes to all matters including spirituality—a culture that's been trained to embrace the attitude, "Have it your way."

For preachers, that means many listeners will unquestioningly presume the rightness of what is right lies within. Gone are the days of an authoritarian stance, "It's true because the Bible says so." The preacher can no longer presume to be telling people how it is or setting people straight. To the contrary, people are seeking more of an experienced guide rather than a lecturer to lead them through the intricacies of life and faith.

"Have It Your Way" Spirituality

The quest for spirituality is a personal affair. Roof concludes, "Today's spiritual quests are the working out of the tendencies deeply rooted in an Emersonian conception of the individual who must find God in herself and himself, and of an experience with the divine affirming that she or he is known and loved in a personal way."[9]

After a recent visit to the local bookstore, I discovered that in postmodern times, spirituality resides in the same book section as self-help literature. To the postmodern mind, spirituality is not the same as religion. Religion speaks of rigidity, structure, and institutionalism; whereas, spirituality is about personal growth and wholeness.

The need to find faith on one's own has given birth to the consumer mentality in which houses of worship are tested in the same way you shop through a mall. The problem is postmodern people can be easily taken in by any group as postmoderns generally lack the framework to make critically discerning choices. Another danger is in churches compromising biblical teaching to form a kind of halfway house of Christian belief and something less than an authentic faith.

Proper biblical preaching can maintain a call to follow Christ without reducing either the content of faith or the level of commitment required. "Many people are misinformed about essential Christianity," Hunter warns. "Once they have been exposed to a distorted, diluted form of Christianity, they are inoculated against the real thing."[10]

An important distinction is drawn in leading people with gradual steps toward Christian faith as opposed to altering the message to make it easier to commit to the Christian faith. It's the difference in breaking down a message to make it clear and accessible versus watering down a message to make it palatable. At the end of the day, the Christian faith should be seen as wholly integrated to every facet of human existence that demands a wholehearted commitment. To minimize the message of God in the age of seekers remains a disservice to the Lord and our listeners.

Knowing versus Experiencing God

Spirituality may begin as an interior voice of the heart but it must find expression in meaningful relationships. Mark Filiatreau sums up this postmodern concern in his critique of J. I. Packer's *Knowing God:* "I realized [the book] was not about knowing God, but about knowing *about* God. . . . *Knowing God* struck me as a careful scriptural exegesis of God's attributes, of which I was already well versed. The distance between God and me was still there."[11]

This need for a relational encounter accounts for the warm reception of such programs as Alpha and *Experiencing God,* which are both interactive and prod participants to dialogue their findings—addressing God, not in abstract theological categories but in the context of relationships.

Postmodern people want to understand God in the context of spirituality and relationship, Filiatreau reminds preachers: "Words like 'Christianity' and 'church' should denote in our minds the living and unpredictable spirit of God and newness of life. . . . Our discourse reflects our experience: Regeneration is too often an abstract doctrine and too rarely a concrete reality."[12]

Is it any wonder that churches emphasizing the presence of the Holy Spirit and the experiential outworking of God comprise some of the fastest growing churches around the world?

By the same token, many growing conservative evangelical churches have retained their focus on biblical teaching while infusing a dynamic and vibrant worshiping community. Authentic spirituality moves the listener beyond self-love to devotion to Christ. This process will involve more than mere words, embodying in demonstrative terms a community of faith and the tangible outworkings of faith.

You Want to Go Where Everybody Knows Your Name

And what about community? As the church moves from rationalism to experiential learning, congregations must think carefully about what it means to be an authentic community of faith. "Karl Rahner noted that community above all 'is the visible sign of salvation that God has established in this seemingly godless world.'"[13]

In the past, the temptation might have been to view the message as the headliner and accompanying praise and worship existed merely as the warm-up act. According to Roof, "Many in this generation have deep-seated yearnings—across all religious traditions and across all social categories. If anything, white Protestants expressed more such yearnings than any other. White Protestantism as a heritage probably suffers more than the others in its loss of transcendent faith and its resulting desacralization of life."[14]

Many churches have attracted large numbers of baby boomers and busters because they've recognized the importance of corporate worship as a means to encounter God. This is not to minimize the role of the sermon but to acknowledge that people are seeking more than cognitive dissemination of information.

"Community, of course, is an elusive term and can mean different things to different people," Roof says. "But in practical terms it refers to a group of people who share their lives and communicate honestly with one another, 'whose relationships go deeper than the masks of composure and who have developed some significant commitment to rejoice together, mourn together, and to delight in each other.'"[15]

Increasingly, churchgoers will ask themselves, "What takes place in the life of the church that I could not achieve simply by reading a book or viewing a video?" These longings for a higher degree of human touch return the focus to community. But how will preaching actually foster community?

Belonging to One Another

One could argue that the "Body Life" movement of the seventies surfaced as a sociological reaction to the institutionalism of the modern church. Loyalty to the institution of the church or to a specific denomination was an accepted value among the pre–World War 2 generation, but not anymore.[16]

In loyalty's absence, it's the sense of community that functions as the glue to hold people together in a meaningful way; both baby boomers and busters crave relationships that deliver a sense of belonging. The biblical communicator will have no trouble encountering the countless passages throughout the New Testament that call the people of God to be intimately connected to one another. In a recent series I conducted on the New Testament principles from the "one another" passages—such as "to belong to," "to serve," "to encourage," "to be devoted to," and "to admonish" one another—a wonderful outpouring of affirmation sprung from the congregation.

Months after the series concluded, people spoke wistfully about how meaningful that emphasis was to them. One person commented, "I was sorry to see it end." As society breaks down and people become more alienated from one another, the church is uniquely poised to address the need for community. In fact, today's churches should supply not only a theological context for belief but also a sociological one.

A Grace-full Community

Community and grace. Is there anything more attractive and winsome than grace in action? Modernity struggled with grace because rationally speaking, it didn't make sense. The parable of the workers in Matthew 20 highlights the tension between grace and human rationality: Casual workers are recruited for the harvest beginning in the morning throughout the day. One would naturally conclude that those who work the longer hours should be compensated with a greater payment. However, the scandal of God's grace is to reward each worker with equal generosity, regardless of the effort. Grace defies all ideas of *quid pro quo*, "do this and get that in return."

As a result, many Christian splinter groups that sprung up in the height of the Enlightenment, such as the Jehovah's Witnesses and the Mormons, were quick to jettison salvation by grace along with other teachings deemed incomprehensible to human rationalism. Salvation based on one's good work is sensible. Grace, like life, is messy. It's best understood when framed in the context of relationship grounded in forgiveness and understanding. The relational focus of grace strikes a responsive chord in postmodern times for the same reasons that modernity rejected it.

To understand just how the absence of grace impacts people's perception of the church, the following is a list of "religious abuses" according to baby boomers:[17]

- obsessive praying, talking about God, quoting Scripture
- thinking the world and our physical bodies are evil
- refusing to think, doubt, or question
- excessive judgmental attitudes
- isolation from others
- unrealistic fears, guilt, remorse, and shame
- thinking only in terms of black and white—simplistic thinking
- excessive fasting and compulsive overeating
- belief that sex is "dirty"
- cries for help: physical and mental breakdown
- attitudes of conflict with science, hospitals, and schools

Do you see some emerging themes in this list? The people of postmodernity reject the "us and them" mentality. Tirades against a godless world will only cement their suspicion of the church's self-superiority. People will insist upon a freedom to think carefully through issues for themselves and are wary of simplistic formulas to resolve life's issues. Today's listeners will struggle with observances that focus upon unconditional adherence. Lastly, people will be suspicious of those with power, in particular, the use of crass emotional and moral manipulation.

Yet, the question arises, "What about the call to uphold the high moral standards of God?" Behavioral motivation will work toward external changes, a quick fix to remedy people's patterns. In preaching, this can be evidenced in the "Do more" messages. People walk away from the worship with a perpetual sense that they aren't measuring up. As someone once said, "You've not been to worship unless you walk away feeling guilty." This is unbiblical and unfruitful.

Romans 2 reminds us, "You, therefore, have no excuse, you who pass judgment on someone else, for at whatever point you judge the other, you are condemning yourself, because you who pass judgment do the same things. . . . Or do you show contempt for the riches of his kindness, tolerance and patience, not realizing that God's kindness leads you toward repentance?"

Increasingly, people will not be intimidated or bullied into faith but must be gently led.

It's a Terrible Thing to Live in Fear

Will legalism within churches continue into the twenty-first century? Undoubtedly. In a time of uncertainty, a few people will find the clarity of legalism desirable. Yet the vast majority will find it untenable. To what extent will people be forced to have their act together before entering one's fellowship? The presence of grace frees the preacher from having to reform individuals or to manipulate listeners but instead to leave that in Christ's hands.

In *The Grace Awakening,* author Charles Swindoll cites S. Lewis Johnson who declared back in 1963, "One of the most serious problems facing the orthodox Christian church today is the problem of legalism. . . . Legalism wrenches the joy of the Lord from the Christian believer. . . . Nothing is left but cramped, somber, dull, and listless profession. The truth is betrayed, and the glorious name of the Lord becomes a synonym for a gloomy kill-joy. The Christian under law is a miserable parody of the real thing."[18]

How often would the casual listener in our churches be left with the impression that the kingdom of God is about what one eats and drinks? When Christianity is reduced to a set of rules or a moral code of conduct, twenty-first-century listeners will be left wanting more.

Churches will have to acknowledge that some decisions are a matter of conscience. Congregations that legislate each minute detail of conduct will be viewed as oppressive. Biblical preaching in the twenty-first century will empower people to think Christianly and make godly choices. As Hebrews 5:14 speaks of training "to distinguish good from evil."

In the film *The Shawshank Redemption,* actor Morgan Freeman portrays Red, a man who has spent his prime wasting away in prison because of a reckless act of violence he committed as a teenager. After forty years of incarceration, Red finally receives his release to enjoy the freedom for which he's longed.

However, he can't seem to free himself from the habit of asking for permission each time he wishes to use the men's room. He's what's called "an institutional man," after all. This newfound life scares him as he's grown accustomed to the structure behind bars. The rigidity is in his DNA. Imprisonment had become safe for Red. He didn't have to exercise his own decision making. Someone else did the thinking for him and now, on the outside, he's faced a prospect more daunting and terrifying than incarceration: freedom.

Red confesses that he contemplates all the various ways to break his parole and return to the security of his prison cell. He sums up his dilemma in one line: "It is a terrible thing to live in fear."

People caught up in legalism are no different than Red—scared to death of the freedom that grace brings. It's much easier to retreat to our cells of dos and don'ts, of black and white categories. But biblical preaching should not protect people by erecting legalistic walls. Instead it can release people by equipping them to discern godly choices on their own. How often have messages blasted people, though, for their failures without offering any constructive measures to help the listener move forward?

Grace-full Preaching

It's been stated, "How something is said is as important as what is said. Rigidity in the pulpit is usually heard in the pew as condemnation. The preacher who seems not to know any personal sin is strong on judgment but weak on grace. Our model is Jesus who said to the unnamed woman taken in adultery, 'Neither do I condemn you. Go and sin no more.'" (John 8:11b).[19]

Too often today's preaching can suggest an elitist mentality that the insiders of the church comprise the "good people" and those on the outside are the "bad people." To certain onlookers, the church's function can be mistaken as bringing in the "bad people" so that they can become "good people." A lack of humility is a clear indicator that postmodern people have failed to grasp the nature of grace.

In truth, grace is a risky proposition. When the message of grace is proclaimed, no one can claim superiority before God and no one is excluded from the invitation into God's presence. But this understanding of grace is fostered in and through the use of language. Postmodernity ushered in the era of political correctness. More than ever before, twenty-first-century people understand the importance of language in either affirming or marginalizing people. According to rhetorical theorist Kenneth Burke, "language has the ability to effect cooperation and create community among people."[20]

Inclusive language needs to be understood in light of our critics, who have leveled charges against the church as promoting white, Anglo males while alienating women, minorities, and the underclass.

"Male preachers, especially, may need to change lenses in order to prepare sermons that reflect a more generous slice of the world," advises Haddon Robinson. "Sermons which are illustrated only by stories about men, quotations from men, and portraits of men receive an increasingly unfavorable response. Neither do they reflect a biblical message."[21]

Speaking to a broader audience requires a sacrifice, he adds: "We give up our freedom to use certain kinds of humor, to call minority groups by names that make sense to us, to illustrate only from books and movies we find interesting, to speak only to people with our education and level of Christian commitment. . . . Sacrificing what comes most naturally to us, though, is what gives us a platform to speak. Just as a legalistic Jew wouldn't regard Paul as credible if Paul ignored the law, so many women, for example, won't regard a preacher as credible if he shows zero sensitivity to their issues."[22]

So a commitment to building community will be reflected not just in the content of the message but in the language as well.

This commitment will take into account the composition of the listening audience too. It's easy to understand how off-putting the terms "unbeliever" and "non-Christian"—or worse yet, "pagan" and "lost"— can sound to the average person. Too often, sermons can unintentionally create an "us and them" mentality. Unchurched people will be sensitive to terminology and tones that convey they're either unwanted or not respected.

I encountered this one Sunday. A young man approached me after a morning message about an eagle living among turkeys. I'd commented that as Christians, we, the eagles, are called to a greater living than hanging around with turkeys.

The young seeker openly queried, "I'm not a Christian. Were you calling me a turkey?" I wasn't trying to put off this guy, but I'd failed to consider how this analogy might be heard in the ears of a seeker.

"I do everything I can to show people I respect them and I'm on their side," Robinson says as a friendly reminder. "I'm careful about terms. Even though you're sure you don't have a bias, a listener may think you do if your phrasing offends them."[23]

People can sense intuitively whether they're accepted or not. Whatever interest a seeker may have in spiritual things, the person will not linger in an environment in which he or she does not feel valued. Fellowships that attract people from the ranks of the unchurched work hard at communicating the truth of God's Word in a way that doesn't belittle those who haven't yet arrived at faith.

Calling people to a decision without alienating them can be a tricky exercise. In approaching an invitation, I like what Australian evangelist John Chapman does. He acknowledges that his listeners are at different places on their spiritual journey. He'll declare, "If this is the first time you've heard the message of Jesus, I'm not talking to you anymore. It's great that you came but I'm now addressing the people who had ample time to consider the claims of Christ."

This device releases people from the pressure of feeling manipulated, that they must decide right now. Likewise, by acknowledging the presence of seekers, the preacher lends assurance that their attendance is appropriate and anticipated. It communicates to non-Christians, "You've come to the right place." If the preaching seeks to build community in a way that will reflect grace and attract those apart from Christ, careful consideration is essential to language and the makeup of listeners.

The Real McCoy

Community grows out of authenticity of living. Grace frees every person to be real, "warts and all." Yet, authenticity in churches will begin in the pulpit and filter down throughout the congregation. Those in leadership will set the tone either for depth or shallowness. The lack of authenticity stands as one of the reasons people cite for leaving the church.

William Hendricks reveals, "There seemed to be a feeling that religious situations too often lack authencity. The truth is not told; people are not 'real.' Christian sermons, books, and conversations too often seemed to avoid the 'bad stuff.' Indeed, religion sometimes seems off in a world of its own. Yet my interviewees felt that if faith is to make any difference in people's lives, it has to face cold, hard reality. It also has to get under the surface to a person's real self, to one's sin and pain and the things one wants to hide."[24]

In our approach to authenticity, the preacher no longer stands above the congregation in a condescending fashion. "Gone are the days when preaching meant an aloof, authoritarian lecture," observes Haddon Robinson. "An impersonal preacher, these days, is almost a contradiction in terms. People have come to expect personal preaching—vulnerability and self-revelation."[25]

The biblical message needs to be presented in relation to the lives of people and importantly, the life of the speaker. Calvin Miller affirms the value of a relational and casual approach, declaring, "The good, healthy sermonic 'I' says, 'Draw up your pew and let's have a coffee-and-doughnuts communication.'"[26]

This approach assumes a willingness to allow people to get close— and that in getting close, they'll sense something of a heart that beats for God, and community will form as people are willing to be vulnerable with one another about their victories and struggles. But this pattern of authenticity begins at the top.

A cautionary note: Don't set yourself up as the model of Christian goodness. When illustrating godly behavior, have the grace to acknowledge someone else in the church, not yourself. When describing how Christians can blow it on occasions, feel free to offer yourself as an example. Such humility and vulnerability will reflect a depth of character that draws others toward greater openness too.

Preaching with authenticity also requires leadership. It means broaching the difficult subjects that are circling in the listener's mind. If the listeners sense the preacher is unwilling to delve in the real issues of life, the sermon will be perceived as a waste of their time. Loscalzo offers, "Milquetoast sermons that dismiss the sticky issues of Christian faith, sermons that water down the demands of the gospel, pabulum preaching pleasing to people's ears but worthless in terms of offering transformed lives will be transparent to the skeptical lenses of postmodernity."[27]

Likewise, Roof's research affirms that baby boomers and postmoderns have failed to make a connection between their belief and the real world. "Many of them never abandoned their beliefs, but often the beliefs seem disjointed from their life experiences. Congregations where the atmosphere helps to bring these two—belief and experience—into some meaningful whole are more likely to capture their loyalties."[28]

Issues like sexuality and sexual conduct, managing finances, growing relationships, and prioritizing one's life are in the forefront of people's minds. Stuart Briscoe believes, "People want to know if the Bible's message can stand up to modern pressures and I want to assure them it can."[29]

If preachers today are to show how the gospel touches every aspect of every being, they must address the touchy subjects with care and thoughtful discourse, reaffirming the authenticity of the Christian faith.

In summary, the community of the church plays an extraordinary role in the reception of the gospel within postmodern times. Frederick Buechner suggests that the model present in a typical AA meeting is worthy of consideration. "[T]he church was born to function like an Alcoholics Anonymous group. Sinners Anonymous, . . . where people 'tell where they went wrong and how, day by day, they are trying to go right. They tell where they find the strength and understanding and hope to keep trying.' Anywhere on earth we go, we can find a group meeting nearby where we can go for help and healing, support and encouragement, 'to listen to the truth and to tell it.' This vision of the church holds a key for today's preaching. By listening to the truth, and telling it, preaching can remain relevant for society while maintaining the distinctive quality that makes it the Body of Christ."[30]

Creation and Connectedness to the World

In my recent travels through San Francisco I was struck in one afternoon by two distinctly different appreciations. Gazing down from a mountain perch, I marveled at the engineering feat of the expansion bridge known as the Golden Gate. This staggering structure caused me to reflect on our human ingenuity: "How incredible are the things we build?" However, earlier that day, I'd strolled through the majestic redwood cathedrals of John Muir State Park, where the forest stirred within me a deep desire to worship as I pondered God's magnificence: "Who is like the Lord?" Both encounters were breathtaking, yet, one led me to boast, "Man, we're something" while the other brought me to my knees, thinking "My God, there is none like You." How often does today's preaching elicit the former response in listeners and not the latter? Have biblical communicators misplaced the understanding that creation has a way of drawing the focus off of self and placing it onto God?

Certainly the reaction against modernity has resulted in a renewed sense of the environment. In centuries past, men and women of God took great pleasure in passing time with the Creator amid nature as a means of enhancing their appreciation of the Lord. Then modernity's focus upon the Word distracted people from what creation might say about God. Now the value of the created order stikes a responsive chord among postmodern listeners. Even a casual glance through any modern art exhibit underscores the prevalence that people sense an alienation in the universe.

"The problem is" authors Middleton and Walsh observe, "that once we become aware that our sense of being-at-home in the world is a construct, not a given, that sense of being-at-home is stripped away from us. The result is a sense of cosmic homelessness."[31]

Modernity's analytic approach to nature served only to heighten the human sense of being "the cosmic orphan."

We've Got to Get Back to the Garden

For many evangelicals, the tension between salvation in Christ and the social gospel still remains. Because of this rift, evangelicals abandoned responsibility for physical provision and human welfare as well as ecological concerns, leaving these duties to those less committed to God's

Word. This sentiment was evidenced in the language. Churches commonly spoke about "saving souls."

In the Enlightenment, Christians adopted a dissecting approach to humanity and yet has anyone ever encountered a person's soul that was somehow unattached to a human body? However, in recent decades, the evangelical church has witnessed a return to the reconciliation of both functions, caring for spiritual as well as social and physical needs. John Stott notes, "It is a whole Christian lifestyle, including both evangelism and social responsibility, dominated by the conviction that Christ sends us out into the world as the Father sent him into the world, and that into the world we must therefore go—to live and work for him."[32]

Along with this new openness to the whole person come these environmental concerns. Over the past decades, critics have commonly viewed the church as only interested in its own backyard. But the message of Christ wanting to redeem the world falls on deaf ears if the listeners targeted see the church turn a blind eye to the environmental problems.

Yet, when concerns are raised about the deterioration of the rain forests and global warming, how many Christians are prepared to say, let's give the preservation of environmental life the same benefit of the doubt. By addressing environmental issues with earnest concern, the church can restore some sense of connectedness between God, the people, and His created world.

In her book *Nature, God and Pulpit*, Elizabeth Achtemeier points to what she calls "the marvelous balance that the Scriptures bring to our understanding of ourselves as human beings." She observes, "We are the creatures made in the image of God, and we cannot be understood apart from that relationship. That relationship implies responsibility, and a part of that responsibility is to care for the earth on behalf of its owner, God."[33]

Achtemeier is calling for preachers to recognize the regency role of humanity under God, to reign and care for the earth in God's name as His image-bearers. As observers agree: "At the same time we are 'merely creatures' and '. . . everything we do on the earth is to point to the sovereignty of the one God and to further the will of the one Lord who made heaven and earth.'"[34]

Your Will Be Done on Earth As in Heaven

While it's true environmental concerns don't resonate with the same sense of urgency as the gospel of Christ, many preachers have come down on the wrong side of these issues. This sends all the wrong messages and leaves groups outside of the Christian faith to call people to environmental consciousness.

In effect, the Christian message can no longer say, "Let's save the people, but the earth can go to hell." For the twenty-first-century listener, a disregard for the environment will be viewed as a callous indifference to all people, both present and future. The God of the Bible never makes Himself out to be some local deity, but indeed, the creator God of the whole universe. It doesn't hurt to remind people of this.

The Creator God, the Cosmic Killjoy

Many people harbor a suspicion that God is out to ruin our fun. The perception is, if God does exist, He wouldn't be overly concerned with rules and regulations. People crave freedom. The common belief is that somehow the prescriptions of the Bible run counter to what's actually best for us.

In the movie *The Devil's Advocate*, Al Pacino portrays the devil who rails against a creator God who gives us natural urges and desires and then instructs us, "Look, but don't touch. Touch, but don't taste. Taste, but don't swallow." The devil is arguing what most people already suspect: that the God of the Bible appears unfair. Preaching can no longer ignore these mental objections, demonstrating both the necessity and wisdom of living as God desires. Connected with the Creator means living according to His parameters.

Gary Richmond, a former zookeeper, relates both a funny and compelling experience when just starting out:

> "Richmond," the supervisor said, "these keys will let you in to care for millions of dollars worth of animals. Some of them could never be replaced, but you could be, if you catch my drift. Some of the animals would hurt themselves if they got out, and more significantly, they might hurt and even kill somebody. You wouldn't want that on your conscience."
>
> I took him seriously, and performed flawlessly for four months. Then something happened with the most dangerous animal at the zoo: Ivan was a polar bear who weighed well over nine hundred pounds and had killed two prospective mates. He hated people and never missed an opportunity to attempt to grab anyone passing by his cage.
>
> I let him out of his night quarters into the sparkling morning sunshine by pulling a lever to his guillotine door. No sooner had he passed under it than I realized that, at the other end of the hall, I had left another door opened. It was the door I would use to go outside if Ivan was locked up inside. Now Ivan could walk to the other end of the outdoor exhibit and come in that door I had left open, and, if he so chose, eat me.
>
> In terror I looked out the guillotine door. Ivan was still in sight. He was a creature of routine, and he always spent the first hour of his morning pacing. His pattern was L-shaped. He would walk from the door five steps

straight out, and then turn right for three steps. He would then rock back and forth and come back to the guillotine door again, which he would bump with his head. He would repeat that cycle for one hour and then rest.

I timed his cycle and determined that I had seventeen seconds to run down the hallway and shut the open door. I staked my life on the fact that he would not vary his routine. He didn't seem to notice the wide open door, which is unusual. Animals tend to notice the slightest changes in their environment.

I decided that when he made his next turn, I would run down the hallway, hoping upon hope that I would not meet Ivan at the other end.

He turned and I ran. With every step my knees weakened. My heart pounded so hard I felt sure it would burst from fear. I made the corner and faced the critical moment. Ivan was still out of sight; I lunged for the door handle. As I reached out for the handle, I looked to the right. There was the bear . . . eight feet away. Our eyes met. His were cold and unfeeling . . . and I'm sure mine expressed all the terror that filled the moment. I pulled the huge steel door with all my strength. It clanged shut and the clasp was secured. My knees buckled and I fell to the floor racked with the effects of too much adrenalin. I looked up and Ivan was staring at me through the window in the door.[35]

Gary Richmond was instructed to be careful when handed the zoo keys. Was the supervisor being harsh and mean when he gave the instructions to guard his actions? Of course not. The supervisor knew the potential danger to everyone if Richmond acted carelessly. God is no different. Just as the natural world functions according to certain guidelines, so too God's instructions are designed to guard against self-destructive and hurtful acts. Or, as the film *Jurassic Park* points out the wisdom of natural laws, Christians need to demonstrate the wisdom of God's order.

There's a song that goes, "I'm free to do what I want any old time." Yet freedom is not found in following our every whim but in living in accordance with the boundaries of both the natural world and God's moral world. In the Enlightenment the physical world was separated from the spiritual world. Today biblical communicators endeavor to show the connectedness between the two realms as being integrated by a creator God and a redeeming Savior. Contrary to popular opinion, living in relation to God brings joy and fullness to life.

Hope beyond Mickey Mouse

What is the attraction about Disney that people flock to its theme parks and buy its merchandise in droves? There's even a saying that goes, "If the lines inside Disney are too long, just stand outside the fence and throw your money over." I thought about this while on a family excursion to one theme park. Had Disney really created the "happiest place on Earth"? Maybe the wholesome family fun and the return of innocence found in this invented children's world is the closest that many people will come to godliness. Disney certainly replicates a world of smiles, goodness, and universal peace all for the price of admission; the Disney experience causes most visitors to wish they lived in a world characterized by goodwill and benevolence rather than evil and mistrust. For some folks Disney World may even seem a modern day Eden, the world as we might wish it could be. Is there hope beyond Mickey Mouse?

The start of the twenty-first century, steeped in relativism and void of universal truth, is characterized as a time of deep uncertainty. Stanley Grenz states, "For the first time in recent history, the emerging generation does not share the conviction of their parents that the world is becoming a better place in which to live."[36]

One danger in addressing postmodern listeners lies in becoming consumed in the ambiguity of the day. This would be the ultimate disaster for the gospel. Postmodern times represent a society deeply entrenched in uncertainty and yet open to the reality of the supernatural. To capitulate to a society that sees nothing as foundational or viable would be a costly mistake.

On the other hand, people of postmodernity are street-smart. They see all the angles and have heard it all before. Reared on television, the postmodern generation is a bundle of useless information and sound bites. Today's listeners approach the issues of life with a muddled self-awareness.

Shows like *Married with Children,* and cartoons like *The Simpsons, The Larry Sanders Show, The Tick,* and *Animaniacs,* plus movies like *Scream, Hot Shots,* and *Naked Gun* are conscious of their genre and often screened as a mild form of self-parody. Written into each show will be lines in which characters step out of character and utter, "Is that really in the script?" or "We can't do that old gag!"

In so doing these shows reflect a self-consciousness of tired and worn formulas, anticipating the audience's awareness. A sophisticated show tips its hat to the savvy viewers, acknowledging that they have seen it all before. As a result, postmodernity teeters on the brink of two ledges: One is uncertainty and the other is a jaded cynicism. A fall from either ledge ends in despair. Into this mix the biblical communicator presents hope in Christ.

More than anything, today's preaching holds out hope in Christ, a hope that can satisfy people's longing for certainty and shatter their cynicism. The tension for postmodern listeners lies between the heart and the mind. The mind tells them that nothing is real or trustworthy, but the heart still longs for the clarity of meaning and purpose. For many, the good news of Christ is quickly dismissed as too good to be true. An example of this can be seen at a wine tasting evening, hosted by Christians to reach out to the community. As people gave their testimonies, a woman professor leaned over to evangelist and theologian Michael Green and whispered, "You know, I don't believe any of this."

Michael then replied, "Yeah, I know, but wouldn't you like to?" With that remark, tears welled up in the woman's eyes.[37] Her head told her "no," but her heart yearned to hear.

"We live in complex and confusing times, and the future promises more of the same. The proliferation of information and the acceleration of change have left most of us struggling to find firm footing. . . . All of these changes may cause us to question Paul's choice of love (as the greatest virtue) and say, 'But the greatest of these is hope.'"[38]

A Hope beyond This World

The strength of hope in the twenty-first century lies firstly in the assurance beyond the grave. In the twentieth century, many preachers abstained from addressing the afterlife because secular humanism dismissed the subject of eternity as pie-in-the-sky ideology. In response to this, William Willimon writes, "one reason the [contemporary] world ignores our preaching is because it rarely hears anything from us it cannot hear from Dear Abby or Leo Buscaglia."[39]

With postmodern times, however, comes a new openness to the possibilities of supernatural existence. Spiritual matters are no longer viewed as irrelevant and unrelated to "real life." In a *Time* article titled "Does Heaven Exist?" (March 24, 1997), one survey revealed that as many as 88 percent of Americans believed they would meet friends and family members in heaven after they die.[40]

In the same article, a recent convert to Roman Catholicism relates that the absence of teaching about heaven created a void in his life. He voiced his complaint, stating, "There was this hope of heaven I thought we all should have. But the priests didn't like to talk about it."[41]

Certainly, the enduring heritage of the Christian faith echoes in the words of Isaiah as quoted by the apostle Paul, "No eye has seen, no ear has heard, no mind conceived what God has prepared for those who love him" (1 Cor. 2:9). The hope of Christ beyond the grave rests at the heart of the gospel message and should be given full voice in these uncertain times.

Into the relativism of the twenty-first century, the pronouncement of an eternal existence becomes unquestionably vital. It was Simone Weil who pointed out, "To be always relevant, you have to say things which are eternal."[42]

We walk and move among people who long to embrace what really matters. What are the things of life that count? A clear advantage for preaching in the postmodern times lies in the disillusionment with life. Dorothy Sayers observes, "In the world it is called Tolerance, but in hell it is called Despair. . . . the sin that believes in nothing, cares for nothing, seeks to know nothing, interferes with nothing, enjoys nothing, hates nothing, finds purpose in nothing, lives for nothing, and remains alive because there is nothing for which it will die."[43]

People no longer buy into the dream that we can reinvent paradise on earth and that "things can only get better." The Australian band The Eurogliders had a hit with the song in which the following chorus rang out, "Heaven must be there. Oh, it's just got to be there. I've never, never seen Eden; I don't want to live in this place." Yet, our society is drawn to focus upon the immediate and therefore their energies become centered in that which ultimately will not last.

A telling commentary on today's society aired on the now axed television show *Millennium*, which is written by influential *X-files* creator Chris Carter. In this episode, a serial killer is stalking clergymen. A confrontation ensues in a cathedral. Frank Black, the tracker, learns that the killer is a disillusioned believer who now views the church as a fraud and faith in God as a sham. Gazing into Frank's eyes the killer detects, "You don't believe either."

Black responds, "I haven't thought about it for a while," neither agreeing nor disagreeing with the troubled person.

The killer then proceeds to rant about the impossibility of God in a world so bleak and tormented. After the serial killer is captured, the final scene gives pause to reflect. Frank and his wife share a quiet moment in their bedroom with this incident, giving them a renewed opportunity to consider why they have not pursued a religious faith.

After silently weighing the value of belief, Frank utters the closing line, "It's true we live in a world in which evil happens, but we can't give up hope."

Carter, both creator of the show and writer of this episode, was speaking for many of this postmodern generation who are holding out for something to give their lives a sense of place. In the disillusionment of the day, the hope of something greater, something lasting can be spoken.

Hope: Dancing to the Music of Faith

The message of hope offers assurance of real living in one's present existence; hope in Christ addresses the restlessness and arbitrary existence of the postmodern world. It's been said, "Faith is hearing the music and hope is dancing to it." Some will tire of the endless possibilities and hunger for a message showing one, clear way.

"The power of religion lies in its capacity to create humanly significant worlds," writes Roof. "In the most basic way, religion provides an anchor, a mooring amidst chaos. 'You have something to hold on to,' one reflective respondent said, 'or else you lose direction in a world where everything seems so relative, so unsure.'"[44]

Baby busters, particularly, will seek a cause worthy of their lives, something in which they can give their lives. Christianity in its full measure offers a challenge to impact the world in a significant way.

Some people have argued that the present culture is immune to commitment. The truth lies more closely in recognizing the deep cynicism of movements and that people are loath to give themselves to a self-serving institution. Commitment in postmodern times is not out of the question. Roof defines the baby boomers as "a generation weighing what commitment means."[45]

One factor in commitment is pinpointed by Robert Nisbet in his book *Twilight of Authority:* "As a society becomes increasingly complex, individuals become overtaxed and unable to integrate all the loyalties in their lives. In order to gain control of their inner world, they are forced to narrow the range of their commitments and interests."[46]

Postmodernity comes with too many choices so people know intuitively that they must choose carefully.

A second factor in commitment is that postmodern people feel as if they've already been burned too many times and that every new solution is equally deceitful and manipulative. As in the title of The Who's song, postmodern people warily say to themselves, "We won't be fooled again."

Preachers bent on the quick fix will be continually disappointed. Commitment to Christ, to a fellowship, and to a ministry will be weighed carefully and tested patiently.

Commonly people will attend our fellowship for well over a year before voicing their allegiance to Christ or taking a step of formal membership. The key will be in cultivating a sense of belonging in the meantime. Without that, a person may never come around.

George Hunter explains, people "generally do not ask about life after death so much as they ask about real life this side of death."[47]

I recall being at a high school assembly in which Christian basket-ballers were scrimmaging the high school team as a point of contact with the teenagers. At the halftime break, one of the Christian players offered his reflection on the value of faith. He stood before this assem-bly of teenagers, some open, some woefully lost, and told them that he came to Christ because the world seemed too complicated and he was tired of having to make decisions. In short, he argued that embracing Christ simplified his life.

I couldn't help but think that the opposite tack might have been more fruitful: Throw down the gauntlet. Tell them that taking a stand for Jesus Christ will be the hardest, the most challenging, yet most satisfying expe-rience of their life.

Tony Campolo does this well as he declares to his readers, "I want you to dream dreams, I want you to have visions, I want you to believe that this same Jesus who died on the cross for your sins two thousand years ago is with you right now. I want you to know that He wants to invade your life, that He wants to use you to do His will. He truly wants to do this—He wants to use you to touch the lives of people who are hurt, to bring joy to people who are sad. He wants to make you into an agent fighting for His great revolution. He wants to begin to change the world through you."[48]

Campolo envisions being part of a spiritual revolution, not an insti-tution. He writes: "We in youth work have mistakenly assumed that the best way to relate to young people is to provide them with various forms of entertainment. For many of us, there is no end to the building of gym-nasiums, the sponsoring of hayrides and the planning of parties. We would do better if we invited our young people to accept the challenge to heroically change the world."[49]

That's precisely the kind of vision that twenty-first-century young people desire.

Many watching the church hear the rhetoric of a revolution, but all they see is a garden party on the front lawn. The evangelical return to social justice or relief concerns fits well into the modern sentiment, "Think globally, act locally." But for many observers outside the church, the people of God are seen to be doing nothing but protecting their own interests. The message of hope in Christ falls on deaf ears unless Chris-tians are perceived as people of hope.

"One of the favorite passages of contemporary Christian apologists is 1 Peter 3:15," comments Philip Kenneson. That verse urges that Chris-tians "always be prepared to give an answer to everyone who asks you to give the reason for the hope that you have."

"To their credit," Kenneson says, "evangelicals, perhaps more than anyone, are poised to give answers; the problem is that no one is asking. Unless we're content to answer questions no one's posing, it seems to me the most urgent apologetic task of the church is to live in the world in such a way that the world is driven to ask us about the hope we have."[50]

Kenneson closes with a quote from Wittgenstein: "The truth can be spoken only by someone who is already at home in it," not by someone who still lives in falsehood and reaches out from falsehood towards truth on just one occasion."[51]

In modernity, after all, the focus is on words and providing answers. In postmodernity, the focus is on truth and living out the hope that is in us.

Some in postmodern times will embrace the message of Christ, providing that the hope in Christ is seen to generate a vision and conviction to make a difference in one's life. Alister McGrath states, "[People] do not feel secure in the world. This awareness of an absence of security is itself a powerful stimulus to look for some grounds of assurance. . . . The apologist [and the preacher] has the task of correlating the gospel with this sense of profound unease, interpreting it and fulfilling it with the presence of the living God."[52]

Generation X author Douglas Coupland writing *Life after God*, a series of fictional encounters with young people today on the streets of Vancouver, leaves readers with these sober words:

> Now here is a secret: I tell it to you with an openness of heart that I doubt I shall ever achieve again, so I pray that you are in a quiet room as you hear these words. My secret is that I need God—that I am sick and can no longer make it alone. I need God to help me give, because I no longer seem to be capable of giving; to help me be kind, as I no longer seem capable of kindness; to help me love, as I seem beyond being able to love.[53]

The postmodern generation can be seen as cynical, hard, indifferent, and jaded. In so few years, they have experienced much harm. They are like teenage runaways: The tough appearance only serves to hide their deep-seated fear, but underneath the exterior lurks a yearning for something profound, meaningful, and beautiful. Biblical preaching must "hold out the word of life" (Phil. 2:16) both for this life and the one to come, and for a broken people whose faith, hope, and love have become rare commodities.

Sense over Sensibility

Since postmodernism truly is the triumph of sense (or what one experiences) over sensibility (what one reasons), will preachers feel pressured to stop making sense all together? No, but bear in mind four post-modern considerations concerning rational thought:

1. People can manipulate rationality to suit their purposes. Ravi Zacharias asks, "While most people will believe something without subjecting it to rational critique, they disbelieve things on the basis that they're rationally inadmissible. They critically attack Christian assumptions using the principles of logic that they don't even hold to."[54]
2. Deep down, people want life to make sense. Absurdity is all right in small doses, but nobody wants to live in it.
3. Postmodern listeners still use reason to understand their world but not exclusively; their experiences and cultural context slant their perceptions of life. Reason alone is not enough.
4. Living in a multicultural society full of complexity, people in the twenty-first century have become accustomed to a world of ambiguity. The people in our society have built up a tolerance for living with contradictions.

In an interview with philosopher Mortimer Adler, the question was posed, "'How do you know there is a real, tangible world outside our minds?' . . . Adler slowly turned his head toward the interviewer and, without cracking a smile, said, 'It's no great mystery. The world outside of my mind never lets me forget it is there. When I run into a wall, reality abruptly stops me. When I throw cold water on my face, reality wakes me up. If I stub my toe or burn myself, reality brings me a taste of pain. If I ever think the external world is not there, reality finds a way to slap some sense into me. The external world is there. I have the bruises to prove it.'"[55]

Some aspects of life can still be shown to be inescapable, no matter how undesirable and unsavory they may be. People living in the post-modern era may be relativistic and wary of reason but certain realities exist that cannot be denied.

Building a Mystery

In the Enlightenment assumption of the all-encompassing nature of reason, the Christian faith was left little room for the supernatural and the unexplainable. McCullough writes concerning modernity, "In place of God, we now have control and explanation. Scientific investigation requires control of relevant variables (often in laboratory settings) in order to test the reliability of theories. . . . And explanation, in turn, supplies the knowledge for further control, and on it goes, as our mastery increases and God seems less and less necessary."[56]

In modernity, unless something could be rationally broken down and dissected, it couldn't be true. As a result many theological tenets were brought under scrutiny such as the sovereignty of God and human responsibility or the Trinity. With modernity came the loss of awe. Everything was analyzed underneath a microscope.

However, postmodern times have moved toward a holistic view of the world and life, and the obsession to rationalize each aspect of God is slowly dissolving. People are more prepared to embrace mystery surrounding a Divine Being and the universe, which accounts for today's growing infatuation with many Eastern beliefs. The Enlightenment paved the way for a greater understanding of our world and yet it also uncovered the limitations of human reason. Human existence could never be fully explained by breaking things down. In the end the Enlightenment quest exposed more questions about life than answers.

So, with the resurgence of mystery, a linear lecturing approach to preaching, characterized by a deductive, point-by-point message will be simple to follow, but less engaging to postmodern listeners.

"We must consider the postmodern idiom if our preaching is to gain a hearing," Loscalzo explains. "The modern pulpit was steeped in a reasoned homiletic, marked by point-making sermons, alliterated outlines, and a third-person descriptive logic. Sermons of the modern era often talked about God, about the Bible, about life, viewing these matters like specimens under a microscope."[57]

Boomers and busters, both of whom were raised on television, and are trained to receive information visually and orally, process information in a more random, less linear fashion. Listeners will want to hear people's stories of how the biblical principles are lived out in contemporary society. Again, Loscalzo says, "the postmodern age is an image-rich age; therefore, postmodern preachers should draw on image-rich narratives and stories to present the gospel and make it clear."[58]

Are You Preaching in Your Right Mind—or Your Left?

Much has been written about the two sides of the brain, the left and right hemispheres. "We learn languages, math and sequential thinking with the left side of our brains. The right brain (the right hemisphere) is more sense-oriented and is responsible for our orientation in space, artistic endeavors, body image, and recognition of faces. The right brain is relational, intuitive, and feeling-oriented."[59]

The left side of the brain processes information in a more analytic, logical, and linear fashion. The right side of the brain tends to be the creative and emotive side, which seeks to grasp the fuller picture of what is being said. Modernity specialized in left brain preaching "just the facts, ma'am" presentations. However, the weakness of verse-by-verse, line-by-line preaching is that while the left side of the brain eats it up, the right side is working overtime saying, "Where does all this fit?" Twenty-first-century preaching would do well to give attention to the right side as well as the left, using narration and real life stories of God's Word lived out. Get in the habit of asking yourself: "To which side of the brain is this message primarily speaking?"

Dennis Hollinger states how this understanding of the brain shapes his preaching: "I haven't abandoned left-brain three-pointers. . . . I've simply added right-brained sermons to my repertoire and tried to ensure that in every sermon some appeal is made to both hemispheres."[60]

Postmodernity favors an approach that incorporated regular appeals to the right side of the brain. For this reason, William Willimon, commenting on his speaking in chapel at Duke University, declares, "The mistake most guest preachers make here is to think, *Oh, I'm at a university. I've got to appeal to their minds.* . . . So when I preach at Duke, I intentionally go for the gut; I want the listener to feel truth."[61]

The Camp David Peace Accords of September 1978, involving Jimmy Carter, Anwar Sadat, and Menachem Begin, wrote a new chapter in history. In U.S. President Jimmy Carter's memoirs, *Keeping Faith*, he recalls how the peace talks had reached a stalemate. Egyptian President Anwar Sadat had approved a peace proposal on the table but Israeli Prime Minister Begin rejected it.

After days of intense and arduous negotiations, all three leaders were tired and ready to head home. This meant that each one would return empty-handed; no peace agreement would be reached that day. As Carter packed his bags, he remembered that he and Begin had agreed personally to sign some of the official photos for their respective families. The emotionally drained Carter and Begin met and were seated on the front porch of Begin's cabin to complete this pleasantry. Carter, wishing to personalize each signing, asked Begin for the names he would like on each photograph. Begin returned the favor. Then Carter went one step farther. Pulling out his wallet, he produced pictures of his grandchildren, giving a brief rundown of each one's unique personality. In reciprocal fashion Begin brought out pictures of his family. As these two world leaders pondered the images of their grandchildren, tears began to well in their weary eyes.

The unspoken question loomed in the air: "What kind of world are we going to leave for them?"

Begin, overcome with emotion, retreated back into the cabin, only to reappear five minutes later with the words, "Bring me the proposal to look at again."

I love this story because it speaks of the unpredictability of what will penetrate a person's heart. It wasn't the debate nor the negotiations but the image of a child that won the day, making the world a safer place. As ministers of God's Word, who can say what will penetrate a person's heart? It may be one word, a gesture, a triggered memory of something lost, or simply the mystery of the human heart.

On certain occasions, it's worth approaching listeners from a completely different angle. Predictability leads to boredom. People can feel battered and annoyed when you keep approaching them from the same slant week after week.

One Mother's Day, I was teaching from Proverbs 31 on the woman of virtue. Obvious point in this message, right? Yet after the service a young woman majoring in women's studies wanted to pray with me. Something in the message compelled her to trust Jesus. I hadn't intended this message to be evangelistic and certainly she'd heard other messages more overtly seeking commitment.

So I asked her, "What made the difference today?"

She looked up and said, "I realized today that God values women in a far greater way than our society ever will."

I was reminded again: You never know the word someone may need to hear. This mystery of the human heart prompts the biblical communicator to consider being less predictable and more creative. The preacher's task is to keep probing until the Spirit's gentle touch opens the listener's heart to concede to God's incomparable truth.

The Demise of the Answer Man

The return of mystery means the biblical communicator need no longer feel obligated to solve everything and present life's difficulties into neatly packaged answers. William Willimon gives some helpful insight in saying, "In sermon preparation, I quickly learned that some of my most unfaithful preaching arose in that moment when, after having studied the biblical text, I asked myself, 'So what?' That's where the trouble starts, in my homiletical attempt to answer the 'So what?' question. . . . My answer to the 'So what?' question will be limited by my present horizons, by conventional ideas of what can and cannot be."[62]

Many preachers fear the loss of authority that comes from confessing, "I don't know" or "I struggle with this as well." However, this level of transparency actually can increase credibility, not diminish it. Listeners will find it refreshing to hear the pastor say, "I don't have a simple solution to this dilemma." The right to speak from the listeners' vantage point is not just a matter of office or knowledge but one of character and trust.

Does the resurgence of mystery signal the demise of theological discourse in preaching? One would hope not. Preaching is always predicated on some form of theological foundation, whether for good or for bad. How you perceive God, and your thoughts of God, become the basis for your attitudes and conduct.

R. C. Sproul writes, "To say that theology is boring is really to say that God is boring. And yet, part of the problem is that the average person in the pew is not likely to get a steady diet of theology that is proclaimed with excitement and relevance."[63]

When preachers engage in direct theological discourse, people need to see the connection between theology and people's real lives. If the comment is made, "The preaching was dry," assume that your listener failed to make the connection between the teaching and his or her world. Then if you engage in direct theological discourse, avoid straight lecture, where God can be seen to be boring if presented as an abstract object as opposed to a living Lord. "The Creator of heaven and earth, the One who has all of history in His hand, the Lord of history, is relevant to everything."[64]

Remember, biblical preaching is more than the passing on of knowledge. It's imparting insight into who God is and to what He calls you. Theological understanding doesn't need to be reduced to a twelve-step program. Generation X author Dieter Zander states, "What [Generation Xers] tell me is 'Don't give me six easy steps to keep joy in my life. I know life is not easy.'"[65]

As opposed to offering an easy plan, clear theological teaching can provide a basis upon which the listener can comprehend God and His purposes regardless of his or her circumstances.

What You Want and What You Need

Twenty-first-century listeners may prefer idols but they lack a God large enough to sustain their lives in complicated times. In the Enlightenment, everything needed to be reduced in terms of human understanding, and the God of the Bible was no exception. Into this context J. B. Phillips penned his classic work, *Your God Is Too Small*. As in the days of Paul with the idol-worshiping Athenians, ours is a world crying out for a "big" God. Sproul comments concerning Mars Hill: "Paul did not compromise the message in order to gain this access. His message was considered relevant precisely because it was not like anything they had heard before."[66]

In the arrogance of modernity people believed that humanity could master the principles of the universe. In postmodern times people recognize how little they really know. The growing Western fascination with Eastern mysticism says something about the disillusionment of deities that can be probed under the microscope or mastered through human intelligence.

Unfortunately, all too often, preachers have contributed to this confusion by presenting a small representation of God. They've gathered to give praise to the god of personal experience, the god of personal prosperity, and the god of self-interest.

The message isn't only unworthy of God but unworthy of people's devotion as well. Ask yourself, "What does the sermon you're about to deliver suggest about God?" Do you use God or approach Him on your own terms? Does He serve your purposes? Is God seen to be petty? People need a big God, a God absolutely worthy of their allegiance and any offering they may bring. "Who is God?" will remain the paramount issue for postmodern times.

Will our preaching strike the appropriate balance between the immanence of God, the immediacy of God's presence, and His transcendence, the exaltedness of a Being who is wholly other?

The narrative of Job shows how God will not be pressed into an apology or explanation. Yet how often have Christians confused the living God with a vending machine? You know the routine. Just follow the instructions, insert the proper amount of coins, make your selection, and out pops what you've asked for, right? Then, when the machine fails to deliver the goods, we kick and shake it and then call for someone to come and repair it. Is that all God is, a cosmic vending machine who exists to do our bidding? Does our preaching allow for unspoken wonder of God or quiet reflection of His awesome Being? Since the God of the Bible can't even be contained in the vastness of the universe, let us restore God to the place of awesome majesty that is rightfully His.

Stanley Grenz argues that the biblical communicator's theology must "give place to the concept of 'mystery'—not as an irrational aspect alongside the rational, but as a reminder of the fundamentally non-rational or supra-rational reality of God. This means that while remaining reasonable, our theology must jettison the unwarranted rationalistic bent of all modern theologies."[67]

John Hannah draws similar conclusions in an article that asks, "Have we sold our heritage for relevance?" He writes:

Could it be that the "evangelical world," which has been so much defined by its opposition to the Enlightenment, has become lost in the very ideas it sought to repel? The emphasis on "getting theology right" and with its reduction of the immensely difficult and complex into quick and easy steps seems to have considerably affected modern evangelical views of the gospel and sufficiency. The stress upon rationality and provability of the evangelical faith has seemingly robbed us of much of the inner dynamic of mystery and wonder, of reverential awe, and of our own littleness. In a quest to make the modern church more important to society, the church is finding itself less appealing in an increasingly apathetic world because it has little to offer that is distinctive. A growing accommodation of the gospel message to immediate felt needs with the hope of attracting the less interested may well cause the church to forget that its true work is about the indescribable miracles of God's grace and that its message is ultimately about something we can neither explain nor cause by self-effort and exertion.[68]

Hannah calls the church back to a Christian message rich in the mystery of God and wonder of His grace. Christian theology in all cultures, throughout all periods of history, should reflect the tremendous mystery that is God. As the world moves out of the modern worldview, preaching can return to the theme of the transcendence of God, not just because it appeals to twenty-first-century listeners but because it's biblical.

The approach to culture will indeed vary from generation to generation. However, the content of the message and the nature of the God proclaimed remains above the reproach of cultural manipulation.

7 | Practices for Engagement

So do you know how you're affecting your listeners? One good gauge is your answer to this telling question: "What's the worst remark someone could make about your preaching?" Are you passionless? Abstract? Boring? Lightweight?

For many who have been raised in an evangelical tradition, the most hurtful answer would be that the preaching was in some way unfaithful to the text or that it failed in its biblical content—because as evangelicals, the Bible is held in high regard.

Yet regard for the Scripture, which is a strength, may also promote a weakness—a neglect of the listeners. Preachers may spend hours poring over the text, but little or no time considering the people who will receive the message.

A key element to Jesus' preaching was the recognition and involvement of the listener, according to Ralph and Gregg Lewis in *Learning to Preach like Jesus*. The lesson he showed: Biblical preaching can no longer solely focus on the message to the exclusion of the listeners.[1]

For this reason, Haddon Robinson has said of the pulpit, "The age of the preacher is gone, the age of the communicator has arrived."

Since the very word "preacher" suggests "having a message," we would do well to think of ourselves by that new name—"communicators." After all, communicators are about a process of imparting information that involves both message and listener; it's that process and the practices of good communicators that will be explored here.

Take a Dialogical Approach

One of these practices involves the use of Socratic dialogue. The philosopher Socrates used question-and-answer dialogue as a method of engaging his pupils in a learning exercise; this kind of give-and-take can certainly help the typical Sunday message.

"One of the most interesting revelations from our research has been how positively baby busters respond to evangelistic efforts that use the Socratic method of training," observes researcher George Barna. "The key to the Socratic method is for the teacher to have mastered the matter under consideration so that he or she may ask probing, directive questions that don't manipulate the student as much as help clarify the truth conclusion sought by the student."[2]

The effective communicator will realize that the task isn't to get the listener inside of his or her head but for the communicator to get inside the head of the listener. This entails anticipating objections and doubts, then surfacing these points in the flow of the message.

It's easily done by simply commenting, "Now, you may be saying to yourself. . . ."

Listeners not only feel as if the message involves them on a personal level, but the dialogical process allows them to work through the issues intelligently, on their own. Then—and this is key to effectiveness—the preacher is not an authority figure, telling someone the way it is, but is more of a guide leading people through the thought processes on these biblical issues. When people are allowed, and even challenged, to interact with what's being said, they'll experience the joy of discovering the truth for themselves. But when people are instructed what to believe and practice, they may deem the message as preachy or of little value.

Ask your listeners questions and see for yourself—you're sure to find that a relaxed dialogue and demonstration of openness puts people at great ease and disarms negativity completely.

A great aid is for the preacher to compose the sermon as an imaginary conversation with another person, in which the congregation is allowed to overhear. Picture in your mind an individual from the church or even an unchurched friend. Then imagine what the interaction might sound like if you were engaged in a conversation on this biblical subject.

Your effectiveness will increase when you understand the concerns on the hearts and minds of your listeners and are able to recognize the issues and problems as they arise in the particular text. You'll develop a stronger bond with the listeners because as they sense your involvement with them, they'll be drawn to you. Your resulting sermon will take on a conversational flavor that's inviting to the listener.

Accompanying this dialogical process is the voice and body language. The speaker can move out from around the pulpit to be seen as open and accessible to listeners; body language in doing this can declare, "I don't want any obstructions between us." In smaller settings I've found it can help to sit on a stool while preaching. You can generate both an informality and relaxed energy that listeners will relate to. Another helpful tip: Ask a friend or loved one to give you honest feedback as to how you come across from the pew: Angry? Uncertain? Distant? Listeners will want someone to engage them, not speak at them, concerning the things of God.

Use Inductive Preaching

Another way of dealing with the suspicions of the twenty-first-century listener is to use inductive, rather than deductive, preaching. The deductive approach, practiced widely over the last hundred years of modernity, involves stating, up front, the central or big idea as a declarative proposition, then proceeding to justify the claim. For example, the message may begin, "When God refines your character into His image, you sometimes feel the heat. . . ." Then the message can proceed to defend the idea that trials can bring discomfort but can be in accordance with God's design for your growth. The deductive message works from the whole (this is what I'm telling you today) to the particulars (this is why), and from the known to the unknown. Inductive preaching, on the other hand, has been described to "lay out the evidence, the examples, the illustrations and postpone the declarations and assertions until the listeners have a chance to weigh the evidence, think through the implications and then come to the conclusion with the preacher at the end of the sermon."[3]

The inductive message postpones the declaration of the big idea to a point later in the sermon so that the listener has the opportunity to arrive mentally at the same conclusion. So inductive preaching works from the particulars to the whole, from the unknown to the known, and employs four valuable elements.

It Involves the Listener in Learning

Again, since postmodern people are loath to take anything on face value and want to be able to investigate and probe ideas, the inductive approach suits them. The approach starts where listeners are, then leads them to draw their own conclusions from the evidence presented.

"Such a process [inductive preaching] involves listeners by giving them a part in the sermon process," contend Ralph and Gregg Lewis. "It enables them to think along with and even mentally anticipate the implications of what's being said. The teaching involves the listener. Thus, the sermon itself becomes part of their experience, part of their familiar inductive learning style. The conclusions that are reached and the assertions made at the end of the sermon, bear the mark of personal conviction, arrived at and tested by personal thought and experience."[4]

Fred Craddock comments on the consequence of not employing inductive preaching: "You leave your listeners in that pitiful box of having only two alternatives of agreeing or disagreeing with you. It's all your work. . . . But in inductive preaching, you unroll your idea in such a way that listeners have to work to get it themselves."[5]

When a preacher actively engages the minds of listeners, not only is their attention captured, but they receive more through the joy of discovery as opposed to having ideas merely handed to them.

It Takes on Dialogical Form

Inductive preaching tends to postpone pronouncements and assertions, instead using questions to stimulate thinking within the sermon. Since this is key to postmoderns, reorient your thinking from believing that the role of the sermon is to give answers, when really it's to raise the right questions.

The practice of a more dialogical approach stems from the realization that people will resist accepting statements as truth on face value and before the claims have been tested.

"Inductive methodology accentuates presence, persuasion, and proclamation more or less in that order," explains Rick Gosnell. "Much of the persuading is done before the Gospel is ever verbally shared." He concludes by saying, "The inductive approach is more geared toward persons who are low in their receptivity to the Gospel."[6]

It Starts the Message Where People Are

Jesus demonstrated this skill with the woman at the well, the healing of the paralytic, the tax collector, and Zacchaeus. In each case, Jesus worked from their understanding to the unrevealed world of the Father.

Paul, on Mars Hill, did the same. He began with his listeners, "Men of Athens, I see that in every way you are very religious" (Acts 17:22). The power of this is not to attempt to fabricate an interest but build on the interest that already exists within the listener.

Christian apologist Alister McGrath identifies six points of contact for the Christian gospel that he sees within the present-day listener: a sense of unsatisfied longing, human rationality, the ordering of the world, human morality, an existential anxiety and alienation, and an awareness of finitude and mortality.[7]

Biblical communicators aren't to impose the human dilemma upon the text but to uncover the human need that exists within each passage. This taps into the idea of exercising intuitive thinking, which occurs when someone comes to accept an idea as true because it resonates with what's already known to be true.

When introducing a new idea Tom Nash contends: "Present your idea as much as possible so that it will fit in with ideas and techniques the audience already holds."[8]

Say, in effect, "This is where you are presently, but let's investigate this idea."

Many preachers already do this well. Take for instance a sermon by Bill Hybels, which addresses the difficult issue of God's holiness. Hybels preached:

> We have a lot of people who can't conceive of a God who would ever punish anybody. That wouldn't be loving. They need to understand God's holiness. . . . If you went to a Cubs game, and Sutcliffe threw a strike down the middle of the plate, and the ump said, "Ball four," and walked in a run, you'd be out there killing the ump, because you want justice.[9]

Using Hybels's example, the effective postmodern preacher would postpone declaring, "God is holy because the Bible says so." Instead, the preacher would demonstrate that people innately crave justice in their own lives; therefore, the justice of God should come as no surprise. Now, people are prepared to entertain the idea and admit, "OK, so maybe God's holiness makes sense."

Experience will determine listeners' view of reality, according to Ralph and Gregg Lewis: "They will pragmatically judge every new idea faced by asking, 'Will it work?' 'Does it square with experience?' . . . Human experience doesn't become the basis of our message, but it can validate what we're saying; it can punctuate the Word in a way our people will readily understand."[10] Increasingly, preachers will need to utilize this kind of intuitive approach to authenticate the truthfulness of God's Word.

People are looking inward for truth. As the world we once knew continues to crumble, listeners will cling to what they can personally affirm from their own experience and insight. When ideas ring true from the Bible, then people will grow to respect the Scripture as authoritative. That means people in postmodern times will need to be informed of the basic tenets of belief that undergird the Christian faith. However, not only will listeners resent the presentation of doctrine in unquestioned terms, but they'll wish to see how each teaching relates both to the big picture of faith and to their own lives.

It Keeps up the Suspense So People Will Follow

Everyone knows the feeling of reading or watching a well-crafted whodunit. A good inductive sermon carries the same force, the element of a story told well where the listener waits eagerly to witness the outcome.

One way this is accomplished is through what Eugene Lowry calls the "process of reversal." Lowry states, "The process of reversal as presented in a sermon can be likened to the action of pulling the rug out from under someone. Often it's necessary to lay the rug before one pulls! Because the [Bible] stories are so well-known it's imperative for the preacher first to cultivate the assumptions Jesus knew would be held by his listeners, and which he then intended to rip away."[11]

This narrative movement will result in what Lowry calls The Aha, Ooops, or Yuck Factor. Take, for example, the parable of the two men who go to the temple to pray. Jesus pits the tax collector against the Pharisee, a clear moral mismatch if there ever was one. But Jesus pulls outs the rug when he declares that the tax collector is the one who went away forgiven by God, not the Pharisee. The listeners are startled because the message challenges their expectation by moving in an altogether different direction than what they'd anticipated. This holds attention as well as causes people to think carefully about the nature of what's being said.

The people of postmodern times consider the Bible old hat. If one can preach using this narrative device, it will prove to be a powerful way to connect God's truth to their lives.

Consider services like Christmas and Easter, when people slouch back in the pews, convinced they already know what will be said before the first syllable is uttered. Turn the tables on their preconceived ideas and shock them into hearing the message afresh.

One Good Friday I decided to take a different tack on Christ's resurrection. I borrowed from Walter Wangerin's tale *The Ragman*, which creatively but accurately unfolds the work of the cross. One week later

I received a sweet note from an attender in her mid-twenties. She said she'd attended services out of guilt, and dreaded hearing "one more Good Friday message." But the message she received took her off guard. The fresh approach enabled her to refocus on Jesus and renewed her Easter joy.

Another way you can sustain suspense is by allowing the dilemma to remain unresolved until the close. A good inductive sermon should awaken a conflict that's real to the listener, then allow the weight of that tension to be felt before beginning the move toward resolution. Tension is the basis behind any good story; and yet is precisely what many sermons lack. Like I tell my homiletics students: Don't show your cards too early. Play 'em close to your chest.

Take some cues in storytelling from fiction writers and moviemakers who have mastered the art of suspense. Be mindful that the inductive method can be implemented for the sermon's central idea, but it can also be used in the formation of the particular points within the message. In other words, each point in the body of the message may be approached either deductively or inductively. The inductive approach within the sermon will serve to hold interest and to enhance listener participation.

Use Storytelling

Now some critics say stories and illustrations are fluff, or at the very least, lightweight, and that solid biblical teaching has traditionally translated itself into propositional teaching focused primarily on lending historical and theological meaning to the text. Yet twenty-first-century listeners enjoy learning in a less linear fashion.

Think about it: How many adults in the church services pay better attention during the children's story time than during the sermon? Stories put us in touch with people on a level of shared humanity. Storytelling can grab the listener's imagination and help people identify with an idea in a way that triggers significance and meaning.

Max DuPree's book *Leadership Is an Art* demonstrates this, and underscores the true importance of storytelling, with the tale of how a Nigerian village entered the modern world:

> Electricity had just been brought into the village where Dr. Frost and his family were living. Each family got a single light in its hut. A real sign of progress. The trouble was that at night, though they had nothing to read and many of them did not know how to read, the families would sit in their huts in awe of this wonderful symbol of technology. The light-bulb

watching began to replace the customary nighttime gatherings by the tribal fire, where the tribal storytellers, the elders, would pass along the history of the tribe. The tribe was losing its history in the light of a few electric bulbs. . . . Every family, every college, every corporation, every institution needs tribal storytellers. The penalty for failing to listen is to lose one's history, one's historical context, one's binding values. Like the Nigerian tribe, without the continuity brought by custom, any group of people will begin to forget who they are.[12]

Stories have power to move people, Leland Ryken writes in his book *Triumphs of the Imagination*, because in hearing a story listeners instinctively place themselves into the setting and action, and experience what the character feels—thus learning on a firsthand basis.[13]

Think about this in your own experience. The reason you scream and shudder while watching a suspenseful movie in the safety of a theater or your own home is because, unconsciously, you identify with the screen characters, imagining yourself being stalked by a deranged killer. In entering the story you live vicariously through the hero and heroine. Their pain becomes your pain. Their victory becomes your victory. Thus, movies with triumphant endings—like *Rocky*—have been dubbed "feel good" movies. You walk away feeling good because you've identified with the lead character's triumph over the odds.

"I don't think it's surprising that parable, anecdote, and storytelling are really the most powerful form of communication," says newsman Peter Thompson. "The audience [is] most easily able to project itself right into the story."[14]

This is where the postmodern preacher would do well to take a page out of a missionary handbook like Don Richardson's *Peace Child*, which offers a classic example of relating the gospel message in biblical context and through story with both relevance and freshness.[15]

In *Peace Child*, Richardson tells how he struggled to communicate Christ to the primitive, cannibalistic Sawi tribe of western New Guinea. Upon initially hearing of the life of Jesus, the Sawi tribe, much to Richardson's chagrin, esteemed Judas Iscariot as the hero of the crucifixion story. The Sawis, Richardson learned, lauded treachery as a high virtue; the greater the betrayal a man devised, the greater the honor bestowed upon him. The esteem of Judas as the hero was clearly not Richardson's intention, and he searched for a fresh approach to unfold the redemptive message of Jesus.

Eventually, Richardson stumbled upon the curiosity of the "peace child" in primitive Sawi culture. This concept involved one tribe raising a baby from a neighboring or foreign, hostile tribe as a symbol of an abiding peace agreement between the two peoples. As the peace child is respected and cared for, the covenant remains intact. Hostilities were conquered by the gift of a child. By reframing Christ as the peace child sent by God into the world, Richardson was able to help the Sawi people see the gravity of the cross. When the Sawis understood they'd violated God's design, they also—for the first time—understood they were now under God's judgment too.

Even in today's enlightened societies, you too must reframe the gospel story in a way that allows people to lay hold of the significance of the Christian message. Think as you sing, "Tell me the old, old story . . .": This is just the way our message is perceived by many listeners—as a tired, old story. But must the message of Christ be drained of any substance and vitality? Reframing the gospel message in contemporary story or by a striking analogy can shine new light on the significance of God's Word to dull or resistant listeners.

A good point to consider here is how moviegoing is nothing more than storytelling with a universal charm. There's a lesson here, too, in the first rule of moviemaking: The audience must like and, in fact, back the lead character. If people don't care what happens to the main character, the film will flop.

Look at the movie *Philadelphia* and how it's remembered for bringing homosexuality into mainstream acceptance. How did the film's director accomplish his formidable task of getting a mass audience to like and root for the movie's hero—a homosexual lawyer who's suing his firm for unfair dismissal?

Casting Tom Hanks in the lead role was a good start. But the most powerful and moving scene of the film is saved for last. As mourners attend a wake for the latest victim of AIDS, Neil Young softly sings a haunting lullaby. On an unattended TV screen, home movies of a healthy, normal boy, enjoying life like any other kid, dance before viewers' eyes. There he is, just a boy on the beach with a sand bucket and cowboy hat. Viewers are compelled to ask, "Is he really any different from you and me?" and then, "What difference should sexual preference make?"

Philadelphia triumphs through an appeal of shared humanity. The power of storytelling shifted people's perceptions as many viewers who objected to homosexuality were led to embrace a gay man's tragedy. That's one point for the other side.

It's a good tip for biblical communicators, then, to remember that a story of someone else's experience told well propels listeners to remember who they are and who they aspire to be. There's an old journalistic adage about the difference between a statistic and a tragedy. Two hundred people killed in a plane crash is a statistic. The loss of one life, an eighteen-year-old girl named Jessica headed to Stanford to study nursing, becomes a tragedy. The story, you see, breathes life into stale facts.

Unfortunately, many in ministry have been led to believe that story-telling is not one of their strengths. They might comment, "I'm no Chuck Swindoll or Garrison Keillor, so why pretend?" But the craft of story-telling is a skill that can be learned and developed with practice—and these six guidelines:

Introduce the Story with Suspense

Spark the interest by previewing the direction the story will take. A star-tling or paradoxical statement can introduce a story. For example, on the hazards of greed, one might begin with, "Sometimes, receiving what you ask for can be your greatest regret."

Another way of introduction is with a rhetorical question: "Have you ever found yourself at a point of despair in which you felt like giving up?"

Yet another approach is a direct lead into a human predicament: "Mary Albright sensed the blood rush from her head the moment she received the news that her only son had just been arrested for posses-sion of heroin."

The opening line establishes a tension with the emotional ingredi-ents to draw in the listener. A strong introduction leads the listener to ask, "What happens next?" A potent introduction will create suspense that will entice the listener to want to hear more: "Frank Lewis felt the slight sting on his wrist only to find a venomous black widow spider had just pierced his arm." Such a carefully constructed opening line raises the interest and the desire to hear more.

Beware stumbling into a tale or anecdote without having carefully thought through how to set the story in motion: A vague or uninterest-ing opening can kill any suspense by actually tipping its hand at the out-set. For example, to begin "This is the story of how Johnny overcame cancer to become a professional baseball player" basically ruins the story by giving the listener too much information too early.

An effective introduction, however, functions to transition the lis-tener's interest into the body of the story and then into the body of the sermon. While maintaining the tension, an introduction sets the action in motion and draws the listener to ask, "I wonder what's next?"

Edward de Bono, an expert on the human mind, states that suspense acts as a means to maintain interest even if what you're watching might be somewhat obscure, like the game of snooker or pool.

"You want to know what's going to happen next," explains a fan. "With snooker, you see the colored balls on the nice green background. You see the serious intent of the player. It's obvious what the player is trying to do: Get the right ball into the pocket. It's obvious that you're going to have to wait only a few seconds. And then the next few seconds. And the next. . . . If the expectation is clear and the time is short, the mind needs to remove the 'will she?/won't she?' uncertainty."[16]

The listener's interest is fueled simply by the mind's desire to know what happens next. By maintaining this kind of suspense in storytelling, the preacher will draw in people who want to hear more.

Summarize Your Point

A story illustrates a specific principle or lesson, and if told properly the listener should grasp the point in a somewhat abstract manner. Once the point is clear, the visible light inside the listener's head flashes, "Yes, I heard that!" If the speaker fails to state the summary, the principle may remain an abstraction.

For instance, a good close might be "So we learn from the story of the gingerbread man that subtle compromise is the road to ruin." Do you see how one carefully constructed sentence can bring clarity to the story and direct the listener to the specific aspect you wish to illustrate? Stories told well carry such force that to ramble on in the close diminishes the impact upon the listener. So the beginning and ending are crucial to telling a story well. An effective introduction and summary can make all the difference.

Use Specifics and Vivid Imagery

Vague and nondescript words fail to paint the mental picture that is necessary in order for the listener to identify with the story. Compare these two lines: "A few years ago" versus "On July 14, 1995." Now notice the difference in saying, "One day a man went to the shop," versus "One balmy August afternoon Bill Spencer strolled into Keating's Hardware store in the little town of Marshall, just north of Bangor, Maine." See the interesting difference when details such as names, dates, and settings are used?

That's why a story using vague generalities doesn't connect with the listener. Mark Galli and Craig Larson state, "'Use specifics' is a fundamental axiom of creative writing courses; it's fundamental because it's vitally important, and it's vitally important because it marks the difference between being interesting and being boring."[17]

Word choice remains critical too. "Economy of words mixed with quality of thought, held together by subtlety of expression," makes the difference, storyteller and pastor Charles Swindoll says. "Practicing a hard-to-define restraint so that some things are left for the listener or reader to conclude on his own. Clear and precise—yet not over-drawn."[18]

When a preacher develops an ear for good communication, he or she will be able to hear whether a phrase strikes like a wrecking ball or dissipates like the morning mist. When hurriedly thrown together in the Saturday night frenzy, the message can count on missing the polish that leaves an idea ringing in the listener's head long after the service has concluded.

"Someone has well said there are no good writers," Calvin Miller comments, "only good editors. In the same way, there are no good preachers, only those who can see things wrong with what will be said. Edit it and then say it well."[19]

It's good to note here that abstractions leave people cold; instead the effective communicator will carve out mental images in the listener's mind. For instance, I have the vivid memory from when I was seven years old in Vienna, Virginia, of having a weather guard at the bottom of a glass door penetrating my heel. The cut went so deep that it almost severed my Achilles tendon. I tried to be brave until I hitched up my pant leg to notice that my white sock was soaked red. Seeing my blood—and a lot of it—is when I lost it.

Hours later I was stomach down on a cold, vinyl table as the attending doctor examined my heel. In all my seven years of living, nothing like this had ever happened; I was completely unprepared to handle the trauma. I didn't understand the medical procedures, or all the poking and prodding.

"Who are these strangers and why are they hurting me?" "Will my foot ever get better?" "What's happening to me?"

Yet, all the time I was to lie there on that table, my mother was present, stroking my head and reassuring me: "The doctors are here to make you better. You're going to be all right. I won't let anything bad happen to you." She brushed away the tears from my cheeks, and I could sense her care and concern and love. Though I couldn't comprehend the circumstance, I trusted my mother's touch.

In re-creating this image of a confused and bewildered boy comforted by the love of his mother, I found the words of the Lord—"I will never leave you nor forsake you"—took on a fresh force. The image moved me from an abstraction to tangible clarity. Such is the strength of an unmistakable image.

Personalize

State how the person, events, or quote relates to you as the speaker. This will bring your own experiences, thoughts, and feelings into the picture, lending an added dimension.

For example, when speaking of Martin Luther's struggle in the face of possible execution at the Diet of Worms, you might quote the famous "here I stand" reply and leave it at that. The speaker, in turn, might relate how he or she was impacted by being in Worms or by Luther's life in particular. (I know that when I rise to my feet to sing the words, "A mighty fortress is our God, a bulwark never failing," goosebumps form on my arms because Luther's words carry the weight of remarkable courage.) So when at all possible move an event or quote into a present reality by indicating the significance as it relates to you.

Maintain the Flow

Too often, a good story is ruined because the action fails to unfold quickly enough to maintain interest. Just as specific information can give a story life, extraneous details can bog it down. A good storyteller understands the balance in maintaining the energy and direction while providing the pertinent details.

"Zealous to be ultra-accurate, we unload so much trivia the other person loses the thread of thought, not to mention his patience," Swindoll says. "Bewildered, he wades through the jungles of needless details, having lost his way as well as his interest. Instead of being excited over the challenge to explore things on his own, lured by the anticipation of discovery, he gulps for air in the undertow of our endless waves of verbiage, cliches, and in-house mumbo jumbo."[20]

Remember, twenty-first-century listeners have grown up on television with remote control units in their hands—and this is an entire generation with attention deficit disorder. In sensing the story's floundering pace, postmodern listeners will lose concentration and simply switch off. As in the case of Edith Bunker of *All in the Family* fame, superfluous details may cause our listeners to think, "Stifle yourself!"

Internalize the Emotional

We ought not just tell a story but relive it for listeners. This point is missed too often, but effective storytellers enact the illustration, using hands, body, and facial expression to make the action come to life. If a story lacked passion and life, without fail, the speaker delivered the account in a deadpan manner.

To retell a story effectively: feel the emotions of the characters, visualize the setting and movement in the events, and allow your gestures and body movement to re-create the environment being described. When a story is told using physical expression, it not only serves to clarify the action but brings to the surface the emotional content as well.

Whether telling a story or preaching a narrative, the preacher needs to match the emotional content of the characters. As a simple exercise ask, "What must the people in this story have experienced?" By getting in touch with the human element, the preacher connects with the heart of the listener.

Martin Buber recalls, "Once my lame grandfather was asked to tell a story about his teacher. My grandfather rose as he spoke, and he related how his teacher used to hop and dance while he prayed. My grandfather became so swept away by his story that he began to hop and dance and show how the master had done. From that hour on he was cured of his lameness. Now that's how to tell a story!"[21]

As a communicator, you no longer stand aloof and detached from the action. You must embody it! When you internalize the emotional content within a story, a rich fabric of passion is revealed in your voice, movement, and expression.

One valuable exercise in developing this skill comes through practicing the story aloud and in front of a mirror. Oral communication is designed for the ear. Just as singers develop an ear to listen critically to the pitch of their own voices, speakers learn to listen to their own speech. With practice, you can develop a keen sense of effectiveness.

One quality that storytelling and humor share in common is timing—maximize your words with pause and cadence. As you hear yourself, ask, "Is my point weak? Convincing? Ambiguous? Compelling?" All good communicators will cultivate the right timing and tone. If the emotional content of the story has been internalized, the emotional expression will be evident in delivery. The internalization of the message, after all, lends itself to the speaker's credibility, which cannot be underestimated in value to postmoderns.

Like most things in life, the more one practices, the better one gets. Storytelling stands as a powerful communication skill for postmodern times. Illustrating with freshness and vitality will make a significant difference both in connecting with and challenging our listeners in the most compelling ways.

Use Audiovisuals, Drama, and Art

When music videos first appeared on the scene, many in the industry viewed the image-making of musicians as a passing fad. One band in the early '80s drew a line in the sand: Journey was enjoying immense popularity when band members announced they would release their new album without a video. After all, they insisted, "It's about the music, man."

After showing utter disdain for such image-making, Journey found its new release floundering on the charts for months. It didn't take long for the band to acknowledge it was wrong: Music videos were here to stay.

But it was too late. Journey's album never recovered and neither did the band. So it goes when a significant shift takes place. Failure to recognize that shift spells catastrophe.

It's no different in the church, observes theologian and author Calvin Miller. Critiquing worship, he wonders: "What will be heard by the worshippers who come within the fellowship? . . . What will be imaged in the sermon? Video paints pictures that the audience is to absorb. These guiding images must be visible, spiritual, and moral encounters. . . . The only important question for the church is, 'Can the church become pictorial in order to live, or will it remain only audio and die?'"[22]

I can appreciate, and even hear, the resistance some might have to such a question: "Well, the church has survived for centuries without all this nonsense—art, drama, mime, role plays, documentaries, dance, and a vast number of other types of audiovisual presentation."

True, the early church flourished in the absence of many things that are now used regularly: electricity, facilities, Sunday schools, biblical commentaries, seminaries, even Willow Creek formats. The use of audiovisuals is, without question, a cultural expression of our time and it too may pass.

Keep in mind, however, that how you communicate God's timeless message will constantly be changing and, yet, God's Word won't.

Does that mean you shouldn't let pass the old methods of communicating that eternal Word? Well, don't confuse the message and the method.

How many more people might you connect to the Word of God if you did use different methods, maybe even show a scene from a film? A movie scene would be familiar to the vast majority of attenders on any given Sunday. But are general moviegoing audiences interpreting such scenes with a godly perspective?

How many folks, for example, would make the connection in viewing the slow-witted Forrest Gump, in the movie by the same name, as a picture of God's gracious response to His creation? The use of this brief clip could provide a powerful illustration of God's immense love to our generation.

Take a look: The movie focuses on Forrest and his love for Jenny, who has spent much of her life lost and wandering. The simple Forrest, Jenny finally realizes, is the one person who has loved her unconditionally, unwaveringly, and devotedly, despite her continual rejection.

After a series of mishaps and ill-conceived flings, fate brings Forrest and Jenny together, and Forrest brings Jenny home. She slowly retreats to her bedroom. Before she reaches the top of the staircase, Forrest musters his courage to ask with his distinctive voice, "Will you marry me? I'd make a good husband, Jenny."

The strength of Forrest's tenderness ignores that she has chased other lovers and run from his affection.

"You would, Forrest," she acknowledges. There is a longing hesitation in her voice.

Sensing this, Forrest replies, "But you won't marry me."

Shaking her head slightly, Jenny mutters, "You don't want to marry me."

Searching for clues, Forrest asks, "Why don't you love me, Jenny?"

She cannot find the words and her eyes merely scan the horizon.

Forrest voices her unspoken thoughts, "I'm not a smart man, but I know what love is."

What Forrest lacks in mind, he makes up for in heart.

This scene never fails to move me as I am reminded how Forrest symbolizes a God-like presence, loving with incredible tenacity beyond reason. What a powerful illustration of God's immense love to our generation! What a redemptive picture of unconditional love!

As the postmodern public endures a media saturation, preachers can bury their heads. But I would opt to critically engage society using its own images and technology. For the following three reasons a video projector and the proper copyright permission in the church could be one of the wisest next investments you make.

Listeners Know the Media

Within our high-tech society, audiovisuals are the waters in which most people swim. Roof affirms a widely held belief: "Perhaps the most important impact of television was that it replaced the word with the image."[23]

Based on the sheer weight of a lifetime of screen watching, researchers now argue that postmodern folks' brains actually process information differently. The average postmodern listener will readily connect with high-tech communication. As one pastor puts it, "This generation is going to have a screen in front of their face. The only question is, 'What will be on that screen?'"[24]

In a smiliar way, during medieval times, the doorways of European cathedrals were adorned with ornate carvings depicting the great themes of the Bible such as creation, salvation, and the final judgment. This wasn't an attempt to cater to the sophisticated art lovers of society. No, it was attempting just the opposite: The majority of the people were illiterate so the pictorial representations of God's truth were a means by which attenders to worship could learn the gospel through images, and not reading.

By using what's familiar to the average listener, you increase your effectiveness and can combat the stereotype of an archaic church too. You'll show how faith can interact in any world, at any time.

Who Else Uses Media to Give the Christian Perspective?

Multimedia preaching can help people develop discernment toward the images that shape both thinking and values. "Hollywood no longer reflects—or respects—the values of most American families," warns Michael Medved in his book *Hollywood vs. America*. "On many of the important issues in contemporary life, popular entertainment seems to go out of its way to challenge conventional notions of decency."[25]

Face it: You cannot afford to be naive. The entertainment industry isn't about amusement alone but more often about manipulation. People are continually bombarded with powerful messages delivered in stealth. Too many church attenders consume hours of TV and movies merely believing they're being entertained. Yet media analysts talk about the "stalagmite effect" in which the constant exposure to ideas and values from movies and TV shape the consciousness of viewers over extended periods of time.[26]

By interacting thoughtfully with what's happening, singling out both the positive and destructive ideas, people can increase their awareness; in time, they'll become critically discerning of the messages they receive.

Remember, the medium is not the threat to God's purposes. The godless ideas are. Only through discerning interaction will our listeners come to distinguish the difference. Your goal should be more than merely capturing attention. You can also educate people to evaluate the underlying, inherent messages and values of nonbelievers.

The Message in Contemporary Imagery and Sound Resonates

On one particular Sunday morning, I'd selected a clip from the movie *Schindler's List*, the Oscar-winning film about the German entrepreneur and hustler Oscar Schindler, who shelters hundreds of Jews from the Nazi holocaust of World War 2.

I chose to show the scene where Schindler and the Jewish refugees had gathered outside a munitions factory. Word of Germany's surrender spread across the land, and the crowd realized Schindler must flee for his own safety. Before he and his wife depart, he's honored with a gold ring by the Jewish workers and families—a token of gratitude for the man who saved their lives. Schindler begins to weep. He has realized, at the end of the war, that his lifelong pursuit of wealth and possessions pales in the light of his compassion toward these Jewish survivors. He's squandered so much, and chased what doesn't really matter.

After showing this scene I read from 2 Peter 3, "Since everything will be destroyed in this way, what kind of people ought you to be? You ought to live holy and godly lives as you look forward to the day of God and speed its coming."

Later, a businessman in our congregation said, "After the Bible reading, it all clicked. You didn't need to say a thing. The point was already clear to me."

It's clear to me too: The combination of imagery about Schindler and God's Word etched a powerful message that day.

In the same manner, the use of art and image can reframe the message from God's Word with arresting force. Paintings, dramas, or a song can break through postmodern people's smugness (the "I've heard it all before" attitude) by appealing to a different dimension of their being.

One might argue that postmodern people have become consumers of images and are accustomed to presentations with both visual and oral accompaniment.

However, one pastor sounds a worthy warning, "If I'm not passionate about God's Word, no amount of technology can correct that deficiency."[27]

Amen.

Many preachers may decry the use of alternative forms of communication such as video and art, arguing that for centuries, God has divinely anointed the proclamation of His Word. Yet the Bible is replete with examples of God's prophets—Hosea, Jonah, and Jeremiah—called to act out or dramatize God's message to His people.

Striking examples are readily found in baptism or the communion service. The Lord's Supper serves as a symbolic act in which the worshiper is called to ingest into his or her own body elements symbolizing the redemptive work of Christ.

Perhaps this explains the very nature of Scripture in that the majority of the Bible comes to us in narrative form, and not in propositional statements. Then again, take a look at nature. Surely God's creativity urges His people toward diversity rather than an immutable approach.

Use Humor

Telling a joke carries a similar pressure to giving an invitation, in that both require a tangible response from the listener—only in the case of humor, the anticipated response is laughter.

Yet, warns Calvin Miller, "Except for the highly skilled ecclesiastical comedian, jokes are risky business."[28] To deliver a punch line, only to be met with a collective groan or silence, can take the wind from any preacher's sails. Maybe that's why so many preachers find it safer to stay within the arm-waving and scowling approach, leaving the humor to Jerry Seinfeld.

Humor that's done well, though, can effectively increase communication—and it can be done. Too often humor from the pulpit serves merely as an icebreaker to loosen up listeners, and may be completely unrelated to the actual message. But humor functions best as a tool to lend insight and to hold interest.

Edward de Bono, who has researched the mind, describes humor as an "asymmetrical" pattern of thinking. It's thinking that lacks symmetry or predictability.[29] Humor directs people to see an idea or object from a different angle or new vantage point, then acts to reinforce what's known to be true on an unconscious level.

For example, Gary Larson of *Far Side* comic fame, commonly employs a device of attributing human qualities to animals. One *Far Side* cartoon depicts a large swimmer scrambling to safety up onto a beach, having just escaped the jaws of a shark. One shark turns to the other shark that pursued the man, and says, "That was a big one!"

The despondent shark who missed his prize catch replies, "I don't want to talk about it now."

It's obvious what Larson is doing—recapturing what takes place when humans lose their catch of the day from the boat.

The humor lies in the absurd twist, so in actuality the audience begins to laugh at self, blind to personal behavior until seen as something else like a shark. The appeal, again, is to allow the postmodern listeners to uncover truth for themselves, and gain insight without being told directly, "Here's what you need to know."

One more advantage to humor is in how it can free up the speaker to make difficult statements. Anyone who's ever heard Howard Hendricks can see how he draws in listeners using laughter just before he unloads on them. One needs to imagine Hendricks telling this in his own animated style:

> I once visited one of my former students to join him for a week of ministry meetings. As soon as I arrived his wife got me aside and said, "Will

you please say something to my husband? He's averaging only five hours sleep a night and is headed for four, and . . . frankly, we can't live with him. He's driving the kids up a wall."

Near the end of the week he and I were traveling in the car together, and as he drove I said to him, "Hey, man, how come you don't smoke?"

We almost went off the highway. "Prof," he finally answered, "I never smoke."

"Yes," I said, "I noticed I hadn't seen you light up a single time all week." By then he was giving me some rather strange looks, as if he thought I had squirrels crawling around in my steeple. "Why don't you smoke?" I asked.

"Prof," he said, "my body is the temple of the Holy Spirit."

"Yeah," I said, "that's right. Fantastic. Good thinking." Then I added, "Is that also the reason you're averaging five hours of sleep a night, headed for four, and driving your family bonkers?"

I wouldn't have jarred him as much if I dropped a two-by-four on his head.[30]

While Hendricks's listeners get a laugh from stories like this, they have no idea he's set them up to drop a two-by-four on their heads about their own priorities. In the grasp of an effective communicator, humor can be used to introduce hard things with subtlety and craft.

Did you ever notice good humor can come straight from the Good Book too? Take for instance, the story of Elijah and the widow at Zarephath.

Allow me to paraphrase. The Lord places his prophet in the first ever "witness protection program." He tells Elijah, "I've made arrangements for future provision through this widow." When Elijah meets the widow, she blurts out, "By the way, my son and I are heading home to eat our last meal and then die."

One could easily imagine Elijah asking, "Are there any other widows around here . . . maybe some . . . wealthy widow . . . one with a large storehouse, perhaps?" But not to be outdone, Elijah comes back with this line: "Listen here, first go back and make me a cake and then you and your son can knock yourselves out with what's left."

Now the widow is thinking "Hey, Mr. Wherever-You're-From, in case you just missed what I said, I'm not throwing any dinner parties or looking to take on any boarders right now, but thank you for the offer. Now if you'll excuse me. . . ."

These wonderful biblical stories possess a touch of the absurd, don't they? A desparate widow to the rescue? When working through the biblical text, look for the humor that underlies the message, but also beware the danger to the overfamiliarity and sobriety associated with such stories.

As with storytelling many preachers have resigned themselves to the idea that they just aren't funny. To all those who feel humorously impaired, Calvin Miller offers this advice: "Better than telling jokes is learning to use anecdotes and stories that have a creative lightness about them."[31]

Instead of going for the roof-lifting howls, go for something more modest. Aim to bring a smile to someone's face and ease some seriousness of the sermon. Some preachers suffer from having all the expression of the automated robots of Disney World except less lifelike, right? If the truth be known, just about everyone has some naturally humorous inclination whether it be a dry wit, a knack for impersonations, a way with words, or a keen observation of human idiosyncrasies.

Whatever the case for you, be intentional in discovering your personal strength and allow it to shine through from the pulpit. Also, be warned: A recipe for disaster comes in attempting to imitate someone else's style or humor. Uncover your own humorous style.

One way is to take note of yourself at parties and social gatherings. Pay attention to what people find amusing in you. Allow the qualities that others enjoy about you into your pulpit delivery.

Another tip is to read humorous writers. Develop a feel for how funny people process life. Perhaps it will never be your strong point but it helps to vary your communication style. It was once put to me this way regarding my preaching, "As much as it is in your power, be funny." Humor communicates insightfully and winsomely in a way that postmodern listeners will find both attractive and compelling.

Become a Good Listener

Most preachers become preachers because they're convinced they have something to say. But listening is, hands down, the most underrated element of biblical preaching. Careful listening is that skill that helps you develop a dialogical feel and conversational tone to your sermon; this evidences that you've grappled with the likely responses of your listeners.

Haddon Robinson assesses proper preaching as follows: "Respond to cues from the audience to tell how you're doing. Study not only content but also people, hearing the spoken and unspoken questions. After speaking, listen intently to find out how you've done."[32]

Remember, listening takes place at all points in the message: before, during, and after the message. The inability to listen and create dialogue has been one of the long-standing criticisms of the church. Traditionally, preaching creates a tone as to suggest a person is being talked at, not spoken to. As Stuart Briscoe puts it, "We pastors are tempted to adopt the 'six feet above contradiction' mindset, isolating ourselves from situations that could contradict or challenge us. Bombast and dynamic rhetoric will be shot full of holes by thinking listeners. I aim to listen not only to what people say to me, but also to what I'm saying to them."[33]

One remedy is to consider forming a focus group—representative listeners who can give you honest, candid feedback. Bill Hybels built his preaching ministry by forming a focus group of key individuals who shared the vision and value of Willow Creek. Each week they would assess the what and how of the preaching process, addressing not just to what was heard but what was felt by the listeners. What was memorable? Was there something that needed to be said and was not? What challenged, confused, or upset the listeners? Whether you ask these kind of questions about your sermons formally or informally, always aim to uncover the issues and concerns on the minds of your listeners.

Listening takes place at all points in the message. You might consider forming a focus group when commencing a sermon series to receive some feedback and uncover what the issues are in the minds of your listeners.

Another means of interacting with your listeners is to conduct imaginary conversations with the various people in the congregation. Imagine how each person would respond to a particular point.

One way of facilitating this listening process is through a "life-situation grid." Don Sunkijian explains:

> Across the top of the grid, I label columns for men, women, singles, married, divorced, those living together. On the side of the grid, I have a row that includes categories for different age groups (youth, young adults, middle-aged, elderly), professional groups (the unemployed, the self-employed, workers, and management), levels of faith (committed Christians, doubters, cynics, and atheists), the sick and the healthy, to name a few. I develop my grid based on the congregation and community I am preaching to. After I've researched my text and developed my ideas, I wander around in the grid looking for two to four intersections where the message will be especially relevant.[34]

Haddon Robinson clarifies the task: "How can we gain an appreciation for lives unlike our own, from cleaning ladies to investment bankers? The same way novelists do: by listening and observing. Pay attention to the people you counsel, the conversations around you in restaurants and stores, to characters in novels and movies, to common people interviewed on the news. Note how these people state their concerns, note their specific phrasing, their feelings, their issues. Get an ear for dialogue."[35]

In short: Learn to listen if you wish to be heard. Adopt some structure of receiving feedback other than the perfunctory "good word, pastor" at the door. Feedback, as a form of listening, will enable you to ascertain the strengths and weaknesses of your unique style and presentation, especially if you increasingly ask, "How can I foster some genuine dialogue in this message?"

With the appropriate input, you'll continually refine and rethink your content, delivery, and tone through the eyes and ears of your listeners; community will be built through good communication, and community will grow through listening.

Make Your Delivery Crisp and Clear

Recently, my children were given *The Wizard of Oz* on video. When I was a kid, I had to hold out eagerly for an entire year to view *The Wizard* on TV. Before the age of television, my parents had to wait for it at the theater and pay for admission.

Today my kids merely punch on the cassette and watch to their little hearts' content, over and over again. I've noted how they fast-forward through the first couple of minutes of the video too. They want to skip the opening credits, a ritual that viewers like me endured years ago.

Sermons could take a cue from the movies in this regard and hit the ground running. You're sadly mistaken if you think most people will listen patiently while you roll some opening credits. It's immediacy that people demand, and instant gratification the masses want.

The first minute of your message is the most critical, requiring you to be both concise and arresting. I don't apologize for spending more time preparing the message's opening than any other part. Why give people an excuse for not paying attention?

The late comedian George Burns explained it this way. Once asked by a preacher, "How can I improve my speaking?" Burns replied: "First, you need a brilliant introduction. Second, you should have a dynamite conclusion. Third, be sure that your introduction and conclusion are not that far apart."

This is not to subscribe to the ten-minute homily. You must fight the enduring stereotype of the preacher droning on and on, and think of an engaging message being like a riveting movie: A good one can't be too long, and a bad one can't be too short.

"Basically, it's not the length of a sermon that makes the congregation impatient for it to stop," contends gifted expositor John Stott. "It's the tedium of a sermon in which even the preacher himself appears to be taking very little interest."[36]

One common sermonic flaw is the preacher's failure clearly to define the thrust of the message. Without some definition, some clarity on the issue tackled, the sermon rambles from one idea to the next like a bumper car with an eight-year-old behind the wheel. What will hold together your sermon for postmoderns is what holds together any motion picture or play—various acts blending to form one overfall assertion.

Try this test: If you can't identify what you're saying in one, clear sentence, it means that you probably aren't clear yourself. You may say some good things, but don't be surprised when no one seems to grasp the thrust of your message. Think about it: When you're uncertain as to what you're saying, you don't know when to stop, do you? How many times have you heard messages like a plane circling the airport, trying to find a place to land? Just when you think the plane is finally making its descent, the pilot takes it back up again for some more circling. A word to the wise: Know what you want to say and say just enough for your listeners to want more. In William Sangster's words, "When you're done pumpin', let go the handle."[37]

One of the greatest compliments you'll ever receive is your preaching appears effortless. Hours of painstaking preparation and planning will make you look like "the natural" with good delivery.

Charles Swindoll offers these five words of advice to the Sunday preacher: "Make it clear, keep it simple, emphasize the essentials, forget about impressing, and leave some things unsaid."[38] One thing to add to this list: Edit at home. Don't enter the pulpit with some vague idea of what you may or may not say, depending upon the mood. Come prepared, having thought through each movement of the message with precision. In the famous words of Haddon Robinson, "Someone suffers every time you preach. Either you suffer in preparing it or the listener suffers in hearing it."[39]

Overall you can improve your effectiveness with greater clarity by knowing what you want to say, and asking yourself, "Who can say 'no' to this invitation?"

Secondly, ask yourself, "Can my listeners make informed decisions?" "Are they clear as to what they're responding to and why?"

The message you craft in response could be the one that prompts someone else to think carefully of how they too can pass along the good news of Jesus Christ.

Conclusion

No Other Place I'd Rather Be

In the movie *Witness*, actors Harrison Ford and Kelly McGillis show us what happens when two cultures collide. Set in Pennsylvania Dutch country, the film is actually a love story between John Book, a big city Philadelphia cop played by Ford, and Rachel, a widowed Amish mother played by McGillis. Throughout the film director Peter Weir depicts the cultural trappings of two equally needy characters attempting to find common ground. The relationship journey is wrought with conflict as the two value systems repeatedly clash. Just when it looks as if love will conquer all, the final scene reveals Detective Book and his Amish sweetheart parting company. The final scene shows Book driving away from Rachel and the rural community even as the locals go about their daily affairs.

My wife still laments this ending. "Why didn't they remain together?" she wondered. "Why couldn't she go or he stay?"

Weir, an Australian working in America, tells something of his own story, we learned later. He understood that when two worlds collide, often people are unable to overcome their differences and ultimately will go their separate ways.

As our present postmodern culture, with its value system, collides with the Christian culture and its message, will the listener and the church go their separate ways? Do you ever stop to think that God has placed you in this time of unprecedented change intentionally?

The pop song "Right Here, Right Now" can help us answer the question. It speaks about the changing times, looking back upon the fall of the Berlin Wall. The songwriter "saw the decade end when it seem[ed] the world could change in the blink of an eye." He was right there, alive and, "watching the world wake up from history."

How many of us engaged in ministry share this same conviction? As we witness climactic movements in our society, we have the opportunity to speak God's message to people in the twenty-first century. Will the church have a voice in postmodern times? Will the message of Christ be communicated with a passion that ignites the lives of listeners?

The way that we evaluate the preaching task in relation to our listeners is critical. For me, addressing postmodern values and unbelief is analogous to dealing with a common cold. If you look for a quick and effective remedy, you won't find one. Anyone can tell you the cure for a cold: "Take lots of liquids and vitamins and get plenty of bed rest." It's a gradual recovery that takes place over time and under the proper care.

Couldn't the same be said of guiding people into Christian maturity from a postmodern morass of relativism and cynicism? We overestimate the force of one sermon, no matter how well crafted, while undervaluing the influence of thoughtful biblical teaching presented over a length of time. It's the steady influence of biblical teaching over time, and the proper care that can restore any person to a place of godly faith, hope, and love.

As our world rises from the slumber of secular humanism and sleep of scientific rationalism, I long to speak the words of life in Christ to a generation in search of a spiritual home.

Communicating God's message to twenty-first-century listeners involves navigating a hazardous path with both opportunities and obstacles. For some, this emergence of postmodernity means closing the shutters and holding on tight in the hope that the tempest soon will pass. For others, the insurgence of postmodern times represents a fresh breeze with a whole new realm of possibility—a long overdue wind that could lift a stale and musty order from our sanctuaries. Whichever the case, each of us as preachers of God's Word will have to decide how to address new generations of the twenty-first century. As for my own preaching approach, the well-known poem by Samuel Shoemaker, "I Stand by the Door," sums it up nicely.

> I stand by the door
> I neither go too far in, nor stay too far out,
> The door is the most important door in the world—
> It is the door through which men walk when they find God.[1]

God has placed you and me in a monumental period in history. If our preaching goes in too far and deep, it may fail to connect with listeners outside. But if it rings hollow with pleasantries, it will be unable to guide people faithfully to the entrance.

An appropriate and necessary place remains near the door, where our preaching may reflect a stance near enough God and close enough to whisper to them the message of Christ, the Anointed One.

As for me, reserve one place near the door.

Notes

Introduction

1. *Contact,* directed by Robert Zemeckis (Warner Brothers, 1997); based on Carl Sagan's 1985 best-selling book by the same title.

2. Diogenes Allen, *Christian Belief in a Postmodern World* (Louisville: Westminster/John Knox Press, 1989), 2.

3. William H. Willimon, "This Culture Is Overrated," *Leadership* (winter 1997): 30.

4. Helmut Thielicke, as quoted by Peter Corney, "Post-modernism and the Gospel," *Grid* (spring 1995): 1.

5. Dean Inge in Willimon, "This Culture Is Overrated," 30.

6. Lesslie Newbigin, *The Gospel in a Pluralist Society* (Grand Rapids: Eerdmans, 1989), 152.

7. Donald A. Carson, *The Gagging of God: Christianity Confronts Pluralism* (Grand Rapids: Zondervan, 1996), 549–50.

8. Os Guinness and John Seel, eds., *No God but God: Breaking with the Idols of Our Age* (Chicago: Moody, 1992), 154.

9. Ibid., 157.

10. Steve Brown, *How to Talk So People Will Listen* (Grand Rapids: Baker, 1993), 9.

11. Lesslie Newbigin, *Truth to Tell: The Gospel As Public Truth* (Grand Rapids: Eerdmans, 1991), 12.

Chapter 1: "Toto, We're Not in Kansas Anymore"

1. Diogenes Allen, *Christian Belief in a Postmodern World* (Louisville: Westminster/John Knox Press, 1989), 3.

2. As quoted in Bryan Appleyard, *Understanding the Present* (New York: Doubleday, 1992), 15.

3. Martin Robinson, "Post What? Renewing Our Minds in a Postmodern World," *On Being* 24, no. 2 (March 1997): 31.

4. Craig Loscalzo, "Apologizing for God: Apologetic Preaching to a Postmodern World," *Review and Expositor* 93, no. 3 (summer 1996): 412.

5. Stanley J. Grenz, *A Primer on Postmodernism* (Grand Rapids: Eerdmans, 1996), 10.

6. Donald A. Carson, *The Gagging of God: Christianity Confronts Pluralism* (Grand Rapids: Zondervan, 1996), 22.

7. Loscalzo, "Apologizing for God," 414.

8. Timothy R. Phillips and Dennis L. Okholm, eds., *Christian Apologetics in the Postmodern World* (Downers Grove, Ill.: InterVarsity Press, 1995), 23.

9. Charles Colson, "The Year of the Neo-pagan," *Christianity Today* (March 6, 1995): 88.

10. Ibid.

11. Peter Corney, "Have You Got the Right Address? Post-modernism and the Gospel," *Grid* (spring 1995): 1.

12. David Goetz, "The Riddle of Our Culture: What Is Postmodernism?" *Leadership* (winter 1997): 56.

13. *Time*, 14 April 1997, 6.

14. Allen, *Christian Belief in a Postmodern World*, 8.

15. Allen in Phillips and Okholm, *Christian Apologetics in the Postmodern World*, 22–23.

16. Clyde Fant and William Pinson Jr., *20 Centuries of Great Preaching* (Waco, Tex.: Word, 1971).

17. Mark Filiatreau, "'Good News' or 'Old News,'" *Regeneration Quarterly* (winter 1995): 1.

18. Michael J. Hostetler, *Introducing the Sermon: The Art of Compelling Beginnings* (Grand Rapids: Zondervan, 1986), 52.

Chapter 2: Postmodernity: Animal, Vegetable, or Mineral?

1. Margot Hornblower, "Great Xpectations," *Time*, 9 June 1997, 62.

2. Os Guinness and John Seel, *No God but God: Breaking with the Idols of Our Age* (Chicago: Moody, 1992), 27.

3. David Cook, *Blind Alley Beliefs* (Leicester, England: Inter-Varsity Press, 1996), 9.

4. Oden in Gene Edward Veith Jr. *Postmodern Times: A Christian Guide to Contemporary Thought and Culture* (Wheaton: Crossway, 1994), 27.

5. Walter Truett Anderson, *Reality Isn't What It Used to Be: Theatrical Politics, Ready-to-Wear Religion, Global Myths, Primitive Chic, and Other Wonders of the Postmodern World* (San Francisco: Harper and Row, 1990), 33.

6. Leighton Ford, *The Power of Story* (Colorado Springs: NavPress, 1994), 37.

7. Martin Robinson, "Post What? Renewing Our Minds in a Postmodern World," *On Being* 24, no. 2 (March 1997): 30.

8. Stanley J. Grenz, *A Primer on Postmodernism* (Grand Rapids: Eerdmans, 1996), 3.

9. Ibid., 7.

10. Packer in David Goetz, "The Riddle of Our Culture: What Is Postmodernism?" *Leadership* (winter 1997): 53.

11. Martin Robinson, "Post What?" 30.

12. David Harvey, *The Condition of Postmodernity: An Enquiry into the Origins of Cultural Change* (Cambridge, Mass.: MIT Press, 1987), 43.

13. Anderson, *Reality Isn't What It Used to Be*, 75.

14. Martin Robinson, "Post What?" 30.

15. Ibid.

16. Anderson, *Reality Isn't What It Used to Be*, 29.

17. Richard J. Middleton and Brian J. Walsh, *Truth Is Stranger than It Used to Be* (Downers Grove, Ill.: InterVarsity Press, 1995), 10.

18. Ibid., 70.

19. Ibid., 71.

20. Martin Robinson, "Post What?" 31.

21. John Shepherd, "Change Is Key to the Future," *The West Australian* (Perth, Western Australia), 27 July 1998, 6.

22. Buttrick in "Apologizing for God," in Craig Loscalzo, *Preaching That Connects* (Downers Grove, Ill.: InterVarsity Press, 1995), 414.

23. Veith, *Postmodern Times*, 83.

24. Kenneth J. Gergen, *The Saturated Self* (New York: Basic Books, 1991).

25. Middleton and Walsh, *Truth Is Stranger than It Used to Be*, 52.

26. Ibid., 53.

27. Veith, *Postmodern Times*, 80.

28. Ibid., p. 82.

29. Ibid.

30. Ibid.

31. Middleton and Walsh, *Truth Is Stranger than It Used to Be*, 58.

32. Ibid., 59.

33. Peggy Noonan, *Life, Liberty and the Pursuit of Happiness* (New York: Random House, 1994), 217.

34. Wade Clark Roof, *A Generation of Seekers: The Spiritual Journeys of the Baby Boom Generation* (San Francisco: HarperSanFrancisco, 1993), 226.

35. Veith, *Postmodern Times*, 195.

36. Haddon Robinson, "When Foundations Tremble," *Leadership* (spring 1993): 140.

37. William D. Watkins, *The New Absolutes* (Minneapolis: Bethany, 1996), 168.

38. Ron Stodgill, "Where'd You Learn THAT?" *Time*, 22 June 1998, 58.

39. David Harvey, *The Condition of Postmodernity*, 52.

40. Tim Keller, "Preaching Morality in an Amoral Age," *Leadership* (winter 1996): 112.

41. Ibid.

42. Grenz, *A Primer on Postmodernism*, 14.

43. Veith, *Postmodern Times*, 195.

44. Martin Robinson, "Post What?" 32.

45. Grenz, *A Primer on Postmodernism*, 14.

46. James Iliffe, "Searching for Reality in a Postmodern Age," *On Being* (September 1996): 37.

47. Anderson, *Reality Isn't What It Used to Be*, 148.

48. Ibid., 152.

49. Veith, *Postmodern Times*, 121.

50. Mike Littwin, "Who's Top Boomer?" *The West Australian* (Perth, Western Australia), 17 June 1996, 18.

51. Neil Postman, *Amusing Ourselves to Death: Public Discourse in the Age of Show Business* (New York: Penguin Books, 1985).

52. Veith, *Postmodern Times*, 81.

53. Ibid., 81–82.

54. Leighton Ford, *Transforming Leadership* (Downers Grove, Ill.: InterVarsity Press, 1991), 226.

55. Joey Horstman, "The Postmodern Yawn," *The Other Side* (May/June 1993): 35.

56. Veith, *Postmodern Times*, 97–98.

57. Anderson, *Reality Isn't What It Used to Be*, 147.

58. Corney, "Have You Got the Right Address? Post-modernism and the Gospel," *Grid* (spring 1995): 1–7.

59. Anderson, *Reality Isn't What It Used to Be*, 144–45.

60. Veith, *Postmodern Times*, 100.

61. Ibid., 99.

62. Ibid., 99–100.

63. Carson, *The Gagging of God*, 47.

64. Iliffe, "Searching for Reality in a Postmodern Age," 38.

65. John Naisbitt, *Megatrends* (New York: Warner Books, 1982).

66. Jan Johnson, "Getting the Gospel to the Baby Busters," *Moody Monthly* (May 1995): 50.

67. Veith, *Postmodern Times*, 144.

68. Ingram in Iliffe, "Seaching for Reality in a Postmodern Age," 37.

69. Roof, *A Generation of Seekers*, 235.

70. Cook, *Blind Alley Beliefs*, 12.

71. Jeff Fountain, "Postmodernity: A Look Ahead," *Reality* 4, no. 20 (April/May 1997): 16.

72. Cook, *Blind Alley Beliefs*, 13.

73. Martin Robinson, "Post What?" 31.

74. Cook, *Blind Alley Beliefs*, 24.

75. Veith, *Postmodern Times*, 178.

Chapter 3: Rules for Engagement

1. Ravi Zacharias, "Reaching the Happy Thinking Pagan," *Leadership* (spring 1995): 27.

2. Calvin Miller, *Marketplace Preaching: How to Return the Sermon to Where It Belongs* (Grand Rapids: Baker, 1995), 137.

3. Buttrick in Larry Dixon, *The Other Side of the Good News* (Wheaton: Bridgepoint Books, 1992), 186.

4. Duane A. Litfin, *Public Speaking: A Handbook for Christians* (Grand Rapids: Baker, 1981), 36.

5. Steve Brown in Michael Duduit, *Communicate with Power* (Grand Rapids: Baker, 1996), 27.

6. John R. W. Stott, *Between Two Worlds: The Art of Preaching in the Twentieth Century* (Grand Rapids: Eerdmans, 1982), 125–26.

7. Donald K. Smith, *Creating Understanding: A Handbook for Christian Communication across Cultural Landscapes* (Grand Rapids: Zondervan, 1992), 21.

8. Hugh Mackay, *Why Don't People Listen?* (Sydney, Australia: Pan Macmillan, 1994), 14–15.

9. Ibid., 11.

10. Calvin Miller, *The Empowered Communicator* (Nashville: Broadman and Holman, 1994), 142–43.

11. Edward de Bono, *I Am Right—You Are Wrong* (London, England: Viking, 1990), 134.

12. Litfin, *Public Speaking*, 36.

13. George G. Hunter III, *How to Reach Secular People* (Nashville: Abingdon Press, 1992), 47.

14. Haddon Robinson, *Biblical Preaching* (Grand Rapids: Baker, 1980), 193.

15. Miller, *The Empowered Communicator*, 146.

16. Robinson, *Biblical Preaching*, 141.

17. Ralph and Gregg Lewis, *Inductive Preaching: Helping People Listen* (Westchester, Ill.: Crossway, 1983), 22.

18. Smith, *Creating Understanding*, 27.

19. Steven R. Covey, *The Seven Habits of Highly Effective People* (New York: Fireside, 1990), 30–31.

20. Tom Nash, *The Christian Communicator's Handbook: A Guide to Help You Make the Message Plain* (Wheaton: Victor, 1995), 96.

21. Mackay, *Why Don't People Listen?* 118

22. Ralph and Gregg Lewis, *Inductive Preaching*, 27.

23. Smith, *Creating Understanding*, 27.

24. de Bono, *I Am Right—You Are Wrong*, 139.

25. Maslow in Litfin *Public Speaking*, 50.

26. Miller, *Marketplace Preaching*, 134.

27. Zacharias, "Reaching the Happy Thinking Pagan," 25.

28. Michael J. Hostetler, *Introducing the Sermon: The Art of Compelling Beginnings* (Grand Rapids: Zondervan, 1986), 68.

29. Ibid., 17–18.

30. Ibid., 24.

31. Mackay, *Why Don't People Listen?* 113–14.

32. Roberta Hestenes, "Teaching So That Adults Listen," *Leadership* (spring 1996): 101.

33. Ibid.

34. Mackay, *Why Don't People Listen?* 94–95.

Chapter 4: Challenging Listeners

1. Craig Loscalzo, "Apologizing for God: Apologetic Preaching to a Postmodern World," *Review and Expositor* 93, no. 3 (summer 1996): 41.

2. Ravi K. Zacharias, "Reaching the Happy Thinking Pagan," *Leadership* (spring 1995): 20.

3. Ibid.

4. Alister McGrath, *Bridge-Building: Effective Christian Apologetics* (Leicester, England: Inter-Varsity Press, 1992), 47–48.

5. Duane A. Litfin, *Public Speaking: A Handbook for Christians* (Grand Rapids: Baker, 1981), 67.

6. McGrath, *Bridge-Building: Effective Christian Apologetics*, 45.

7. Calvin Miller, *Marketplace Preaching: How to Return the Sermon to Where It Belongs* (Grand Rapids: Baker, 1995), 131.

8. Loscalzo, "Apologizing for God," 416–17.

9. Miller, *Marketplace Preaching*, 19.

10. Ravi Zacharias, *Can Man Live without God?* (Dallas: Word, 1994), 21.

11. Zacharias, "Reaching the Happy Thinking Pagan," 23.

12. Gordon MacDonald, *When Men Think Private Thoughts* (Nashville: Thomas Nelson, 1996), 27.

13. Paul Vitz, "The Psychology of Atheism," *Truth* 1, (1985): 30.

14. John R. W. Stott, *Basic Christianity* (Downers Grove, Ill.: InterVarsity Press, 1974), 18.

15. Brennan Manning, *The Ragamuffin Gospel* (Portland, Ore.: Multnomah, 1990), 24–25.

16. Tim Keller, "Preaching Morality in an Amoral Age," *Leadership* (winter 1996): 113.

Chapter 5: Obstacles

1. Peter Corney, "Have You Got the Right Address? Post-modernism and the Gospel," *Grid* (spring 1995): 7.

2. Alister McGrath, *Bridge-Building Effective Christian Apologetics* (Leicester, England: Inter-Varsity Press, 1992), 425.

3. Gregory A. Boyd and Edward K. Boyd, *Letters from a Skeptic* (Wheaton: Victor, 1994), 79.

4. Bill Hybels, Haddon Robinson, and Stuart Briscoe, *Mastering Contemporary*

Preaching (Portland, Ore.: Multnomah, 1989), 30.

5. George G. Hunter III, *How to Reach Secular People* (Nashville: Abingdon Press, 1992), 43.

6. Lesslie Newbigin, *Truth to Tell: The Gospel As Public Truth*, (Grand Rapids: Eerdmans, 1991), 32.

7. Hybels, Robinson, and Briscoe, *Mastering Contemporary Preaching*, 38.

8. Achtemeier in Calvin Miller *Marketplace Preaching: How to Return the Sermon to Where It Belongs* (Grand Rapids: Baker, 1995), 128.

9. Robinson, *Biblical Preaching*, 103.

10. Mark Filiatreau, " 'Good News' or 'Old News,'" *Regeneration Quarterly* (winter 1995): 15.

11. Dr. Tom Nash, *The Christian Communicator's Handbook*, 138.

12. Ravi K. Zacharias, "Reading the Happy Thinking Pagan," *Leadership* (spring 1995): 20.

13. Donald A. Carson, *The Gagging of God: Christianity Confronts Pluralism* (Grand Rapids: Zondervan, 1996), 44.

14. Ibid., 45.

15. Wade Clark Roof, *A Generation of Seekers: The Spiritual Journeys of the Baby Boom Generation* (San Francisco: HarperSanFrancisco, 1993), 202.

16. Ibid., 209.

17. Ibid., 245.

18. Francis A. Schaeffer, *How Should We Then Live?* (Westchester, Ill.: Crossways, 1976), 25–26.

19. Carson, *The Gagging of God*, 45.

20. Ravi K. Zacharias, *Can Man Live without God?* (Dallas: Word, 1994), 126.

21. Timothy R. Phillips and Dennis L. Okholm, *More than One Way?* (Grand Rapids: Zondervan, 1995), 160.

22. Ibid., 153.

23. Charles Colson, *A Dangerous Grace* (Dallas: Word, 1994), 82.

24. Philip Yancey, *The Jesus I Never Knew* (Grand Rapids: Zondervan, 1995).

25. Carson, *The Gagging of God*, 257.

26. R. C. Sproul, *The Holiness of God* (Wheaton: Tyndale House, 1986), 73–74.

27. James W. Sire, *Why Should Anyone Believe Anything at All?* (Downers Grove, Ill.: InterVarsity Press, 1994), 146.

28. Cook, *Blind Alley Beliefs*, 6.

29. Loscalzo, "Apologizing for God," 409–10.

30. Kenneson in Phillips and Okholm, *Christian Apologetics in the Postmodern World*, 166–67.

31. Loscalzo, "Apologizing for God," 409–10.

32. Sire, *Why Should Anyone Believe Anything at All?* 168.

33. Carson, *The Gagging of God*, 177.

34. Newbigin, *Truth to Tell*, 47.

35. Ibid., 32–33.

36. Donald W. McCullough, *The Trivialization of God: The Dangerous Illusion of a Manageable Deity* (Colorado Springs: NavPress, 1995), 32.

37. Ed Dobson in Robinson, "When Foundations Tremble," 140.

38. Robert McKee, *Story* (New York: Reagan Books, 1997), 12.

39. Newbigin, *Truth to Tell*, 33.

40. Phillips and Okholm, *Christian Apologetics in the Postmodern World*, 19.

41. McGrath, *Bridge-Building: Effective Christian Apologetics*, 81.

42. Middleton and Walsh, *Truth Is Stranger than It Used to Be*, 105.

43. Ibid., 106.

44. Corney, "Have You Got the Right Address?" 2.

45. Richard J. Middleton and Brian J. Walsh, *Truth Is Stranger than It Used to Be* (Downers Grove, Ill.: InterVarsity Press, 1995), 107.

46. Robinson in Hybel, Briscoe, and Robinson *Mastering Contemporary Preaching*, 23.

47. Iliffe, "Searching for Reality in a Postmodern Age," *On Being* (September 1996): 37.

48. Andres Tapia, "Reaching the First Post-Christian Generation," *Christianity Today* (September 12, 1994): 20.

49. Phillips and Okholm, *Christian Apologetics in the Postmodern World*, 120.

50. Ibid., 381.

51. Ibid., 381–82.

52. Ford, *The Power of Story*.

53. Robert McKee, *Story*, 334.

54. Walter Truett Anderson, *Reality Isn't What It Used to Be*, 202.

55. Dixon, *The Other Side of the Good News*, 122.

56. Zacharias, *Can Man Live without God?* 26–27.

57. Dixon, *The Other Side of the Good News*, 157.

58. Hunter, *How to Reach Secular People*, 46.

59. Jo Wiles, "How to Raise Drug-Free Kids," *Reader's Digest* (December 1997): 98.

Chapter 6: Inroads

1. Kenneth L. Woodard, "On the Road Again," *Newsweek*, 28 November 1994, 61.

2. Marty in Wade Clark Roof, *A Generation of Seekers: The Spiritual Journeys of the Baby Boom Generation* (San Francisco: HarperSanFrancisco 1993), 226.

3. Ibid., 158.

4. Alan J. Roxburgh, *Reaching a New Generation: Strategies for Tomorrow's Church* (Downers Grove, Ill.: InterVarsity Press, 1993), 59.

5. Walter Truett Anderson, *Reality Isn't What It Used to Be: Theatrical Politics, Ready-to-Wear Religion, Global Myths, Primitive Chic, and Other Wonders of the Postmodern World* (San Francisco: Harper and Row, 1990), 191.

6. Roof, *A Generation of Seekers*, 147.

7. Carson, *The Gagging of God: Christianity Confronts Pluralism* (Grand Rapids: Zondervan, 1996), 208.

8. Roof, *A Generation of Seekers*, 8.

9. Ibid., 256.

10. George G. Hunter III, *How to Reach Secular People* (Nashville: Abingdon Press, 1992), 44.

11. Mark Filiatreau, " 'Good News' or 'Old News,'" *Regeneration Quarterly* (winter 1995): 15.

12. Ibid.

13. John Dever, "As the Church Moves into the Twenty-First Century: Some Extended Observations," *Review and Expositor* 93, no. 1 (winter 1996): 19.

14. Roof, *A Generation of Seekers*, 236.

15. Ibid., 252.

16. Leith Anderson, *A Church for the Twenty-First Century* (Minneapolis: Bethany, 1992), 158.

17. Roof, *A Generation of Seekers*, 207.

18. Charles R. Swindoll, *The Grace Awakening* (Dallas: Word, 1990), 76–77.

19. Amy Mears and Charles Bugg, "Issues in Preaching in the Twenty-First Century," *Review and Expositor* 90, no. 3 (summer 1993): 347.

20. Ibid., 343.

21. Steve Brown, Haddon Robinson, and William Willimon, *A Voice in the Wilderness: Clear Preaching in a Complicated World* (Portland, Ore.: Multnomah, 1993), 72.

22. Haddon Robinson, "Preaching to Everyone in Particular," *Leadership* 15, no. 4 (fall 1994), 99.

23. Brown, Robinson, and Willimon, *A Voice in the Wilderness*, 79.

24. William Hendricks, *Exit Interviews* (Chicago: Moody, 1993), 260–61.

25. Bill Hybels, Haddon Robinson, and Stuart Briscoe, *Mastering Contemporary Preaching* (Portland, Ore.: Multnomah, 1989), 129.

26. Miller, *Marketplace Preaching: How to Return the Sermon to Where It Belongs* (Grand Rapids: Baker, 1995), 114.

27. Craig Loscalzo, "Apologizing for God: Apologetic Preaching to a Postmodern World," *Review and Expositor* 93, no. 3 (summer 1996): 413.

28. Roof, *A Generation of Seekers*, 192.

29. Briscoe, Hybels, and Robinson, *Mastering Contemporary Preaching*, 79–80.

30. Dever, "As the Church Moves into the Twenty-First Century," 344–45.

31. Richard J. Middleton and Brian J. Walsh, *Truth Is Stranger than It Used to Be* (Downers Grove, Ill.: InterVarsity Press, 1995), 145.

32. John R. W. Stott, *Issues Facing Christians Today* (London: Marshall Pickering, 1990), 15.

33. Achtemeier in Mears and Bugg, "Issues in Preaching in the Twenty-First Century," 346.

34. Ibid.

35. Gary Richmond, *A View from the Zoo* (Waco: Word, 1987), 25–27.

36. Grenz, *A Primer on Postmodernism*, 13.

37. Brown, Robinson, and Willimon, *A Voice in the Wilderness*, 88–89.

38. Dever, "As the Church Moves into the Twenty-First Century," 348.

39. Brown, Robinson, and Willimon, *A Voice in the Wilderness*, 145–46.

40. David Van Biema, "Does Heaven Exist?" *Time*, 24 March 1997, 49.

41. Ibid., 46.

42. Guinness and Seel, *No God but God*, 169.

43. Colson, *A Dangerous Grace*, 93.

44. Roof, *A Generation of Seekers*, 237.

45. Ibid., 185.

46. Joe Seaborn, "Whatever Happened to Authority?" *Preaching* 12, no. 4 (January-February 1997): 42.

47. Hunter, *How to Reach Secular People*, 46.

48. Tony Campolo, *You Can Make a Difference* (Waco: Word, 1984), 36.

49. Campolo as quoted in Paul Borthwick, *Youth and Missions* (Wheaton: Victor, 1988), 12–13.

50. Phillips and Okholm, *Christian Apologetics in the Postmodern World*, 169.

51. Ibid.

52. Alister McGrath, *Bridge-Building: Effective Christian Apologetics* (Leicester, England: Inter-Varsity Press, 1992), 70.

53. Douglas Coupland, *Life after God* (New York: Pocket Books, 1994), 359.

54. Ravi K. Zacharias, "How to Reach the Happy Thinking Pagan," *Leadership* (spring 1995): 20.

55. William D. Watkins, *The New Absolutes* (Minneapolis: Bethany, 1996), 225.

56. Donald W. McCullough, *The Trivialization of God: The Dangerous Illusion of a Manageable Deity* (Colorado Springs: NavPress, 1995), 17.

57. Loscalzo, "Apologizing for God," 412.

58. Ibid., 413.

59. Dennis Hollinger, "Preaching to Both Brains," *Preaching* 11, no. 4 (July-August 1995): 35.

60. Ibid.

61. Willimon, *A Voice in the Wilderness*, 119.

62. Ibid., 15–16.

63. R. C. Sproul, "The Object of the Contemporary Relevance," *Power Religion* (Chicago: Moody, 1992), 319.

64. Ibid.

65. Tapia, "Reaching the First Post-Christian Generation," *Christianity Today* (September 12, 1994) 20.

66. Sproul, "The Object of Contemporary Relevance," 320.

67. Grenz, *A Primer on Postmodernism*, 13.

68. Hannah in John H. Armstrong *The Coming Evangelical Crisis* (Chicago: Moody, 1996), 168.

Chapter 7: Practices for Engagement

1. Ralph and Gregg Lewis, *Learning to Preach like Jesus* (Westchester, Ill.: Crossway, 1989), 16.

2. George Barna, *Evangelism That Works* (Ventura, Calif.: Regal, 1995), 113–14.

3. Ralph and Gregg Lewis, *Learning to Preach like Jesus*, 43.

4. Ibid.

5. Fred B. Craddock, "Inductive Preaching: An Interview with Fred B. Craddock," *Ministry* (July 1998): 16.

6. Timothy R. Phillips and Dennis L. Okholm, *Christian Apologetics in the Postmodern World* (Downers Grove, Ill.: Inter-Varsity Press, 1995), 379.

7. Alister McGrath, *Bridge-Building: Effective Christian Apologetics* (Leicester, England: Inter-Varsity Press, 1992), 51–73.

8. Dr. Tom Nash, *The Christian Communicator's Handbook*, 168.

9. Hybels, *Mastering Contemporary Preaching*, 33.

10. Ralph and Gregg Lewis, *Learning to Preach like Jesus*, 41.

11. Eugene Lowry, *The Homiletical Plot* (Atlanta: John Knox Press, 1975), 56–57.

12. Max DuPree, *Leadership Is an Art* (Melbourne, Australia: Australian Business Library, 1989), 71–72.

13. Ryken in Mark Galli and Craig Brian Larson, *Preaching That Connects* (Grand Rapids: Zondervan, 1994), 82.

14. Peter Thompson, *The Secrets of the Great Communicators* (Sydney, Australia: ABC Books, 1992), 37–38.

15. Don Richardson, *Peace Child* (Ventura, Calif.: Regal, 1974).

16. Edward de Bono, *I Am Right—You Are Wrong* (London: Viking, 1990), 140.

17. Galli and Larson, *Preaching That Connects*, 82.

18. Charles Swindoll in Marshall Shelley, *Changing Lives through Preaching and Worship: 30 Strategies for Powerful Communication* (Nashville: Moorings, Library of Christian Leadership, 1995), 57.

19. Miller, *Marketplace Preaching: How to Return the Sermon to Where It Belongs* (Grand Rapids: Baker, 1995), 159.

20. Swindoll in Shelley, *Changing Lives through Preaching*, 58.

21. Buber in Jack Canfield and Mark Victor Hansen, *A Second Helping of Chicken Soup for the Soul* (Deerfield Beach, Fla.: Health Communications, 1995), xvii.

22. Miller, *Marketplace Preaching, 115*.

23. Roof, *A Generation of Seekers*, 54.

24. Ed Rowell, "Where Preaching Is Headed," *Leadership* (winter 1997): 97.

25. Michael Medved, *Hollywood vs. America* (New York: Harper Perennial, 1992), 10.

26. Ibid., 245.

27. Rowell, "Where Preaching Is Headed," 97.

28. Miller, *Marketplace Preaching*, 105.

29. de Bono, *I Am Right—You Are Wrong*, 87.

30. Howard G. Hendricks, *Teaching to Change Lives* (Portland, Ore.: Multnomah, 1987), 46–47.

31. Miller, *Marketplace Preaching*, 106.

32. Haddon Robinson in Shelley, *Changing Lives through Preaching and Worship*, 39.

33. Briscoe, *Mastering Contemporary Preaching*, 144–45.

34. Sunkijian in Haddon Robinson, *A Voice in the Wilderness*, 75.

35. Ibid., 76.

36. Stott, *Issues Facing Christians Today*, 292.

37. Swindoll in Shelley, *Changing Lives through Preaching*, 58.

38. Ibid.

39. Robinson, *A Voice in the Wilderness*.

Conclusion: No Other Place I'd Rather Be

1. John Guest, *In Search of Certainty* (Ventura, Calif.: Regal, 1983), 10.

Bibliography

Allen, Diogenes. *Christian Belief in a Post-modern World*. Louisville: Westminster/John Knox Press, 1989.

Anderson, Leith. *A Church for the Twenty-First Century*. Minneapolis: Bethany, 1992.

Anderson, Leith, Ed Dobson, Os Guinness, and Haddon Robinson. "When Foundations Tremble." *Leadership* (spring 1993): 134–42.

Anderson, Walter Truett. *Reality Isn't What It Used to Be: Theatrical Politics, Ready-to-Wear Religion, Global Myths, Primitive Chic, and Other Wonders of the Postmodern World*. San Francisco: Harper and Row, 1990.

Apokis, Con. "Have You Met the New Audience?" *Grid* (spring 1995): 7–8.

Appleyard, Bryan. *Understanding the Present*. New York: Doubleday, 1992.

Armstrong, John H., ed. *The Coming Evangelical Crisis*. Chicago: Moody, 1996.

Barna, George. *Evangelism That Works*. Ventura, Calif.: Regal, 1995.

Barrett, C. K. *The First Epistle to the Corinthians*. New York: Harper and Row, 1968.

Begley, Sharon. "Science of the Sacred." *Newsweek*, 28 November 1994, 56–59.

Bellah, Robert N., Richard Madsen, William M. Sullivan, Ann Swidler, and Steven M. Tipton. *Habits of the Heart*. New York: Harper and Row, 1985.

Blackaby, Henry T., and Claude V. King. *Experiencing God*. Nashville: Broadman and Holman, 1994.

Bloesch, Donald G. *The Future of Evangelical Christianity*. Colorado Springs: Helmers and Howard, 1988.

Bloom, Allan. *The Closing of the American Mind: How Higher Education Failed Democracy and Impoverished the Souls of Today's Students*. New York: Simon and Schuster, 1987.

Booher, Dianna. *The Confident Communicator*. Wheaton: Victor, 1990.

Borthwick, Paul. *Youth and Missions*. Wheaton: Victor, 1988.

Boyd, Gregory A., and Edward K. Boyd. *Letters from a Skeptic*. Wheaton: Victor, 1994.

Brown, Steve. *How to Talk So People Will Listen*. Grand Rapids: Baker, 1993.

Brown, Steve, Haddon Robinson, and William Willimon. *A Voice in the Wilderness: Clear Preaching in a Complicated World*. Portland, Ore.: Multnomah, 1993.

Burnham, Frederic B., ed. *Postmodern Theology: Christian Faith in a Pluralist World*. New York: Harper and Row, 1989.

Campolo, Tony. *You Can Make a Difference.* Waco: Word, 1984.

Canfield, Jack, and Mark Victor Hansen. *A Second Helping of Chicken Soup for the Soul.* Deerfield Beach, Fla.: Health Communications, 1995.

Carson, Donald A. *The Gagging of God: Christianity Confronts Pluralism.* Grand Rapids: Zondervan, 1996.

Chappell, Bryan. *Christ-Centered Preaching.* Grand Rapids: Baker, 1994.

Colson, Charles. "Postmodern Power Grab." *Christianity Today* (June 20, 1994): 80.

Colson, Charles. "The Year of the Neopagan." *Christianity Today* (March 6, 1995): 88.

Cook, David. *Blind Alley Beliefs.* Leicester, England: Inter-Varsity Press, 1996.

Corney, Peter. "Have You Got the Right Address? Post-modernism and the Gospel." *Grid* (spring 1995): 1–7.

Coupland, Douglas. *Life after God.* New York: Pocket Books, 1994.

de Bono, Edward. *I Am Right—You Are Wrong.* London: Viking, 1990.

Derrida, Jacques. *Positions.* Trans. Alan Bass. Chicago: University of Chicago Press, 1981.

Derrida, Jacques. *"Speech and Phenomena" and Other Essays on Husserl's Theory of Signs.* Trans. David B. Allison. Evanston, Ill.: Northwestern University Press, 1973.

Dever, John. "As the Church Moves into the Twenty-First Century: Some Extended Observations." *Review and Expositor* 93, no. 1 (winter 1996): 11–26.

Dixon, Larry. *The Other Side of the Good News.* Wheaton: Bridgepoint Books, 1992.

Dockery, David S., ed. *The Challenge of Postmodernism: An Evangelical Engagement.* Grand Rapids: Baker, 1995.

Duduit, Michael. *Communicate with Power.* Grand Rapids: Baker, 1996.

Duduit, Michael, ed. *Handbook of Contemporary Preaching.* Nashville: Broadman, 1992.

Fernando, Ajith. *The Supremacy of Christ.* Wheaton: Crossway, 1995.

Filiatreau, Mark. "'Good News' or 'Old News.'" *Regeneration Quarterly* (winter 1995).

Ford, Kevin Graham, and Jim Denney. *Jesus for a New Generation.* Downers Grove, Ill.: InterVarsity Press, 1995.

Ford, Leighton. *The Power of Story.* Colorado Springs: NavPress, 1994.

Ford, Leighton. *Transforming Leadership.* Downers Grove, Ill.: InterVarsity Press, 1991.

Fountain, Jeff. "Postmodernity: A Look Ahead." *Reality* 4, no. 20 (April/May 1997): 13–17.

Freedland, Jonathan. "Welcome to the Nineties." *ELLE* (November 1994): 36–39.

Galli, Mark, and Craig Brian Larson. *Preaching That Connects.* Grand Rapids: Zondervan 1994.

Gergen, Kenneth J. *The Saturated Self.* New York: Basic Books, 1991.

Goetz, David. "The Riddle of Our Culture: What Is Postmodernism?" *Leadership* (winter 1997): 52–56.

Grant, Reg, and John Reed. *The Power Sermon.* Grand Rapids: Baker, 1993.

Grant, Reg, and John Reed. *Telling Stories to Touch the Heart.* Wheaton: Victor, 1990.

Grenz, Stanley J. *A Primer on Postmodernism.* Grand Rapids: Eerdmans, 1996.

Grenz, Stanley J. *Revisioning Evangelical Theology: A Fresh Agenda for the Twenty-First Century.* Downers Grove, Ill.: InterVarsity Press, 1993.

Grenz, Stanley J. *Theology for the Community of God.* Carlisle, Pa.: Pasternoster Press, 1994.

Guest, John. *In Search of Certainty.* Ventura, Calif.: Regal, 1983.

Guinness, Os. *The American Hour: A Time of Reckoning and the Once and Future Role of Faith.* New York: Free Press, 1993.

Guinness, Os, and John Seel, eds. *No God but God: Breaking with the Idols of Our Age.* Chicago: Moody, 1992.

Harvey, David. *The Condition of Postmodernity: An Enquiry into the Origins of Cultural Change*. Cambridge, Mass.: MIT Press, 1987.

Hauerwas, Stanley. *After Christendom?* Nashville: Abingdon Press, 1991.

Hauerwas, Stanley, and William H. Willimon. *Resident Aliens: Life in a Christian Colony*. Nashville: Abingdon Press, 1990.

Hawtrey, Kim. "The New Apologetics." *Impact Bulletin* no. 24 (October-December 1996): 1.

Hendricks, Howard G. *Teaching to Change Lives*. Portland, Ore.: Multnomah, 1987.

Hendricks, William. *Exit Interviews*. Chicago: Moody, 1993.

Hestenes, Roberta. "Teaching So That Adults Listen." *Leadership* (spring 1996): 100–104.

Hollinger, Dennis. "Preaching to Both Brains." *Preaching* 11, no. 4 (July-August 1995): 35.

Hornblower, Margot. "Great Xpections." *Time*, 9 June 1997, 54–62.

Horstman, Joey. "The Postmodern Yawn." *The Other Side* (May/June 1993): 34–35.

Horton, Michael Scott, ed. *Power Religion*. Chicago: Moody, 1992.

Hostetler, Michael J. *Introducing the Sermon: The Art of Compelling Beginnings*. Grand Rapids: Zondervan, 1986.

Howe, Frederic R. *Challenge and Response: A Handbook of Christian Apologetics*. Grand Rapids: Academie Books, 1982.

Hunter, George G., III. *How to Reach Secular People*. Nashville: Abingdon Press, 1992.

Hunter, James Davison. *Culture Wars: The Struggle to Define America*. San Francisco: HarperCollins, 1991.

Hybels, Bill, Haddon Robinson, and Stuart Briscoe. *Mastering Contemporary Preaching*. Portland, Ore.: Multnomah, 1989.

Iliffe, James. "Searching for Reality in a Postmodern Age." *On Being* (September 1996): 34–38.

Johnson, Jan. "Getting the Gospel to the Baby Busters." *Moody Monthly* (May 1995).

Kaiser, Walter C., Jr. "The Crisis in Expository Preaching Today." *Preaching* 11, no. 5 (September-October 1995): 4–8.

Keller, Tim. "Preaching Morality in an Amoral Age." *Leadership* (winter 1996): 110–15.

Lewis, Ralph, and Gregg Lewis. *Inductive Preaching: Helping People Listen*. Westchester, Ill.: Crossway, 1983.

Lewis, Ralph, and Gregg Lewis. *Learning to Preach like Jesus*. Westchester, Ill.: Crossway, 1989.

Litfin, Duane A. *Public Speaking: A Handbook for Christians*. Grand Rapids: Baker, 1981.

Logan, Samuel T., Jr. *The Preacher and Preaching*. Phillipsburg, N.J.: Presbyterian and Reformed Publishing Co., 1986.

Long, Thomas G. *Preaching and the Literary Forms of the Bible*. Philadelphia: Fortress, 1989.

Loscalzo, Craig. "Apologizing for God: Apologetic Preaching to a Postmodern World." *Review and Expositor* 93, no. 3 (summer 1996): 405–18.

Loscalzo, Craig. *Evangelistic Preaching That Connects*. Downers Grove, Ill.: InterVarsity Press, 1995.

Lowry, Eugene. *The Homiletical Plot*. Atlanta: John Knox Press, 1975.

Lundin, Roger. *The Culture of Interpretation: Christian Faith and the Postmodern World*. Grand Rapids: Eerdmans, 1993.

Lyon, David. *Postmodernity: Concepts in Social Thought*. Minneapolis: University of Minnesota Press, 1994.

Lyotard, Jean-Francois. *The Postmodern Condition: A Report on Knowledge*. Trans. Geoff Bennington and Brian Massumi. Theory and History of Literature, vol. 10. Minneapolis: University of Minnesota Press, 1984.

McCullough, Donald W. *The Trivialization of God: The Dangerous Illusion of a Manageable Diety*. Colorado Springs: NavPress, 1995.

McGrath, Alister. *Bridge-Building: Effective Christian Apologetics*. Leicester, England: Inter-Varsity Press, 1992.

MacIntyre, Alasdair. *After Virtue*. 2d ed. Notre Dame, Ind.: University of Notre Dame Press, 1984.

Mackay, Hugh. *Why Don't People Listen?* Sydney, Australia: Pan Macmillan, 1994.

McKee, Robert. *Story*. New York: Reagan Books, 1997.

Mears, Amy, and Charles Bugg. "Issues in Preaching in the Twenty-First Century." *Review and Expositor* 90, no. 3 (summer 1993): 341–50.

Medved, Michael. *Hollywood vs. America*. New York: Harper Perennial, 1992.

Middleton, Richard J., and Brian J. Walsh. *Truth Is Stranger than It Used to Be*. Downers Grove, Ill.: InterVarsity Press, 1995.

Miller, Calvin. *The Empowered Communicator*. Nashville: Broadman and Holman, 1994.

Miller, Calvin. *Marketplace Preaching: How to Return the Sermon to Where It Belongs*. Grand Rapids: Baker, 1995.

Miller, Calvin. *Spirit, Word, and Story: A Philosophy of Marketplace Preaching*. Grand Rapids: Baker, 1989.

Moore, Peter C. *Disarming the Secular Gods: How to Talk So Skeptics Will Listen*. Downers Grove, Ill.: InterVarsity Press, 1989.

Naisbitt, John. *Megatrends*. New York: Warner Books, 1982.

Nash, Dr. Tom. *The Christian Communicator's Handbook*. Wheaton: Victor, 1995.

Natoli, Joseph, and Linda Hutcheon, eds. *A Postmodern Reader*. Albany, N.Y.: State University of New York Press, 1993.

Newbigin, Lesslie. *Foolishness to the Greeks: The Gospel and Western Culture*. Grand Rapids: Eerdmans, 1986.

Newbigin, Lesslie. *The Gospel in a Pluralist Society*. Grand Rapids: Eerdmans, 1989.

Newbigin, Lesslie. *Truth to Tell: The Gospel As Public Truth*. Grand Rapids: Eerdmans, 1991.

Niebuhr, H. Richard. *Christ and Culture*. New York: Harper and Row, 1951.

Oden, Thomas C. *After Modernity . . . What? Agenda for Theology*. Grand Rapids: Academie Books, 1990.

Phillips, Timothy R., and Dennis L. Okholm, eds. *Christian Apologetics in the Postmodern World*. Downers Grove, Ill.: InterVarsity Press, 1995.

Phillips, Timothy R., and Dennis L. Okholm. *More than One Way?* Grand Rapids: Zondervan, 1995.

Piper, John. *The Supremacy of God in Preaching*. Grand Rapids: Baker, 1990.

Pitt-Watson, Ian. *Preaching: A Kind of Folly*. Philadelphia: Westminister Press, 1976.

Postman, Neil. *Amusing Ourselves to Death: Public Discourse in the Age of Show Business*. New York: Penguin Books, 1985.

Richardson, Don. *Peace Child*. Ventura, Calif.: Regal, 1974.

Robinson, Haddon. *Biblical Preaching*. Grand Rapids: Baker, 1980.

Robinson, Martin. *The Faith of the Unbeliever*. Crowborough, England: Monarch Publications, 1994.

Robinson, Martin. "Post What? Renewing Our Minds in a Postmodern World." *On Being* 24, no. 2 (March 1997): 28–32.

Robinson, Martin. *To Win the West*. Crowborough, England: Monarch Publications, 1996.

Roof, Wade Clark. *A Generation of Seekers: The Spiritual Journeys of the Baby Boom Generation*. San Francisco: HarperSanFrancisco, 1993.

Rowell, Ed. "Where Preaching Is Headed." *Leadership* (winter 1997): 95–98.

Roxburgh, Alan J. *Reaching a New Generation: Strategies for Tomorrow's Church*. Downers Grove, Ill.: InterVarsity Press, 1993.

Rye, James. *The Communicator's Craft*. Leicester, England: Inter-Varsity Press, 1990.

Schaeffer, Francis A. *How Should We Then Live?* Westchester, Ill.: Crossway, 1976.

Seaborn, Joe. "Whatever Happened to Authority?" *Preaching* 12, no. 4 (January/February 1997): 42–43.

Shelley, Marshall, ed. *Changing Lives through Preaching and Worship*. Nashville: Moorings, 1995.

Sire, James W. *Why Should Anyone Believe Anything at All?* Downers Grove, Ill.: InterVarsity Press, 1994.

Smith, Donald K. *Creating Understanding: A Handbook for Christian Communication across Cultural Landscapes*. Grand Rapids: Zondervan, 1992.

Sproul, R. C. *The Holiness of God.* Wheaton: Tyndale House, 1986.

Stivers, Dan R. "Much Ado about Athens and Jerusalem: The Implications of Postmodernism for Faith." *Review and Expositor* 91, no. 1 (winter 1994): 83–102.

Stott, John R. W. *Between Two Worlds: The Art of Preaching in the Twentieth Century.* Grand Rapids: Eerdmans, 1982.

Swindoll, Charles R. *The Grace Awakening.* Dallas: Word, 1990.

Tapia, Andres. "Reaching the First Post-Christian Generation." *Christianity Today* (September 12, 1994): 18–23.

Thompson, Peter. *The Secrets of the Great Communicators.* Sydney, Australia: ABC Books, 1992.

Unger, Merrill F. *Principles of Expository Preaching.* Grand Rapids: Zondervan, 1955.

Van Biema, David. "Does Heaven Exist?" *Time,* 24 March 1997, 44–52.

Veith, Gene Edward, Jr. *Postmodern Times: A Christian Guide to Contemporary Thought and Culture.* Wheaton: Crossway, 1994.

Watkins, William D. *The New Absolutes.* Minneapolis: Bethany, 1996.

Wells, David F. *God in the Wasteland: The Reality of Truth in a World of Fading Dreams.* Grand Rapids: Eerdmans, 1994.

Wiles, Jo. "How to Raise Drug-Free Kids." *Reader's Digest* (December 1997): 93–102.

Willimon, William H. "This Culture Is Overrated." *Leadership* (winter 1997).

Willimon, William H. *The Intrusive Word: Preaching to the Unbaptized.* Grand Rapids: Eerdmans, 1994.

Woodard, Kenneth L. "On the Road Again." *Newsweek,* 28 November 1994, 61–62.

Yancey, Philip. *I Was Just Wondering.* Grand Rapids: Eerdmans, 1989.

Yancey, Philip. *The Jesus I Never Knew.* Grand Rapids: Zondervan, 1995.

Zacharias, Ravi K. *Can Man Live without God?* Dallas: Word, 1994.

Zacharias Ravi K. *Deliver Us from Evil.* Dallas: Word, 1996.

Zacharias, Ravi K. "Reaching the Happy Thinking Pagan." *Leadership* (spring 1995): 18–27.

Graham Johnston is senior pastor of Subiaco Church of Christ in Western Australia and an adjunct lecturer in homiletics with the Australian College of Ministries. He holds degrees from Gordon-Conwell Theological Seminary and Dallas Theological Seminary.